DISCARDED

LITERATURE AND HISTORY
OF
AVIATION

LITERATURE AND HISTORY
OF
AVIATION

*Advisory Editor:* JAMES GILBERT

# THE SKY'S THE LIMIT

## The History of the Airlines

CHARLES J. KELLY, Jr.

New Introduction by Charles J. Kelly, Jr.

ARNO PRESS
A NEW YORK TIMES COMPANY

Reprint Edition 1972 by Arno Press Inc.

Introduction Copyright © 1972 by Charles J. Kelly, Jr.

Copyright © 1963 by Charles J. Kelly, Jr.
Reprinted by permission of Charles J. Kelly, Jr.

Reprinted from a copy in The State Historical Society of Wisconsin Library

LC# 70-169423
ISBN 0-405-03766-X

Literature and History of Aviation
ISBN for complete set: 0-405-03789-9
See last pages of this volume for titles.

Manufactured in the United States of America

Feb. 28, 1963

Dear Mr. Kelly:

I had hoped to write to you before this to thank you for sending me the copy of your book, "The Sky's the Limit," but I wanted to finish reading it and it arrived at a time when I was unusually hard pressed with plans and obligations. I was able to read only a chapter or two before leaving the United States, and two or three more on the flight across. I finished the reading, here in Europe, last night.

Ordinarily I glance at the books I receive in the mail, possibly read a few paragraphs, and put them out of the way more or less permanently. It is seldom that I have read a book from start to finish, as I have yours. I found it fascinating. I was deeply impressed with the quality of the writing, with the broad coverage, with your perception in regard to individuals, and with your attempt to state both sides of a situation objectively-- a combination rarely encountered in books produced these days. Very few people will realize the amount of research and thought that you have put into this book.

Naturally your book is, and will continue to be, a controversial one; and naturally, in the broad areas you have covered, some inaccuracies will be found. Stimulating thinking is bound to have its vulnerabilities, and to create its oppositions. I found most challenging your suggestions in regard to airline policy and regulation (I agree with many of them), and I admire your ability to bring out in brief sketches so much of the character of the individuals you touch and to connect this character with the organizations on which it has impinged.

As you say in your prologue, every figure involved would tell the story somewhat differently, particularly as it relates to him. It is impossible, of course, for any man to give a balanced account of any other man, or even of himself. There are instances where I might change emphasis somewhat, but I think you have done amazingly well--better than in any parallel work I know of. I particularly like your trying to find something decent relating to a man to balance off the qualities you disapprove of.

With best wishes,

*Charles A. Lindbergh*

INTRODUCTION TO THIS EDITION

I am pleased that Arno Press is publishing the series LITERATURE AND HISTORY OF AVIATION, including *The Sky's The Limit*, and I am particularly gratified that Charles Lindbergh has permitted the use of his letter to me in connection with this edition, for surely there is no other single individual whose range of knowledge, participation, and contribution is so extensive. My chief regret is that I will not have an opportunity to amend the original text, but this new introduction does at least permit some reflection of the changed perspectives.

Ten years is a long time in the history of the airlines and the industry today shows many changes. There is a new generation of chief executives and a new generation of equipment. The famous old faces are gone, the titans of the trade, their passings noted in varied ways. Of the major figures in this book, only C. E. Woolman of Delta has since died, but of those retired, regrettably only Rickenbacker of Eastern has as yet published his memoirs; and the literature of the airline industry cannot be complete without the invaluable source material of these illustrious men. W. A. Patterson retired from United with the graceful gesture of severing his ties completely — no directorship, not even the usual courtesy office — so as not to impede his successor. Even so, the steps of the mighty are hard to follow, even for hand-picked successors, for Patterson's choice as United's president was preemptorily fired last year, to be replaced by the head of United's hotel subsidiary. Rumor has it that Najeeb Halaby is having difficulty freeing himself of the long shadow of Juan Trippe in the halls of Pan American. Howard Hughes is gone from TWA and has been willing to accept a default judgment in excess of 100 million dollars to preserve his privacy by avoiding a court appearance. Those who feel Howard Hughes, for all his idiosyncrasies, is erratic in his business judgments, should consider his decision to sell his controlling interest in TWA when the stock was above 90 (it later fell below 15). From the seclusion of a perpetually curtained top floor of a Nassau hotel, Hughes continues his involvement in aviation through his control of Air West, a regional carrier; and some even feel Hughes is contemplating a return to TWA. C. R. Smith left American to become Secretary of Commerce in the Johnson Administration, and thereafter became a partner of the Lazard investment banking firm and so continues an active business career out of the airline industry, leaving American in the hands of George Spater, formerly of the Chadbourne law firm.

With the new generation of executives, there is also a new generation of equipment — the "jumbo jets," the 450-passenger Boeing 747, and the 350-passenger McDonnell-Douglas and Lockheed airbusses. It is no secret that the new generation of equipment poses serious problems. Whereas the original jets nearly doubled the speed of their prop predecessors, thereby sharply increasing productivity, the jumbos do not offer comparable advantages to offset their much higher purchase price (approximately 25 million dollars for a 747 versus 6 million dollars for a 707). The chief advantage of the jumbos is a somewhat lower operating cost per seat mile flown and an alleged customer appeal. It often appears that airline managements place too much emphasis on "passenger appeal." For example, a major airline proudly announced its airbus order with the assertion that more man-hours of computer time had been involved in analyzing this decision than had been spent in building the pyramids. Curious as to the alternatives considered, I asked the chief financial officer of the airline whether it would not have been much more economic to order extended versions of existing aircraft, such as the Boeing 727, wherein the cost savings might be as much as 50 per cent. He told me that such a comparison was never seriously considered, because management believed that the passenger appeal of the wider fuselage would outweigh any such cost considerations.

That decision carries serious consequences, for the airlines have nearly 3 billion dollars of 747s on order and perhaps as much as 5 billion in orders for airbusses. Financings of such magnitude present a very real problem for an industry that lost about 200 million dollars in 1970, especially so since the increased capacity of the jumbos far exceeds the increase in passenger traffic. Nor are these huge dollar amounts necessarily good for the aircraft manufacturers. Just as cost overruns on the early jets forced General Dynamics out of the commercial aircraft business and so damaged Douglas that a merger with McDonnell was the only means of survival, so today Lockheed faces bankruptcy from problems associated with the development of its Tri-Star airbus.

With so many current financing and operational problems already facing them, it is probably fortunate for the airlines that the U. S. Supersonic Transport program has been cancelled. The SST was not an economic vehicle, and it was so expensive that massive government assistance was required. The federal subsidy program was defeated in Congress, despite the support of the Nixon Administration; the issue of pollution of the atmosphere was a factor in the decision. The pollution issue, as developed in Congress, was somewhat superficial; however, there is a very real ecology issue in the literal sense: the use of man's technology out of relation to his environment. It does not make sense to subsidize the airlines with tax revenues to fly uneconomic airplanes at supersonic speeds when the passengers cannot get to town from the airport.

Our national transportation policy is as fragmented and chaotic as ever; cities strangle with automobile traffic while urban mass transit is neglected. Existing modes of transport all have very finely developed constituencies and lobbies, both in and out of government; whereas new alternatives have relatively little support. As a consequence, the larger questions of appropriate national policy are not faced, while official debate continues on more limited issues, often with regrettably petty bickering. As before, the airlines continue to blame their problems on the Civil Aeronautics Board for granting excessive competition on major routes and for permitting supplemental carriers to offer low-cost charter flights; while the CAB counters that the airlines' problems are their own fault, for ill-advised and excessive aircraft purchases — the same old arguments. Of course, the numbers are bigger: in dollars, miles flown, passengers carried. Giant computers analyze and re-analyze masses of data, but the human element remains to confound and complicate, for in the last analysis, decisions are made by men.

So, the faces change, the aircraft change, but the fundamental issues remain very much the same.

Charles J. Kelly, Jr.<br>1971

*THE SKY'S THE LIMIT*

# THE SKY'S
## THE LIMIT

### The History of the Airlines

CHARLES J. KELLY, Jr.

Coward-McCann, Inc.   NEW YORK

COPYRIGHT © *1963* BY CHARLES J. KELLY, JR.

*All rights reserved.*
*This book, or parts thereof, may not be reproduced in any*
*form without permission in writing from the Publisher.*
*Published on the same day in the Dominion of Canada by*
*Longmans Canada Limited, Toronto.*

*Quotations from* The Spirit of Saint Louis *by Charles A. Lindbergh,*
*by permission of Charles Scribner's Sons.*

*Library of Congress Catalog*
*Card Number: 63-8209*

*Manufactured in the United States of America*
*Van Rees Press • New York*

*To the memory of my Father,
    who saw the beginnings of Flight;
        and*
*To my Daughters,
    who will see its future*

# Contents

| | | |
|---|---|---:|
| *Prologue* | | 9 |
| **Part One: THE BOLD BEGINNINGS** | | |
| I | First Flights and Patent Fights | 15 |
| II | The Wing as a Weapon | 23 |
| III | "Nor Dark of Night": The U.S. Air Mail | 30 |
| IV | The Flight of the Lone Eagle | 43 |
| **Part Two: CONSOLIDATION AND THE GROWTH OF GOVERNMENT CONTROL** | | |
| V | Boeing and the Birth of United | 51 |
| VI | From Barnstormers to Bankers | 59 |
| VII | Wall Street and Washington | 69 |
| VIII | The New Deal | 83 |
| IX | Reconciliation, Regulation and Subsidy | 97 |
| **Part Three: ACROSS THE OCEANS** | | |
| X | Instruments of Empire | 105 |
| XI | Juan Trippe in the Caribbean Laboratory | 113 |
| XII | From China Clippers to the North Atlantic | 130 |

## Part Four: WORLD WAR II: AIR TRANSPORT COMES OF AGE

XIII  Achievements of the Air Transport Command — 143

## Part Five: POSTWAR POLITICS

XIV  The "Chosen Instrument": Pan American vs. the World — 153
XV  The Challenge of New Competition — 168
XVI  The Fateful Climax of the Air Coach Controversy — 180

## Part Six: ADVENT OF THE JETS

XVII  The Equipment Race — 187

## Part Seven: JET AGE GIANTS

XVIII  The Example of United — 199
XIX  American: Heir of the AVCO Empire — 212
XX  Eastern: Rickenbacker, Rockefeller and the American Merger — 227
XXI  TWA and the Enigma of Howard Hughes — 243
XXII  The Stormy Career of National Airlines — 264
XXIII  Northwest and the Great Circle Run to the Orient — 273
XXIV  Delta: A Crop Duster's Progress or Virtue Rewarded — 277
XXV  Continental and the Furor over Fares — 280

## Part Eight: A DARK HORIZON

XXVI  Technical Triumph and Financial Failure — 283
XXVII  Policy or Politics? — 292

Acknowledgments — 303
Bibliography — 305
Index — 309

*A section of illustrations follows page 160*

## *Prologue*

The soaring sound of a jet in the sky is commonplace today. Only a few young boys, or old pilots, even bother to look up. Yet, the story behind that sound is one of the great adventures of history. In the short span of one lifetime, aviation has progressed from the first faltering flight at Kitty Hawk in 1903 to the dominant means of distance transportation.

Commercial aviation is doubly fascinating, combining the age-old dreams of Icarus and Midas, man's search for wings with his quest for wealth. It adds to adventure the spice of avarice. Beneath the surface of the airlines' achievement lies a never-ending struggle for profit, power and prestige. Today, at the very peak of their technical capabilities, the airlines face serious financial difficulties. How this paradox came to pass can be understood only in the complex interrelationships of men, money, planes and politics.

Throughout, this is a story of men—men in aspiration and

achievement, in competition and conflict. As in all human relations, facts are disputed, motives are unclear, and gossip is often confused with truth. Doubtless every figure in this book would tell the story differently, particularly in so far as it relates to him. However, I shall be satisfied if, despite my errors as to his role, he believes that I have caught the general character of others.

There is also another aspect to the story—the economic and political effects of advancing technology. In essence, the airlines are shaped by the aircraft available to them. However, each advance in performance reopens that basic conflict of our society: economic efficiency versus economic freedom. The most efficient utilization of bigger, more expensive planes seems to require consolidations. Yet such concentrations of power are contrary to our most basic national beliefs in competition and free enterprise. For a half a century, this argument has swung back and forth.

This story really begins with the Wright brothers' airplane and the bitter patent fights to determine control of its future development. Backed by Morgan, who deplored the sorry state to which cutthroat competition had reduced the railroads, the Wrights favored a public utility approach along the pattern of the telephone industry. Opposition was intense and powerful, including Glenn Curtiss, Alexander Graham Bell, Henry Ford, and the jealous scientists of the Smithsonian Institution. In 1916, frustrated by government indifference, embittered by patent litigation, and saddened by his brother's death, Orville Wright sold out to a syndicate of automobile men who anticipated the huge aircraft production demands of World War I. There followed a series of ill-advised decisions which produced thousands of already obsolete British DH-4 "Flaming Coffins," the surplus of which glutted the market for the next decade.

Despite the inadequacies of the war-surplus planes, several

rugged, independent men began flying the mail over short, unconnected routes. Soon Lindbergh's thrilling transatlantic flight and the success of Bill Boeing's gamble to build improved airplanes for his airline demonstrated the potential of advanced aircraft. Seeking more profitable employment for the new vehicle, Wall Street financiers, with the active assistance of the "big business" philosophy of the Hoover Administration, shaped the motley collection of embryo airlines into three great national systems. In the process, several of the smaller pioneers believed themselves unfairly cut out. With the advent of the New Deal, they demanded a chance to get back into the game. The ensuing political vendetta, together with sharply increased competition at the depth of the depression, undermined the structure of the industry and drove it to seek government protection and subsidy.

Then came World War II where military necessity expanded air transport to every corner of the globe. In the postwar days, the availability of cheap war-surplus aircraft, coupled with the profitable prospect of airline growth, once again tempted newcomers to try to carve out a place for themselves. The resulting hostilities and political intrigues plagued the industry for the next decade—culminating in a fateful, and seemingly suicidal, showdown. The interlopers were finally excluded, but at the expense of irrational expansion of competition among the scheduled airlines. A simultaneous series of orders for an impoverishing number of new jets increased airline capacity beyond any foreseeable future demand.

In the face of such self-inflicted overcapacity, many executives and economists now argue for a series of consolidations, reducing the industry once again to a few giant airline systems. However, such evolution will first require thorough reappraisal of our national transportation policy. The government regulatory framework conceived in the days of the DC-3 is now just as obsolete. The airlines have long since outgrown any need for special, separate treatment to protect them from the domination of other forms of transport. Furthermore, the scandalously mounting local service airline subsidy (presently $85 million annually) cannot be resolved without reference to available alternatives, such as express bus connections and restored railroad service—coordination which the presently fragmented government regulatory bodies cannot provide.

Inevitably, such fundamental changes will be accompanied by the old charges, countercharges and vituperations. The siren song of politics will be heard and arguments will be presented in terms of little companies versus big; monopoly versus competition; socialism versus free enterprise. As the dispute approaches its inexorable climax (hearings are already in progress on the merger of American–Eastern, and Pan American–TWA will likely follow), it is helpful to look back over the years and recognize that the problem is not really new but has, in fact, been fought and refought in various forms in every decade since the Wright brothers' first flight.

*THE SKY'S THE LIMIT*

*PART ONE*

# The Bold Beginnings

*CHAPTER 1*

# First Flights and Patent Fights

Orville made the first flight. One hundred and twenty feet. A man could throw as far. A boy could run as fast. A horse could carry more. But the world would never be the same again.

After that brief flight, the world began to shrink. Slowly at first, so slowly that people hardly noticed it, but twenty-four years later—when Lindbergh demonstrated that the Atlantic was only 30 hours wide, instead of a week—the whole world had to recognize what had happened on that hill at Kitty Hawk.

The honor of the first flight was determined by the flip of a coin. The day was cloudy, with a bitter wind; depressions in those desolate dunes were filled with dark pools of rain water, rippled by wind and edged with ice. Wearing his usual business suit, high, stiff collar and tie, Orville Wright lay face down on the bottom wing of his flimsy machine, his face only inches from the blowing sand, and pulled the launching lever.

It is ironic and perhaps symbolic that man's age-old dream of flight, one of history's great scientific achievements, should be accomplished by two poor, obscure bicycle mechanics with no formal scientific education whatever. Their first flight took place on the barren, windswept dunes of the North Carolina coast, with one assistant and four curious lifeguards as the only other witnesses. Every part of their plane and motor, every piece of their equipment, was designed and built by them, in their spare time. Their only financial backing was the meager surplus of their bicycle-repair business. Offers of financial help were refused; as Wilbur wrote to his father: "Others have kindly offered to help bear the expense of these experiments, but we have refused to accept money, because we would be led to neglect our regular business too much if the expense of experimenting did not exercise a salutary effect on the time devoted to them."

Almost from the moment of the airplane's birth, the government was destined to play a dominant part in its development. The Wrights, like uncounted parents before and since, were somewhat overwhelmed by their offspring—and were uncertain as to the proper course for their future. Undependable, short-ranged and slow, the early flying machine had little commercial value, except perhaps for exhibition or stunt flying. Nor were the Wrights themselves commercially inclined. Solemn, shy, lifelong bachelors, the brothers had neither appetite nor aptitude for financial affairs. To leave themselves "free to pursue scientific studies," they sought to sell all their rights to the airplane to the government for $25,000 (they earlier considered asking only $10,000) to avoid the necessity of "assuming business responsibility" or "exploiting our invention commercially."

At the time the government was the logical market, for the airplane had obvious military implications, despite the inadequacy of its performance. But dealing with the government is never as simple as it sounds, and for the Wrights, the normal complications were compounded. The predictable antipathy of the military mind toward a new concept was reinforced by the hangover of the Langley Affair.

Head of the Smithsonian Institution, Samuel Pierpont Langley was one of the foremost American scientists at the turn of the century. His interest turned to flying, and from his position at the Smithsonian, he rallied the support of the more articulate and politically persuasive scientists of his day to prevail upon Congress and the War Department for a research grant. With $100,000 of Army funds (the largest government research grant up to that time), as well as technical and financial assistance from the Smithsonian and other institutions, Langley proceeded to build a flying machine. His preparations received great attention and publicity. The press followed every move. Finally the great day arrived—December 8, 1903, just one week before the Wrights' first flight at Kitty Hawk. Langley planned to launch his machine from a catapult arrangement on a barge in the Potomac River. A large crowd assembled as the barge was towed into place. Bands played, children shouted, skyrockets were set off. With a flourish, Langley cut the restraining cords. The machine quivered, slid slowly down the launching track, and toppled into the river.

The fickle public turned on Langley with a vengeance. Congressmen cried "Folly and Waste." Ridicule and abuse poured out on everyone connected with the project: Langley, the Smithsonian, the War Department—and the whole, crazy idea of flying machines. The following week the story of the Wrights' flight at Kitty Hawk was buried on the newspapers' back pages—or not even reported at all.

Incredible as it seems today, official reaction to the Langley experience was so strong that for four long years the Army refused to believe that a flying machine existed—and obstinately refused even to observe a demonstration. Disappointed and disgusted, the Wrights took their airplane to Europe, where their flights were received with wild acclaim. As reports of the European successes filtered back to this country, they could no longer be ignored. When the Army finally decided that there might be some military use for the flying machine, the Wrights were the only men in the world who knew how to make one. But the Army couldn't just buy a plane from them; procurement regulations specified that the contract had to be advertised and bids accepted from all interested parties.

Money has always been regarded as a corrupting influence, and there is something particularly corrupting about government money. So it was with the aviation industry. With the first government contract came the first authentic aviation son-of-a-bitch (a relationship which has continued to exist in varying forms from that day to this). To the Army's surprise and discomfort, forty-one bids were received. Government lawyers gathered in hasty conference and concluded that obviously frivolous bidders could be eliminated by requiring a 10-percent performance bond. Thirty-nine bidders promptly withdrew, leaving only the Wrights and Augustus M. Herring. All during their long years of sales efforts, the Wrights' terms had been public knowledge—$25,000, with delivery in 200 days. When the two formal bids were opened, Herring's bid was $20,000, with delivery in 180 days.

Herring was already well known as a fake and fraud. He had first worked for Chanute, helping to build gliders; he had also worked with Langley—and had been fired by both. Undaunted, Herring had filed baseless patent applications covering the work of both of his former employers. Following the same tactics, Herring visited the Wrights during some of their gliding experiments at Kitty Hawk in 1902. Subsequently he wrote them that he knew their secrets and that extensive litigation could be avoided if they would give him a one-third interest in their invention. Rebuffed, he went to Langley and offered to sell him the Wrights' secrets. To Langley's credit, he too threw Herring out. Predictably, Herring turned up once again with the prospect of a government contract. He brazenly informed the Army contracting officers that they were obligated by law to accept his bid as the lowest submitted.

The problem was referred to Secretary of War William Howard Taft, who determined that the difficulties should be resolved by accepting both bids. Taft believed that, in the fullness of time, Herring's fraud would be exposed when he could not deliver. However, by statute, the government was precluded from accepting bids without sufficient appropriations available to pay for all such contracts accepted. Taft explained the problem to President Theodore Roosevelt, who, with statesmanlike grace, placed his emergency fund at the disposal of the War Department to satisfy the necessary legal guarantee.

Thus prepared, Taft proceeded to call Herring's bluff. To everyone's surprise, Herring signed the contract without a qualm. He then immediately presented himself to the Wrights and laid out his proposition: the Wrights should make two airplanes, sell one to the Army under its contract, and the other to Herring for $15,000. Herring would then deliver the second airplane to the Army and receive the $20,000 under his contract. Firm in the integrity of their Baptist heritage, the sons of Bishop Wright would have no part of any such transaction. Even then Herring's preposterous confidence remained unshaken. When the delivery date for the contract arrived, Herring appeared in Washington and delivered a suitcase containing what he claimed to be all the parts necessary to produce an airplane. The final disposition of the suitcase is unrecorded, but Herring persisted in his underhanded career and soon joined forces with the Wrights' chief rival.

Glenn Curtiss, a flashy motorcycle racer as well as a gifted mechanic, had become interested in flying soon after the Wrights' success. Both a pilot and a builder, he made many record flights, as well as some significant technical contributions, including the tricycle landing gear and floats. Most important, Curtiss designed a better aileron—infringing on the basic Wright patent. He achieved the desired effect by means of a hinged flap instead of twisting the wing tip, as the Wrights had done. The question was: Had Curtiss discovered a new, patentable principle or merely improved upon an existing concept? ·

In addition to Curtiss, a number of other less able inventors were busily copying the Wright design—and amateur aviators were killing themselves in steadily increasing numbers. (It's fascinating to note that, even though they generally flew the most hazardous test flights themselves, none of the great early inventors, such as the Wrights, Curtiss, Sikorsky, or Martin, were killed in crashes.) Fearing the effect which the accidents would have on public acceptance of aviation, the Wrights begged the government to take some action to stop the infringements, but to no avail. At last, worn out by their futile and frustrating experiences with the government, the Wrights finally became convinced that the only way to achieve sound development for their device was to control its use themselves, through strict enforcements of their patents. They had previously considered their patents primarily as a means of securing scientific recognition, and it was with great reluctance that they abandoned their former hope "to make our patents freely available to mankind."

For support, they turned to that titan of private financial strength and stability, the great J. P. Morgan. Morgan's ideas of business fitted in well with the Wrights' plans. Above all else, he deplored unsound development and what he considered

## The Bold Beginnings [ 21

wasteful competition. A few years before, he had reorganized the railroads, which had been laid low by cutthroat competition. He had just completed the organization of U.S. Steel, to consolidate and regulate the steel industry. To Morgan's orderly mind, it would be most unfortunate if the vast potential of the Wrights' invention was to be impaired by the incompetence and bickering of irresponsible men. With Morgan's backing, the Wrights planned to develop the airplane along public-utility concepts, as had already been done with Bell's telephone.

But the Morgan alliance was not a popular one. Wall Street and the "trusts" were under heavy political and journalistic attack—and Morgan was the prime target. In spite of the economic success of the great industrial concentrations, there was a powerful and growing public suspicion of private business power as an instrument of social inequality and oppression. In the view of the muckraking press, the Wrights had "sold out" to the Wall Street "monopolists"—and popular support swung to Curtiss as the symbol of opposition to a patent monopoly.

Allied with Curtiss was a curious group, and for a variety of motives: Henry Ford, who always hated bankers, particularly Morgan; Alexander Graham Bell, who ironically already enjoyed a secure monopoly position for his telephone; and the Langley followers at the Smithsonian, who wished to restore their prestige by discrediting the Wrights.

The ensuing patent suits were lengthy and bitterly fought—but were eventually decided in the Wrights' favor in a definitive decision by Judge Learned Hand. Curtiss' attorneys (recommended to him by Ford) advised him that his position was hopeless unless some means could be found to invalidate the Wrights' patent.

Desperate to prove that those patents lacked priority, Curtiss then hit upon a scheme to try to make Langley's original machine fly. The Smithsonian Institution was an eager participant in the deceitful enterprise. The Langley machine was shipped to

Curtiss' plant and hidden away in a courtyard which had been walled in and roofed over to prevent observation. There, Curtiss rebuilt it in accordance with the Wright principles, installing a more powerful engine and a more efficient propeller. With these modifications and improvements, a few short, erratic flights were achieved, although the plane was still unstable. Nevertheless, these flights were touted by Curtiss and the Smithsonian as evidence against the priority of the Wrights' claims. After the flight, the rebuilt Langley machine was immediately returned to the secret courtyard, where it was restored as nearly as possible to Langley's original structure. The machine was then sent to the Smithsonian and displayed as: "The first man-carrying airplane in the history of the world capable of sustained free flight."

The scheme did not deceive the courts, but Orville was outraged and subsequently sent their original plane to the Science Museum in London for permanent display. Many years passed before the Smithsonian agreed to publish an official apology for its disgraceful conduct. Finally on December 17, 1943, at the instigation of President Franklin Roosevelt, the Smithsonian made public apology at a dinner honoring Orville Wright on the fortieth anniversary of the brothers' first flight. Orville then agreed to return their airplane to this country, but wartime conditions prevented the return for five more years. After the war, on December 17, 1948, the plane was installed in the Smithsonian Institution as "the world's first heavier-than-air machine in which man made free, controlled and sustained flight." Orville Wright was not present at the ceremony. He had died the preceding year.

## CHAPTER II

## *The Wing as a Weapon*

Ignored by the military, its commercial future clouded by patent disputes, the airplane languished in the land of its birth. In Europe, however, military aviation was already far advanced before the start of World War I. As the fighting progressed, the airplane played an ever-increasing role, but, with seemingly invincible ignorance, our military planners refused to recognize the obvious. Before our entry into the war, this country ranked fourteenth among the nations of the world in aviation appropriations, trailing even China, Spain, and Bulgaria.

However, our unpreparedness was not entirely the fault of fatuous "Colonel Blimps" in the War Department; our political leadership was at least equally to blame. Despite the fact that his foreign policies increasingly involved the risk of war, President Wilson seemed to lack the political courage to make the necessary preparations. The Army General Staff grew increasingly apprehensive. Desperately short of the practical necessities—rifles, machine guns and cannon—what meager appropriations were forthcoming the general staff rationed out for proven weapons. Either blinded by his idealism or with singularly cynical self-interest, Wilson postponed all military preparations until after the 1916 Presidential election, and campaigned on a Peace Platform as "The man who kept us out of war."

Well before the 1916 elections, realistic thinking could see that war was at hand—and that many airplanes would be needed. Battle experience had clearly demonstrated the necessity of airpower. United States pilots were already in action, flying as volunteers with the glamorous Lafayette Esquadrille of the French L'Armée de L'Air. Rapid build-up to large-scale production would be needed almost immediately, and the few appropriation-starved aircraft designers of this country were in no condition to provide either the facilities or production-trained management. Only the automobile industry seemed to have the right combination of mechanical background and production experience.

Early in 1916, Thomas Chadbourne, an imaginative and venturesome New York lawyer, brought several automobile executives from the Simplex Company together with bankers Richard F. Hoyt of Hayden Stone & Company, and Harvey D. Gibson of the Manufacturers Trust. With their financial backing arranged, Chadbourne's group approached Orville Wright. Saddened by Wilbur's recent death from typhoid, hurt by his country's treatment, and himself a sick man, the inventor of the airplane sold out—at the brink of aviation's first great development.

Soon thereafter, Chadbourne's group acquired the aircraft business of Glenn L. Martin, merging the two into a new entity, the Wright-Martin Aircraft Corporation, in 1917. Before long, the Curtiss company was similarly acquired by automobile man

John North Willys, with Chadbourne and Hoyt again participating in this syndicate. (Eventually Martin broke away and reopened his own company. The remaining corporate activities were subsequently merged as Curtiss-Wright, ironically combining the names of aviation's most bitter antagonists.)

In the Wrights' home town of Dayton, Ohio, another powerful unit was being formed under the leadership of an able and energetic promoter, E. A. Deeds. While at the National Cash Register Company, Deeds had known its brilliant engineer, Charles F. Kettering. About this time, Henry Leland of Cadillac was trying to develop a self-starter for his automobile, to replace the hand crank. A close friend of Leland's had been killed by a backfire, and Leland had a strong personal interest in an electric self-starter. Kettering's cash-register motor seemed to be the answer. With Leland's help, Deeds and Kettering started the Dayton Electric Laboratory Company in an old barn. Even before Delco was in production on the self-starter, the agile mind of Deeds foresaw the wartime profit possibilities in aviation. With Harold Talbott (later Secretary of the Air Force under President Eisenhower), Leland of Cadillac, Howard Coffin of Hudson Motor Car, and Jesse Vincent of Packard, Deeds organized the Dayton-Wright Airplane Company, paying Orville a small fee for the use of his name.

Soon this country was at war—with no plan or program for the use of airpower in its general staff, with no airplane factories, and with its only aviation companies in the hands of bankers and automobile men of no aeronautical experience whatever.

Into this vacuum stepped Howard Coffin, now of Dayton-Wright. While Coffin admittedly knew nothing of airplanes, he did know production and engines from his Detroit automobile days. And production seemed to be what was needed most. Accordingly, President Wilson appointed Coffin chairman of the

Aircraft Production Board. Coffin immediately selected his old friend and business associate Deeds to work with him in controlling the production of aircraft within this country.*

Supremely confident of their own abilities, Coffin and Deeds scorned the efforts and proposals of existing U.S. aircraft designers. Instead, they determined to mass-produce one standard aircraft engine, which would then be mated to combat-proven European airplanes. Claiming justification by the urgency of the need, Coffin and Deeds passed out the government contracts to their own companies and those of their friends and associates. To select suitable European designs for production in U.S. factories, a mission was promptly dispatched to Europe, headed by a former U.S. Steel attorney, Reynal Bolling, selected for his background in important negotiations, rather than for any experience or training in the aeronautical field. Bolling's mission was additionally handicapped by a total lack of policy guidance or statement of requirements by our military staff. (As evidence of the lack of imagination existing in our military over the use of airpower, all available Army airplanes were assigned to the Signal Corps, rather than to a combat arm.)

Discussions were begun with British, French, and Italian governments, but the British negotiations progressed fastest, since the British were willing to let the question of royalties and license fees await final determination until the end of the war. On the other hand, the ever-practical French insisted upon a fixed price in advance. This attitude infuriated Bolling, who exploded that he'd "be damned if he'd pay the French an admission fee to get into their war."

Meanwhile, in this country the automobile men were busy with the design of the so-called "Liberty" engine, confident

---

* It is interesting to consider how often automobile men are selected for significant civilian positions within the military establishment. Charles E. Wilson of General Motors served as Secretary of Defense under President Eisenhower, and Robert S. McNamara of Ford was similarly selected by President Kennedy.

that their engine could readily be fitted to any of the European airframes which Bolling might bring back. Serene in their self-assurance and accustomed to the high-pressure salesmanship of the automobile industry, Coffin and Deeds declared that they would "fill the skies with planes" within a year and thus "assure victory" for the Allies.

Difficulties developed rapidly. The European planes selected by Bolling were already obsolete. United States designers, frustrated at the indifference of our government before our entry into the war and distrustful of the motives of the automobile men suddenly in power, were enraged at the selection of foreign designs, while official Washington refused to look at such superior models as Glenn Martin's bomber or Grover-Loening's fighter. Furthermore, the adaptation of the Liberty engine to foreign planes was almost uniformly unsuccessful. The weight added to the airframe by the engine and the necessary design alterations adversely affected aerodynamics, and the hybrid aircraft did not achieve expected performance. Apparently influenced by their automotive training and background, the designers of the Liberty engine had placed the drive shaft at the bottom of the V-8 block, a condition necessary in automobile design to permit the drive shaft to pass below the body of the automobile; however, in aircraft design, such drive-shaft placement greatly increases the ground clearance needed for the propeller, necessitating extra-long landing gear. The only aircraft to reach volume production in this country was the DeHavilland DH-4, first produced by Dayton-Wright and later by other companies. But only a few of these aircraft were shipped to Europe, and none saw combat before the Armistice.

At the end of the war, the U.S. aircraft production program presented a sorry picture, particularly in the light of the earlier boastful claims to fill the skies with planes. Out of the welter of charges and countercharges, it is unlikely that a full, dispassionate story can ever be pieced together. In any case, the incontrovertible facts are that Coffin and Deeds awarded over $1,000,000,000 in aircraft contracts in less than two years, a large majority of which went to their former associates in the automobile industry. In return, the aircraft-production program failed to produce American-built aircraft in combat.

As for Coffin and Deeds, their own companies, Delco and Dayton-Wright, benefited particularly. The largest single military expenditure was for the Liberty engine, produced by several manufacturers, but all contracts specified that the engine must use the Delco ignition system. Subscribers' capital was never fully paid in to the Dayton-Wright Company, most of the financing being provided by advances from the government. Similar situations appeared in other favored aviation enterprises organized by friends and associates of Deeds and Coffin. The vast difference between costs and results, when coupled with what appeared to be obvious favoritism and profiteering, produced accusations, bitterness, shame and embarrassment on all sides.

The scandal soon became so heated that President Wilson realized that a full-scale investigation would be necessary to quiet public outcry. To counteract charges of partisanship, he appointed his recent Republican Presidential opponent, Charles Evans Hughes, a distinguished lawyer and subsequently Chief Justice of the Supreme Court, to head the investigation. After hearing the evidence, Hughes recommended court-martial for Deeds, primarily for his conflict of interest in failing to divest himself of his substantial stock ownership in Dayton-Wright and Delco. (Coffin was a civilian, not subject to military discipline.) Another subsequent investigation was instituted, this time clearing Deeds of criminal charges, although his associate, Jesse Vincent, was now indicted.

Despite the impropriety of Deeds' and Coffin's actions, it is neither fair nor wise to place the blame for the whole situation entirely on the automobile men. An industry that had not produced 200 planes between the Wright brothers' flight in 1903 and the declaration of war in 1917, was suddenly called upon to produce 30,000 planes in one year. No industry could possibly expand so rapidly. Of greater long-range significance was the fact that the decision to build foreign aircraft designs in automobile factories deprived a native U.S. aviation industry of deserved development. Moreover, the subsequent release on the public market of the already obsolete war-surplus planes at less than 1 percent of their cost destroyed the postwar market for nearly a decade.

The search for scapegoats and individual profiteers tended to obscure the real issue: the sorry state of U.S. aviation. Surely part of the blame must lie with our military planners, who ignored the airplane and its potential so long that the automobile executives came to power in a policy vacuum. Coffin, Deeds and their cohorts could not have made their ill-advised decisions had the military planners done their job instead of always seeking to preserve the *status quo*. In the light of history, the larger fault lies in a military system where responsibility for a weapons' policy rests in the hands of men whose power and prestige may be diminished by any innovation (as it does to this day); and in a government which lacked the political courage to prepare for the war which its foreign policies risked.

CHAPTER III

*"Nor Dark of Night"*: *The U.S. Air Mail*

The U.S. Mail! Even today there is still something adventurous in the sound—a distant memory of the dusty riders of the Pony Express; grizzle-bearded stagecoach drivers fingering their shotguns; fearless engineers at the throttle of the Fast Mail train. And last of that gallant line—the Air Mail pilot, leather-helmeted, goggles streaked with oil, grimacing out of his open cockpit into the stormy sky.

In the appropriation-starved days following World War I, the Air Mail contributed far more than romance, it kept aviation alive in this country.

On the morning of November 11, 1918, President Woodrow Wilson told the American people: "The Armistice was signed this morning. Everything for which America fought has been accomplished." Clearly such was not the case. Instead of a world "safe for democracy," there came the sad spectacle of cynical old men squabbling over the defeated body of the enemy. The noble vision which had seemed to justify the sacrifices of the war was suddenly reduced to the series of sordid compromises in the Treaty of Versailles.

Then came the various procurement scandals. Military aviation, which had once seemed a series of daring combats between "knights of the air" engaging each other in chivalrous duels, was revealed to have been handled by what appeared to be a group of selfish, incompetent men who had needlessly sacrificed lives in their ignorance and greed. The flow of government funds to the aviation industry stopped almost completely. Unlike other industries with a fully developed peacetime function, aviation had no commercial demand upon which to fall back.

In the ill-advised wartime aircraft procurement program, this country had produced not only the wrong kind of planes, but it had also produced far too many of them. The hastily built factories which did not produce aircraft in time to see combat, nevertheless had more than fulfilled any foreseeable commercial demand in this country for years to come. Curtiss' JN-4's, the famous "Jenny," and DeHavillands could be purchased, unused, for as little as $300, whereas any new aircraft manufactured at that time would cost at least $15,000. A few native American designers who sincerely wished to stay in the aircraft manufacturing business—Boeing, Martin, and Grover Loening *—implored Congress not to release the flood of surplus planes. The potential sale price was scarcely equal to the cost of the sales effort itself, and by making aircraft available so cheaply, the government was destroying the only remaining market for the aircraft industry. Nevertheless, surplus sales continued.

As yet there were no regulations or requirements for pilot's licenses. Any boy with a few dollars, a hankering to fly, and a

---

* Curtiss, disgusted by the wartime procurement procedures, retired to his farm in 1919.

willingness to risk his neck, could buy an airplane and fly it away. And so there came the "barnstormers," youngsters with surplus planes, working anywhere—county fairs, commercial expositions, any farmer's pasture; wing walkers, parachute jumpers, girls in tights who hung from the wings of low-flying planes. Aviation, as an industry, was dying. The former automobile manufacturers quickly converted their airplane factories to the production of automobiles. (Even Captain Eddie Rickenbacker, then America's most famous pilot, could find no appealing job in his field, and like others, turned his energies to the automobile business.) With a market swamped with surplus planes, the Air Mail was the only organized activity in a position to assist in aviation development and progress.

The Air Mail began in 1918, when Congress alloted $100,000 to the Post Office Department for Air Mail experiments, initially between Washington and New York. The Post Office Department held out high hopes for the new service, promising that a letter mailed in Washington in the morning would be delivered in New York that afternoon (an efficiency of service that has not been realized to this day).

Every effort was made to inaugurate the service as soon as possible. Three Curtiss JN-4 training aircraft were detailed from the Army. Difficulties developed at once. The aircraft arrived in their packing crates. For two days disappointed pilots worked around the clock, assembling their planes.

Dawn broke clear on the 15th of May, 1918, and anxious officials of the Post Office Department gathered at the tiny polo field in Washington between the tidal basin and the Potomac River. The first take-off was scheduled for 10:30, and most of official Washington, including President and Mrs. Wilson, was present. With great fanfare, Post Office trucks delivered the first sack of Air Mail. To everyone's chagrin, it was discovered that the first batch of Air Mail stamps had been printed upside down.

*The Bold Beginnings* [ 33

(At the time it was embarrassing, but that first batch of stamps was considered such an oddity in the world of stamp collectors that today a single specimen is valued at $4,500.)

The mail was stowed in the waiting plane and all was in readiness for the take-off precisely on schedule. Eager for favorable publicity, Post Office officials urged President Wilson to step forward and examine the plane for the benefit of newspaper photographers. Wilson's participation was noticeably lacking in enthusiasm. His hand was still bandaged from a severe burn he had received the previous week when ambitious Army officers had urged him to examine a tank and he had placed his hand on a hot exhaust manifold.

The picture-taking concluded, President Wilson stepped back, and the waiting Air Mail pilot was ordered to take off. The band struck up; the pilot shouted "Contact!" Vigorously, and with mounting embarrassment, mechanics swung the lifeless propeller. Mortified Post Office officials heard President Wilson say to his wife: "We are losing a lot of valuable time here." Suddenly it was discovered that someone had forgotten to fill the gas tank. Refueled, the pilot took off, circled low over the field, waved to the crowd, and climbed on course—in the wrong direction. With a terrible sense of frustration, the Superintendent of the Air Mail watched the Jenny disappear over the horizon. Two hours later the lost pilot called in from nearby Maryland. The first Air Mail was driven ignominiously back to Washington by car.

Despite its inauspicious beginning, the Air Mail was soon amazingly successful. Within a short time it was completing nearly all of its schedules. Actually, the original wartime purpose was not only the transportation of mail, but also and more important, the training of pilots. The personnel still was inexperienced (two more pilots got lost following the coastline in the next week of operation); the equipment was only what the Army could spare; but in spite of all obstacles the system prospered.

By December 1918, encouraged by 100-percent completion of all New York–Washington schedules for the previous ninety days, the Postmaster General ordered the inauguration of New York–Chicago service. The Superintendent of the Air Mail protested the decision, knowing that the aircraft were inadequate to undertake such a flight in the middle of winter. But in presenting his new budget requests for Congressional approval, the Postmaster General had committed himself to certain Congressmen to begin New York–Chicago service, and felt that his reputation—not to mention future appropriations—was at stake. Ordered to proceed, the Superintendent resigned in protest.

On December 12, 1918, reluctant Air Mail pilots set out simultaneously from New York and Chicago. Both planes were soon forced down by bad weather. Too much was demanded of the Air Mail and its flimsy, undependable open-cockpit planes—mostly rebuilt DeHavilland DH-4's with the Liberty engine, and already obsolete before the end of the war. Pilots hated the plane, primarily because the unreliable engine caused frequent crash landings. With the fuel tank between the engine and cockpit, any damage risked an explosion, giving the DH-4 its nickname, "Flaming Coffin." * Limited in capacity, too heavy to climb out from small fields, poor in visibility, its landing gear weak, the DH-4 was inadequate in every respect.

Under the prevailing conditions, it was not surprising that the Air Mail could offer scant improvement over the railroad. But the longer the distance that the planes flew, the greater their speed advantage. Accordingly, the Post Office Department was eager to extend its service over the broad expanses of the West. On September 8, 1920, the first transcontinental mail

* During 1921 alone, the Army Air Service recorded 330 DH-4 crashes, with 69 fatalities.

flight between New York and San Francisco was completed. But still the airplane flew only by day and the total time savings over the train schedules were relatively insignificant.

"It's a matter of life or death, for the lead we gain by day over the ships and railways is lost each night." Thus wrote the poetic French pilot, Antoine de Saint-Exupéry, in his classic *Night Flight,* describing the inauguration of Air Mail service in South America. So it was also in this country; for until night flying was possible, full utilization of the Air Mail could not be attained.

Even before a transcontinental flight had been completed in daytime, the Post Office Department made plans for night service. Once again, part of the motivation was political. Warren G. Harding had been elected President on the slogan "Back to normalcy." The Air Mail had been inaugurated by the prior Wilson Administration, and outgoing Democrat officials feared that the new Republican Congress would reduce appropriations drastically. Accordingly, it made a last desperate effort to demonstrate its potential by inaugurating a transcontinental night flight.

The audacity of the night flight can scarcely be appreciated today. There were then no radio beams to guide the lonely pilots; there were no weather stations or reports; all the navigation aids we accept so casually today were unknown. Radio communication, blind-flying instruments, even that irreducible minimum of lighted airways, were still far in the future. There were no emergency landing fields in case the obsolete wartime engines failed in the darkness. And the experiment was being attempted during the worst weather of the year.

At 4:29 A.M. on March 4, 1921, a biplane rose out of the clammy darkness of San Francisco Bay, struggled upward and eastward, topping the jagged Sierras at 12,000 feet, then glided down through the dawn to Reno. From Reno to Rawlins for gas and oil; from Rawlins to Cheyenne, and on to North Platte, Nebraska. It was 8 P.M. in North Platte when Jack Knight took off. At 2,000 feet the river was distinguishable, but the surrounding countryside was a sea of darkness relieved only by the lights of occasional towns. Along the route a few public-spirited citizens had lighted bonfires, hoping that the unseen ship, buffeted by the winds above them, would be cheered and directed by the light. After nearly four dark and rough hours, Knight landed in Omaha, hungry, tired, and eager for his replacement.

The next pilot was nowhere to be found. Ahead lay 435 miles of unfamiliar territory from Omaha to Chicago. The weather was getting worse, but Knight agreed to go on. After a cup of coffee, he was off again into a strong north wind spitting snow, with only an automobile map to guide him. Beyond Des Moines the wind shifted. Knight could only estimate its effect and attempt a rough compensation. Soon he was in fog, flying by dead reckoning. At last through the murk he saw the steady glint of a railroad track. Now down to 200 feet, following the guiding glimmer, he flew on to Iowa City. Low on fuel, he circled the dark and unfamiliar town, searching for the airport. The ground crew knew that the west-bound flight had been forced down in Chicago and assumed that the east-bound flight had given up also. Only a night watchman remained at the field to light a welcoming flare. Knight's tank was dry as he rolled to a stop near the flickering flame. Together, Knight and the watchman refueled the aircraft by hand from five-gallon cans. Then he was on his way again. The fog was lifting in the morning sunrise as he landed at Maywood Field, Chicago, where other pilots waited to carry the mail on to Cleveland and eventually to Hazelhurst, Long Island, 33 hours and 20 minutes from San Francisco.

The time seems slow to us today, but at that time no train could come within days of it. The successful night flight had demonstrated the possibilities of the Air Mail. Harding recommended larger appropriations to Congress. Regular night service did not begin until the completion of the lighted airway, nearly five years later. But the first night mail proved the feasibility of the service and paved a way for the beacons that were to make night flying routine. Some regard it as the most significant step in the development of commercial aviation.

By 1925, the Air Mail had clearly demonstrated its practicality. But the price was high. Of the 40 mail pilots first engaged by the Post Office Department, 31 lost their lives during the period of government operation, primarily from inadequate equipment and facilities. However, improvement was forthcoming; partially from an unexpected source, the controversial Billy Mitchell.

The only general officer in the military service who was also a pilot, Mitchell agitated for more rapid development of U.S. aviation, commercial as well as military. In his campaign Mitchell lost no opportunity to criticize the policies of the General Staff. Acutely sensitive to ridicule in peacetime, the Army suffered deeply at Mitchell's hands. Stories of official absurdity were rampant. Typical of the petty level of harassment was the series of orders dealing with the question of whether or not Air Service officers would be required to wear spurs on their boots while flying.

To demonstrate its military significance, Mitchell challenged that an airplane could sink a battleship, specifically the captured German flagship *Ostfriesland*. So great was the Navy's confidence that Secretary of the Navy Josephus Daniels declared that he would be willing to stand "bareheaded" on the bridge of the *Ostfriesland* while Mitchell attacked it with a bombing plane. Mitchell's new Martin bombers dropped six bombs, splitting open the hull of the *Ostfriesland* and sinking her immediately. (Daniels was not aboard.)

Emboldened by success, Mitchell redoubled his attacks. The officers of the Army General Staff claimed that Mitchell was destroying the morale of the Army. The ranking admirals stated that he was undermining public confidence in the nation's "First line of defense." Many prominent industrial leaders, particularly in the steel industry with its vast shipbuilding interests, feared the effect of Mitchell's theories on the economy generally and their industry in particular.*

Believing himself the leader of a crusade against entrenched hypocrisy and self-interest, Mitchell became more and more intemperate and extreme in his attacks. At the culmination of the struggle he issued a public statement charging that the officers of the General Staff were incompetent to hold office. With Mitchell's glove in its face, the Army had no choice but to proceed with a court-martial. Conviction was inevitable, and Mitchell used his trial testimony to enumerate, point by point, the inadequacies in our aviation program.†

A series of tragic military aircraft crashes seemed to bear out Mitchell's charges. Fearing that public confidence in our aviation policies had been impaired, President Coolidge appointed his old Amherst College classmate, Dwight Morrow, to conduct a public investigation of U.S. aviation. Morrow, who was widely respected, had left the practice of law to become a Morgan partner (and was soon to become the father-in-law of Charles A. Lindbergh). After hearing extensive testimony, Morrow concluded that, while Mitchell's charges were perhaps overstated, more rapid progress should be made. As a step to this end,

---

* When one considers the composition of the group of forces in league against Mitchell, it is intriguing to reflect upon the admonitions contained in President Eisenhower's farewell address as he left the Presidency, in which he warned the nation against a military-industrial clique wherein high governmental officers and industrial leaders with a vested interest in certain weapons' development might, however sincerely and unconsciously, lead the nation in ways of error.

† For instance, Mitchell remarked that the Hawaiian Islands were particularly vulnerable to aerial attack from a carrier strike force. Defense coordination was impossible as long as neither the commanding Army general nor Navy admiral would speak to the other or even attend the same social functions. The Japanese Naval Attaché in Washington attended Mitchell's trial, busily taking notes, and the Japanese attack in December 1941, took place almost exactly as Mitchell had predicted.

Morrow recommended the transfer of the Air Mail service from government to private hands to stimulate development.

It had always been the intention of the Post Office Department to transfer operation of the Air Mail to private companies when regular cross-county service over the lighted airway had attracted a sufficient volume of mail to demonstrate the practicability of the service. Gradually, as the country prospered, businessmen began to once again look at the commercial possibilities of the airplane. Clearly, the gypsy pilots, barnstormers, and local charter and sight-seeing services, had no real future. At best they could provide only a novelty attraction. But an Air Mail contract over a regular route might be a different story.

Ironically, one of the loudest voices raised against the government Air Mail service was that of the railroads, which did not want the government competing with them in carrying mail. (Today, with the airlines on the point of carrying not only Air Mail, but also all first-class mail as well, and in addition capturing almost the entire long-haul passenger market, present railroad managements might well wish that their predecessors had not argued the case quite so vigorously.)

The various pressures were transmitted to Congress and to the person of Representative Clyde Kelly of Pennsylvania, who had made his reputation as the "Voice of the railway mail clerks" by continued advocacy of their cause. Congressman Kelly therefore seemed a logical sponsor for a bill under which the government might hand over the Air Mail service to private operators, and thus cease to compete with the railroads in the carrying of mail. The resulting bill, known as the Air Mail Act of 1925, was duly passed, authorizing the Postmaster General to "encourage commercial aviation and to contract for the Air Mail service."

There remained, however, the question of the allocation of such mail contracts. Within two months after the passage of that Air Mail Act, over 5,000 inquiries were received from prospective airline operators. The great majority of such inquiries came from the barnstormers and gypsy pilots—colorful, daring men who liked airplanes and adventure and equally disliked business and office routine. A worthy and attractive group, but not the type required for the stability and development of a national airline system.*

Post Office officials were reluctant to turn over the system they had developed to irresponsible or unequipped agents. Accordingly, initial contracts were to be only for short-haul, "feeder" routes. Until the private operators had proven themselves, the Post Office Department would not turn over the main transcontinental or "Columbia" line.

The initial group of private Air Mail contractors produced a curious conglomeration of personalities and motivations. The first contract awarded, Civil Air Mail Route #1, from Boston to New York, went to Colonial Airways (now part of American). Prophetically, the guiding hand of this group was Juan Trippe, later to head Pan American World Airways. Trippe had a vision of the future of aviation, one that he was to realize in remarkable fashion. The other participants in the original Colonial group were men of social prominence, wealth and civic interest, who wished to see aviation prosper and to participate in the new venture.

Civil Air Mail Route #2 from Chicago to St. Louis (also later incorporated into American) was awarded to the Robertson Aircraft Corporation, organized by Frank Robertson and his brother William, a World War I fighter pilot. The Robertsons hired three former government Air Mail pilots for its initial

---

* The pilots of this period were notoriously uninhibited and hard living. One veteran recalls that Lindbergh was the only pilot of the period who did not drink, and that occasional mail flights were flown by pilots too drunk to walk to their aircraft. Considering the conditions under which he flew, a pilot's need for liquid courage is somewhat more understandable.

service, among whom was a young barnstormer named Charles Augustus Lindbergh. The route from Chicago to Dallas, CAM #3 (today a Braniff component), went to National Air Transport, a group organized by Clement Keys, a successful Wall Street promoter.

CAM #4 from Los Angeles to Salt Lake was won by Western Air Express, largely a product of the energy and civic mindedness of Los Angeles *Times* publisher Harry Chandler and a group of local industrialists. Air Mail service already linked San Francisco with New York, and Chandler resented the fact that Los Angeles was being deprived of its just opportunity to participate in the progress of aviation and the development of the West. Operational management of Western Air Express was in the hands of a former automobile racer named Harris M. Hanshue. CAM #5 went to Varney Air Service, operating between Elko, Nevada, and Pasco, Washington, later to be incorporated into the United system. CAM #8, between Los Angeles and Seattle, went to Vernon Gorst's Pacific Air Transport, also another of the components of United. CAM #9, from Chicago to Minneapolis, was won by its present operator, Northwest. CAM #10, from Atlanta to Jacksonville (now Eastern's route), went to Reed Chambers, a World War I ace, ranking second only to Eddie Rickenbacker.

The shortest and initially the most profitable route was CAM #11, between Cleveland and Pittsburgh (after a series of mergers, this route became part of Capital, and was more recently acquired by United), which was awarded to Clifford Ball, a former Hudson-Essex automobile dealer from McKeesport, Pennsylvania. Ball entered the airline business almost by accident. He was not a pilot and had little interest in aviation, but through a real estate deal he had acquired part of an airport near Pittsburgh. Several of the barnstormer pilots using the field could not pay their rent, and Ball foreclosed on their only assets, their planes. With an airfield and some airplanes,

Ball entered a bid on an Air Mail route, apparently without any clear idea of what would happen if he were to win a contract.

At the time the most significant awards were CAM #6 and #7, between Detroit, Chicago and Cleveland, won by Henry Ford, then probably the most influential of all business leaders. In the minds of most Americans, if Henry Ford went into the airline business, its future seemed assured. Actually, however, these routes were soon sold to United, and Ford's real contribution was to be the famous Ford Trimotor transport, then still several years away from full development.

The next major steps in the history of air transportation were to be taken by a poor young Air Mail pilot and a wealthy Seattle sportsman.

CHAPTER IV

## The Flight of the Lone Eagle

*M*ay 21, 1927; Le Bourget Field, Paris. A sudden silver shimmer in a searchlight's beam triggered the imagination of the world. Lindbergh had made it—alone—nonstop—from New York to Paris.

Blond, blue-eyed, slim and straight, he had been raised in the woods and lakes of northern Minnesota, the son of a bitterly independent Progressive Party Congressman. From his earliest days he had dreamed of flight; a dream which the family's limited financial resources seemed to make an impossibility. All through his college days the dream persisted. By skimping, saving, working at whatever job offered him a chance to be near airplanes, Lindbergh finally soloed. Then followed a period of barnstorming through the country for a living, flying war-surplus "Jennies" out of cow pastures. His fearlessness was legend. He developed an act in which he stood on the top wing of a looping airplane, to the delight of the crowds and the horror of his fellow pilots. At Kelly Field in Texas, he won the silver wings of the Army Air Service. From there he joined the Robertson Company as a pilot on Civil Air Mail Route #5, between St. Louis and Chicago. By the age of twenty-five he was chief pilot.

Flying the lumbering, unreliable old DH-4's along the St. Louis–Chicago route, Lindbergh longed for something better. The Robertson system was typical of the airline operations of those days. Actually it had established the best record of all the lines serving Chicago, with over 90 percent of its schedule completed. In his autobiography, *The Spirit of St. Louis,* Lindbergh describes those days:

> Plowing through storms, wedging our way beneath low clouds, paying almost no attention to weather forecasts, we more than once landed our rebuilt Army war planes on Chicago's Maywood Field when other lines canceled out, when older and perhaps wiser pilots ordered their cargo put on a train.

On the short runs between relatively nearby cities competing with the crack mail trains, the Air Mail saved but a few hours at most. And the cost in life was high. But for Lindbergh and the other pilots there was the sense of contributing to something significant, something of the future:

> We pilots of the mail have a tradition to establish. The commerce of the air depends upon it. Men have already died for that tradition. Every division of the mail routes has its hallowed points of crash where some pilot on a stormy night, or lost and blinded by fog, laid down his life on the altar of his occupation. Every man who flies the mail senses that altar and consciously or unconsciously, in his way, worships before it, knowing that his own next flight may end in the sacrifice demanded.

The chief obstacle to the fulfillment of the promise of the airlines was inadequate equipment. Better planes, safer equipment were available, but the airline companies lacked the means or the desire to finance the necessary purchases. Most of the airline operators then flying were former World War I pilots, operating on a shoestring. A few were men of no aviation knowledge who nonetheless saw an opportunity to get government subsidies with minimum financial outlays. The Robertson Aircraft Corporation, for which Lindbergh flew, was an example of a sincere and dedicated group of men who lacked the capital to accomplish their objectives. Lindbergh's company was "paid by the pounds of mail we carry, and often sacks weigh more than the letters inside. Our operating expenses are incredibly low; but our revenue is lower still. The corporation couldn't afford to buy new aircraft. All our planes and engines were purchased from Army salvage, and rebuilt in our shops at Lambert Field." Facilities available to mail pilots in those days were not provided by the government but were the responsibility of the individual companies themselves. Lindbergh wrote:

> We've been unable to buy full night-flying equipment for these planes, to say nothing of lights and beacons for the fields we land on. It was only last week that red and green navigation lights were installed on our DH's. Before that we carried nothing but one emergency flare and a pocket flashlight. When the dollars aren't there, we can't draw checks to pay for equipment. But it's bad economy, in the long run, to operate a mail route without proper lights. That has already cost us one plane. I lost a DH just over a week ago because I didn't have an extra flare, or wing lights, or a beacon to go back to.

A low fog had come in, obscuring the ground entirely. Lost, unable to land, low on fuel, Lindbergh had circled above the overcast, hoping for a hole to appear. When his engine ran dry, he loosed his safety belt and rolled over the cockpit side into the dark night sky. His parachute landed him in a cornfield. Wagon tracks led him through the darkness to a farmyard. With the farmer's help, he searched for the wreck of his plane, finally finding it two miles away in another cornfield. "Splinters of wood and bits of torn fabric were strewn all around. The mail compartment was broken open and one sack had been thrown out; but the mail was undamaged—I took it to the nearest post office to be entrained."

Nor was this experience an isolated example. Similar occurrences were taking place daily on the various routes served by private Air Mail companies at that time. Conditions in the industry were in a vicious circle. The low mail revenues did not seem to justify the capital expense of better equipment. Without better equipment, service could not improve—and revenues stayed low. Clearly, passengers could not endure such risks of travel in any worthwhile number. Perhaps a few daring young men might strap on parachutes and take the chance, often holding the mail sacks on their laps. But until better equipment and facilities became available, there was little hope for progress.

To Lindbergh, the limited range of the old equipment was a major factor retarding the growth of aviation:

> I'm annoyed at the thought of landing. It's a round-about method anyway, this flying the mail to Chicago to get it East. Why shouldn't we carry it direct to New York from St. Louis? True, there aren't enough letters in that wilted sack to pay for a direct service, but the mail will grow in volume as aircraft improve and people learn to use them. The more time we save, the more letters we'll get. If we flew direct, we could wait until the business day closed before collecting St. Louis mail, and still land in New York City before offices opened the next morning. Such a service would really be worth the cost of extra postage. We might even be able to fly from St. Louis to New York, nonstop, eventually. Not with these salvaged Army DH's—they can't reach Chicago against a headwind without refueling—but with new planes and new engines ...

To Lindbergh, it seemed, the key to progress was to demonstrate the efficiency of new aircraft. Range, speed and payload—these were the factors that could make aviation's success; such planes could be built, yet few people realized it. Development by the military was at a standstill. Appropriations were meager,

## The Bold Beginnings [ 47

and the ignorance and pride of the General Staff had already destroyed the career of General Billy Mitchell. If the famous Mitchell could not make the brass hats understand, how could the unknown Lindbergh convince hardheaded and conservative businessmen? He wrote:

> Businessmen think of aviation in terms of barnstorming, flying circuses, crashes, and high costs per flying hour. Somehow they must be made to understand the possibilities of flight. If they could see the real picture, it wouldn't be difficult to finance an airline between St. Louis and New York, even at the price of new airplanes. Then commercial pilots wouldn't have to fly old Army war planes or make night landings with flares instead of floodlights.

Thus meditating during his night mail runs, Lindbergh gradually determined that he would find some way to demonstrate the possibilities of the airplane to the businessmen and financiers of St. Louis. Then, "... they'd see how swiftly and safely passengers could fly. There are all kinds of records I could break for demonstration—distance, altitude with load, nonstop flights across the country." With a suitable plane, Lindbergh knew he could prove its utility. "It could break the world endurance record and the transcontinental, and set a dozen marks for range and speed and weight. Possibly—my mind is startled in its thought—I could fly nonstop between New York and Paris."

On the evening of May 19, 1927, there was a drizzle of light rain over Long Island, typical of the spring season, but crucial in the lives of three pilots who waited only for clear weather to attempt to fly the Atlantic for the Orteig Prize.

Raymond Orteig, a Frenchman who owned the Brevoort and Lafayette hotels in New York, had offered $25,000 for the first nonstop flight between New York and Paris. Two of the planes competing were large, well-equipped aircraft with trained and experienced crews with major financial backing: one to be flown by Clarence Chamberlain and the other by Lieutenant Commander Richard Byrd of North Pole fame. The last of the trio was Lindbergh with his little single-engined Ryan monoplane, *The Spirit of St. Louis*. There was something particularly daring and romantic about the handsome youth risking the perilous journey alone. And there was a quiet efficiency about him also. When asked how he dared to fly with his single engine, he replied: "None of the trimotors can make it with an engine out. Having three of them just triples the risk."

Despite the local drizzle, weather reports indicated a chance of clearing over the Atlantic. Still doubtful, Byrd and Chamberlain decided to wait, but Lindbergh leapt at the chance; he worked through the night on navigation calculations and his final preparations for the trip. A little before 8 o'clock on the morning of May 20th, Lindbergh staggered the overloaded *Spirit of St. Louis* off the runway at Roosevelt Field into the gray dawn.\*

As his wheels touched the runway at Le Bourget, a jaded, disillusioned world had a new hero. Probably no man in our history has ever been subjected to such personal popular acclaim. Upon his return to this country, Lindbergh was overwhelmed with a torrent of praise and worshipful attention. His triumphal return to St. Louis was followed by a visit to Dayton, Ohio, to meet Orville Wright. He then returned to New York and secluded himself on the Long Island estate of Harry F. Guggenheim (president of the Guggenheim Fund, whose generous and imaginative philanthropy, during a low period of government appropriations, made significant contributions to the development of aviation). There in three weeks of intense activity, Lindbergh produced the manuscript of the story of his flight, *We*.

---

\* Clearly beaten, Byrd and Chamberlain subsequently attempted different destinations; Byrd crash-landed off the French coast, while Chamberlain and his crew made it from New York to Germany. Nevertheless, the real purpose was gone. Today their flights are only footnotes to Lindbergh's fame.

## The Bold Beginnings   [ 49

In an effort to utilize Lindbergh's popularity as a positive force in the development of aviation, Guggenheim arranged with the U.S. Department of Commerce for a tour of the nation which would bring Lindbergh to each of the 48 states. The purpose of the tour was to stimulate popular interest in aviation and to demonstrate the safety and punctuality of professional flying. Flown with his characteristic precision, Lindbergh's performance had been practically perfect. During the tour he covered 22,350 miles in 260 flying hours. He made scheduled stops in 82 cities and was late only once, when fog prevented his landing in Portland, Maine. He made 147 speeches, all of them concerned solely with the progress in aviation. He was guest of honor at 69 dinners and was driven 1,285 miles in parades. Unquestionably the tour was a high point in the development of American aviation. The cities Lindbergh visited were filled with aviation enthusiasm and activity. Those he missed were determined to provide suitable airports and facilities so that their regions of the country would not be left behind in the great era of progress.

In November, 1927, President Coolidge presented Lindbergh with the Hubbard Gold Medal of the National Geographic Society, saying:

> ... with a clear conception of public service, he determined to capitalize his fame, not for selfish aggrandizement, but for the promotion of the art he loves. This courageous, clearheaded, sure-handed youth, whose character has withstood the glare of publicity and the acid tests of hero-worshiping adulation became an apostle of aeronautics... because of what he has done, aeronautic plans for 1928 indicate an activity far beyond any dreams six months ago.

In many ways, Lindbergh's greatest contributions to aviation were still to come: his ocean survey flights for Pan American; his engineering work on the long-range Clippers; his World War II service as consultant and combat test pilot (many Navy and Air Force fighter pilots owe their lives to Lindbergh's work on fuel conservation). However, none of these activities, important as they were to be, had nearly the worldwide impact of his first Atlantic flight. The imagination of the world responded, as it has not since (even to the first astronaut), to the inspiration of the slim young man conquering ocean, storm and sky.

PART TWO

# Consolidation and the Growth of Government Control

CHAPTER V

## Boeing and the Birth of United

At the northwest tip of the United States, the melted snows from the Olympic Mountains raced down in torrents through tall evergreen forests to the smooth waters of the Duwamish River. Near the mouth of the river on Puget Sound, an earnest young man stood on the deck of his yacht examining the bare ribs of a boatyard he had just purchased. He had bought it to build yachts in, a new one of his own first of all. Hardly a profitable venture, but Bill Boeing could afford it, since much of the rich timberland in those mountains belonged to him.

Lumbering held little interest for his restless, inquisitive mind. Bored with the prosaic aspects of an established business at which he had already proven his ability, Boeing turned to yachting, and then to the designing and building of yachts themselves. But even as his dream vessel took shape on the ways of his boatyard, his thoughts were elsewhere. Ever since he had seen the Frenchman Louis Paulhan race Glenn Curtiss in Los Angeles five years before, Boeing had wanted to fly.

Tall, reserved, and seemingly aloof, his intent eyes owlish and shy behind huge, round dark-rimmed glasses, a clipped mustache over his thin, unsmiling lips, Bill Boeing looked more like a schoolteacher than a wealthy young sportsman. Raised in Minnesota where his German-born father had substantial timber and iron properties in the rich Mesabi Range, Boeing's upbringing had been strict. After his father's death he was sent to prep school in Switzerland. His mother remarried, but Boeing never returned to his family home. Financially independent, Boeing left Yale in 1903, after his junior year, and moved to the Northwest to go into the lumber business for himself. He was successful from the first, and rapidly increased his fortune. Unsatisfied and restless, he roamed the Pacific Northwest, seeking outlets for his imagination in fishing, hunting, and sailing.

Four years passed as Boeing's aviation interest grew. Weekends on his yacht, cruising Puget Sound, he talked flying to his friends between rubbers of bridge. Finally, in 1914, Boeing went to Los Angeles to learn to fly. Glenn Martin ran a flying school there in the daytime and built airplanes at night in a nearby shed. As soon as Boeing had soloed, he bought the plane from Martin and returned to Seattle.

The plane didn't last long. One of Boeing's friends stalled on a steep bank and crashed into Lake Washington. Unhurt, the chagrined pilot swam ashore, but the plane was reduced to splintered wreckage. Immediately Boeing ordered another. Martin replied that he couldn't get around to it for six months or so. Impatient, angry at Martin's delay, Boeing determined to build his own.

The boatyard had it ready in less than six months—by June, 1916. Generally based on the earlier Martin, the new Boeing

## Consolidation and the Growth of Government Control [ 53

had several innovations. On its first taxi test it felt so good that the eager Boeing pulled back on the stick. It flew.

In the summer of 1916, it was clear to Boeing, as well to many others, that the United States would soon be at war. He cleaned out the last of the boat business, hired engineers and designers, and set up an airplane factory in his boatyard to help build war planes. As soon as his factory was ready, Boeing went to Washington to offer his services.

Military aircraft production was then in the hands of the automobile men Coffin and Deeds, who had never heard of Boeing or his airplane factory. They felt that time was too short and production too desperately needed to experiment with the unknown and unproven. So Boeing's shop, financed entirely with his own funds, stood idle and empty, while Coffin and Deeds made government money available to their automobile associates to build airplane factories.

Eventually Boeing was permitted to subcontract some Curtiss training planes, but the end of the war stopped military production completely. Then came painful days, laying off the trained work force so carefully assembled. The sight of the empty factory was depressing, and no new production orders would be forthcoming.

The Post Office had discussed the possibilities of an Air Mail service, but war-surplus planes were plentiful. Little work of a new production nature could be expected from the Air Mail for some time. Without government contracts, most wartime airplane builders went looking for other markets in fields unrelated to aviation. The automobile people quickly converted their government-built airplane plants. But Bill Boeing wanted to stay in aviation and he was willing to risk his own money.

A flying boat seemed to offer the best possibilities for commercial sale. Landing fields were scarce in the rugged country of the Pacific Northwest, but water was plentiful. The resulting

Boeing B-1 was a fine airplane, but there were no buyers. Finally Boeing used it to fly from Seattle to Vancouver to catch outbound ocean liners with the latest mail—thus starting the first private commercial mail service in this country. (That B-1 stands in Seattle today as a monument to that effort.)

Economic conditions in the aircraft industry grew steadily worse. Somehow Boeing kept the doors open, and at last he was able to subcontract some fighters for the Army. Knowing he could design better, safer, more efficient planes, Boeing searched for some idea, some market for the superior ones he longed to build.

By 1926, the U.S. Air Mail had been contracted to private companies on feeder routes for nearly a year. But the Air Mail service had not done much to stimulate the aircraft industry generally. Most operators still used war-surplus planes, or at least war-surplus Liberty engines. The Postmaster General was at last ready to accept bids on the main transcontinental, "Columbia," route. Despite the obvious desirability of a through coast-to-coast service, the Postmaster General ruled that the route be split in two sections—San Francisco to Chicago, and Chicago to New York.

News of the prospective invitation for bids first reached Seattle in *The New York Times*. Up earlier than her husband, Mrs. Boeing read the news and placed the carefully folded paper at her husband's place at the breakfast table.

Things were going badly at the factory. At times Boeing had been forced to pay his men partially in company stock.* Perhaps this was the opportunity he had been waiting for. The operation of an airline, as such, held little appeal for Boeing. For him, the fascination lay in creating airplanes themselves. But if he could demonstrate the practical and economic value of improved

---

* An enterprising foreman picked up substantial amounts of this stock from disgruntled Boeing workers at neighborhood bars on payday. A wealthy man today, he allegedly remains one of the major individual Boeing stockholders.

## Consolidation and the Growth of Government Control  [ 55

aircraft by operating an airline route, American aviation could break out of the rut of surplus equipment.

Boeing pondered the problem on the way to the office. Later that morning he called his top staff together and asked them to evaluate the costs for flying the mail from San Francisco to Chicago on two bases: first, assuming the use of existing aircraft; then, on the basis of the proposed performance of the new Boeing mail plane, as yet unbuilt and untried. The differential seemed promising, and Boeing was willing to take the gamble. He submitted a bid at approximately one-half the going rate.

Everyone in the air transport business had expected that the San Francisco–Chicago route would be won by Western Air Express. Western was experienced and efficient, perhaps the most efficient line then flying. When Boeing's bid (less than half that of Western's) was accepted, the disgruntled losers waited to see the rich Seattle sportsman lose his fortune flying the mail.

Within five months Boeing had designed and built a fleet of twenty-five Boeing B-40's. Big, rugged biplanes designed expressly for mail service, the B-40's were placed in service almost as soon as they were rolled out of the factory doors. To almost everyone's surprise, Boeing made money from the start. The secret was the performance of his new B-40. Behind the plane was a new engine, and behind the engine—Frederick Rentschler.

Rentschler had been an engine man from his boyhood days in Hamilton, Ohio, where his father had started a machinery plant. Educated at Princeton at the same time that Bill Boeing was struggling through Yale, he afterward returned to Hamilton and worked as a molder in the foundry of the Hooven-Owen-Rentschler Company. When World War I broke out, Rentschler enlisted and was commissioned to lieutenant in the Army Signal Corps aviation arm. Knowledgeable in metals and engines, he was assigned to the Wright-Martin Aircraft plant at New Brunswick, New Jersey, to test airplane engines then being built for the Allies.

By the end of the war Rentschler was one of the leading American authorities on airplane engines. He was then invited to head the new Wright Aeronautical Corporation, recently formed (from the ruins of Dayton-Wright) and plentifully financed by New York capital. Confident, intense, and hard-driving, young Rentschler, scarcely thirty years old, put together an impressive staff of designers and builders. He soon made Wright the primary source of power for military and commercial aviation.

The outstanding achievement of the company was the Wright "Whirlwind" air-cooled radial engine. More reliable than the old Liberty, the Whirlwind delivered more power per pound, without the dead weight and nuisance of radiators and coolants. (When asked for the secret of the success of his airlines, Bill Boeing replied that his planes were carrying mail over mountains instead of radiators and cooling water, thanks to Rentschler's engine.)

Good as the Whirlwind was for its time, Rentschler felt that he could build a better one, but the bankers on his board of directors objected to spending more money for the development of new engines when their company already had the best in the field. Frustrated in his desire to improve the design and chafing under the domination of the New York bankers on his board, Rentschler resigned and looked about for new backing and new opportunities.

He found both in the Niles-Bement-Pond Company, machinery builders and owners of the idle Pratt & Whitney tool plant in Hartford. The persuasive Rentschler talked them into letting him have the Pratt & Whitney plant and name, together with $1,000,000 in working capital. Then Rentschler took his pick of the engineering staff he had built at Wright and went to work on a new engine. (In addition to the brilliance of his own

## Consolidation and the Growth of Government Control  [ 57

engineering staff, Rentschler also had the support and backing of the Navy, which was eager to see engine improvement take place and also to achieve a second, and competitive, source of engine supply in this country.) The first Pratt & Whitney "Wasp" engine exceeded all expectations, developing nearly twice the horsepower of the Wright Whirlwind. The Navy ordered all the Wasps Pratt & Whitney could build.

Boeing, whose acquaintance with Rentschler dated from World War I days, followed his friend to Hartford and switched to Wasp power for all Boeing designs. In fact Boeing had to use all of his skill to persuade Rentschler to divert twenty-five Wasp engines from the original Navy order to power the Boeing B-40 mail planes.

The success of the Wasp engine was so great that Boeing found himself more and more closely allied with the fortunes of Pratt & Whitney. Whenever Boeing traveled East, he and Rentschler got together to exchange ideas. One night, after a long philosophical discussion, Rentschler advanced a new proposal to Boeing: why not merge Pratt & Whitney with Boeing Aircraft and Boeing Air Transport to form a vertical, integrated aviation company? They took their idea to Joseph Ripley at the National City Company, the underwriting affiliate of the National City Bank (where Rentschler's brother Gordon was soon to be president). Ripley, today's senior partner of Wall Street's Harriman, Ripley & Company, likes to describe himself as the "corporate midwife at the birth of United." To preclude a personality conflict over the corporate name, Ripley set up a new holding company, United Aircraft and Transport Corporation, swapping its stock for Pratt & Whitney, the Boeing Airplane factory at Seattle, as well as Boeing Air Transport. The aggressive Rentschler became president of the new company, with the more retiring Boeing as chairman.

To round out the United Aircraft and Transport holdings, Rentschler added the Hamilton Propeller Company, and later the Standard Steel Propeller Company, when the new metal blades became an issue in patent litigation. At that time no one could conceive of an airline operation overseas in anything but a flying boat, so Rentschler bought Sikorsky Airplane Company, the leading designer of flying boats and amphibians. National City provided new outside capital. Almost overnight, United became the dominant factor in U.S. aviation.

## CHAPTER VI

## *From Barnstormers to Bankers*

Nostalgic old sailors tell of the sad transformation from the days of "Wooden ships and iron men." So, too, old pilots might talk of the change from "Wooden planes and iron men" to "Aluminum planes and money men."

For the airlines, future growth required public passenger travel. Passengers demanded safety and dependability. New and better equipment was obviously necessary. Lindbergh's thrilling flight and the unexpected financial success of Boeing's airline had demonstrated the technical advances and economic possibilities of improved airplanes. But such new aircraft were also much more expensive than their wooden, war-surplus predecessors. No airline company, however skilled or venturesome its pilots, could continue without substantial capital—and that meant Wall Street and the underwriters.

Actually, the late twenties was the ideal time in which to be seeking new capital. The stock-market boom was in full swing;

everybody in the country seemed eager to help finance almost any new venture. The success of radio and the automobile were the financial keystones of the twenties—and now aviation seemed to offer another similar opportunity. As the role of Wall Street increased, the leadership of aviation gradually passed from the daring individualists of the early days to the less romantic, but equally important, financial and corporate executives.

The first major concentration of power was United—and United was soon in conflict with another emerging giant, Clement Keys' North American Aviation. Keys was a careful, precise, and scholarly individual and native of Canada, where he had taught history before moving to the United States. He settled in New York and joined the editorial staff of the *Wall Street Journal,* later becoming financial editor of the magazine *World's Work.* With his accumulated knowledge and understanding of the financial community, Keys founded an investor's service which he soon expanded into an investment banking house. When automobile man John North Willys bought into the Curtiss company in 1916, he brought Keys along as financial vice-president. The Armistice ended the flow of military appropriations to the aviation industry, and Willys was anxious to get back to his automobiles.

Deprived of government appropriations and with Willys' support withdrawn, the Curtiss company was a hollow shell. Keys bought control for almost nothing. In the lean years that ensued, he kept Curtiss alive with a few orders from the War and Navy departments. But Keys was primarily a financial promoter and had no appetite for the daily routine of manufacturing executive. He often said: "Ten percent of aviation is in the air, and ninety percent of it is on the ground." For him, the 90 percent was organization and finance. From his control of Curtiss, he conceived the idea for the creation of a

## Consolidation and the Growth of Government Control [ 61

giant holding company, North American Aviation, combining manufacturing units as well as a system of airlines.

The first step was National Air Transport, which won the New York–Chicago position of the transcontinental Air Mail route at the same time that Bill Boeing won the Western end. To finance the operation, Keys set about raising $2,000,000. His financial associates in New York, already air-minded and eager for new investment opportunities in this rapidly growing industry, pledged $1,000,000—and more was readily available. However, Keys believed that the other million should be raised in Chicago, to provide a balance in control of the new organization—and perhaps to prevent dominance by his New York associates. (With his own assets limited, Keys always sought several sets of investors to play off against each other in order to keep himself in the driver's seat.)

Through influential friends he arranged a luncheon to which the major figures of Chicago's industrial and financial circles were invited. Before them, in glowing terms, he outlined his plans for National Air Transport. But Chicago's economy rested on railroads and slaughterhouses, and the hardheaded businessmen of that city could see no future in an airline. The dismal luncheon concluded, Keys sat disconsolately, going over the list of attendants with members of the Chicago Chamber of Commerce. One of the Chamber's bright young men casually observed that nearly every man present at the luncheon had a son who had been a pilot in World War I. Keys' inventive mind instantly seized upon the opportunity. He arranged a lunch for the sons on the following day. Guests included Philip Wrigley, Lester Armour, Philip Swift, Earle Reynolds, Marshall Field II, and other men of similar fortune and quality. In less than ten minutes the necessary financing was arranged.

For some unexplained reason, Keys maintained National Air Transport purely as a mail operation, devoting all passenger development to another of his projects, a hybrid air-rail system,

Transcontinental Air Transport, where passengers flew by day and took the train by night. Part of the reason for this split operation was a fear of flying over the Alleghenies (and part was doubtless the influence of the Pennsylvania Railroad which held a major stock interest). However, the success of Boeing's operation between San Francisco and Chicago made a through transcontinental airline system desirable. If the Boeings could clear the Sierras and the Rockies, the Alleghenies should be no barrier.

During 1929, United carried 6,100 passengers to Chicago in the new trimotored Boeing "Flying Pullman." Most were dumped there, because National Air Transport's single-engined mail planes made no provision for passengers. It was increasingly evident that air travelers would not be satisfied with the antiquated railroad precedent of transferring from one system to another in Chicago. (Interestingly enough, nearly thirty years later the railroad promoter Robert Young won an important proxy fight in which his telling slogan was: "A pig can ride from coast to coast without changing trains, but you can't.") Keys' failure to develop a passenger operation made United determined to extend its own.

Rentschler opened United's drive to reach New York in June, 1929, by absorbing Ford Air Services, operating from Chicago to Cleveland via Detroit, and with the additional right to extend its line to Buffalo. With this potential threat of a competitive service via the Ford routes, Rentschler approached the directors of National Air Transport with a proposal to merge. Keys would have no part of such a deal; however, his control was not complete. Operational authority rested largely in the hands of the enthusiastic young financiers who had put up the Chicago quota of the original National Air Transport capital after their elders had cold-shouldered the idea. Chief of the Chicago group was Earle H. Reynolds, the largest individual stockholder, who was also NAT's president. He and his associates owned approxi-

## Consolidation and the Growth of Government Control [ 63

mately one third of the company—and United's proposal seemed appealing.

On April 4, 1930, Rentschler declared war, announcing in *The New York Times:* "From an economic point of view, the air between the coasts is not big enough to be divided." While Keys and Rentschler were denouncing each other in the press, Rentschler's financial agent, Joseph Ripley, was quietly negotiating with the Chicago group. Soon Rentschler backed up his threat with the statement that he had acquired one third of National Air Transport shares through an exchange agreement with certain unnamed shareholders. He then went over the heads of the Keys group and asked all NAT shareholders for proxies for the April 10th meeting, then only five days away. Stocks of both companies traded wildly on the New York Exchange. Time was too short to permit the Renstchler forces to stage a full-scale proxy campaign, but they had a plan to gain time. They intended not to vote the stock under their control, precluding a quorum, thereby postponing the meeting until they had time to line up a majority of shareholders for their reorganization and merger plan.

They reckoned without the legal and financial skills of the North American group. Keys had been a Wall Street reporter for many years, and he had learned his lessons from the railroad barons of the past. Perhaps recalling Jay Gould and his fertile printing press which ground out additional stock in the Erie Railroad whenever Gould's control was challenged, Keys hastily called a director's meeting. The bylaws were quickly amended to reduce the quorum requirements from one half to one third, and to make doubly sure that Rentschler would not capture control, Keys arranged to issue 300,000 new shares of NAT stock and swap them for shares in North American Aviation, the holding company which Keys controlled beyond challenge.

Apparently out-maneuvered, Rentschler turned to the courts. He challenged the legality of Keys' changes in the bylaws and secured an injunction restraining the exchange of the new shares with North American. While Rentschler was in court, his agent, Ripley, lined up NAT shares wherever he could find them. Within a week Ripley had secured 57 percent of the then outstanding NAT stock. This time Rentschler called a special meeting of stockholders.

Keys' associates could see the handwriting on the wall and agreed to an armistice. Ripley sweetened the financial terms, and the Keys group capitulated. United could now fly direct from San Francisco to New York; the first transcontinental airline.

At the time, the loss of NAT did not seem too important to Keys. He still had Transcontinental Air Transport, the combination air-railroad service, as well as Curtiss, and he had recently acquired Elmer Sperry's gyroscope company, which gave promise of helping the airplane conquer weather. (Jimmy Doolittle, flying as a test pilot for Sperry, had been photographed standing nonchalantly on the wing of his airplane, which was being flown only by the unattended Sperry autopilot.) However, the multiplicity of these ventures and Keys' perennial shortage of capital forced him to bring in outside assistance. The partner he chose was General Motors—and General Motors was eventually to devour him. But at the time the deal made sense. Keys wanted money and General Motors wanted an opportunity to expand its aviation activities.

General Motors had already acquired stock in the American Fokker Company. Anthony Fokker, a Dutchman by birth, had offered his talents to the Allies early in World War I. His offer rejected, he went to work for the Germans—and produced the finest fighter planes of the war. We in this country, ever alert to our own shortcomings, sometimes fail to recognize the problems of our enemies. While our military aircraft procurement in

## Consolidation and the Growth of Government Control [ 65

World War I was poorly handled, Germany was also plagued with incompetence in high office. Fokker was clearly the outstanding German designer, but because he was not a native German, he was not favored in the inner circles of the German High Command. As engine performance improved, the more powerful Mercedes aircraft engines were diverted to Fokker's native German competitors in an effort to improve their performance in relation to Fokker's. (The famous Fokker triplane was a result of this policy, since Fokker had to go to the triplane design to achieve competitive rate of climb and maneuverability with a lower-powered engine.)

Eventually Fokker was able to convince the German General Staff that aircraft procurement should be determined by a competitive trial of the various models, their performance to be tested by a group of fighting pilots recruited from the front. Even then, intrigue played a hand. The various German aircraft designers, including Fokker, found it necessary to maintain luxurious quarters, amply furnished with wine and women, for the pilots on the trial board.

At the Armistice, Fokker smuggled his tooling and some disassembled planes across the border in sealed railroad boxcars. Safe in Holland, he designed transports for the Dutch airline KLM. Soon the U.S. air attaché asked Fokker to visit this country (much as German rocket scientists came here after World War II), where Fokker quickly designed a trimotor transport around the new Wright Whirlwind engines. The plane was an immediate success, and General Motors saw a good opportunity to buy in. Its interest awakened by the Fokker transaction, General Motors was eager to participate in Keys' North American Aviation, which soon added Eastern Air Transport and Western Air Express, as well as strong minority positions in Allison, Bendix, and Douglas, to its holdings. For General Motors, the North American deal was not only a good investment—but more important, it gave General Motors a chance to catch up to its archrival, Henry Ford.

For all his genius, Henry Ford was a man of curious complexes and idiosyncrasies. Probably the most influential individual in American industry at the time, Ford had entered aviation apparently inadvertently. His friends were an odd assortment, few of them wealthy or renowned. One such was Joe Brooks, Ford's fiddling crony. One night after a fiddling session, Brooks confided his worry over his son Harry, who could think about nothing but aviation. Brooks asked Ford to take an interest in the boy.

Through young Harry Brooks, Ford met William Stout. Himself a remarkable inventor with achievements in many fields, Stout had become absorbed in aviation before the war. As chief engineer of the aircraft division of Packard Motor Car Company, Stout had worked on an aircraft design to go with the Liberty engine then being built by Packard. By 1918, Stout had become technical adviser to the Aircraft Production Board in Washington.

At the end of the war, Stout drew up a design for an all-metal commercial airplane. To finance this experiment, he sent 100 letters to leading businessmen, briefly outlining his idea and asking them for $1,000 apiece, saying: "You may never get a cent of your money back but you will have had one thousand dollars worth of fun. It's a gamble, but you can afford it. I think it is your duty to go in. Let's call it a gift to progress." Amazingly, 60 of the 100 responded, including such major industrial figures as Ford, Walter Chrysler, William Knudson, Fred Fisher, and Robert Stranahan. With their backing, Stout developed the first all-metal transport aircraft in this country.

Through Stout, Ford became more and more interested in the possibilities of the airplane. Ford had said that the secret of success in life was to see how much you could give for a dollar instead of how much you could get, and the possibility of a new and better airplane whetted his interest. At first his reaction was dubious. "That thing will never amount to anything until you can get it to back up." But, before long, Ford bought out Bill Stout for $1,000,000. All of Stout's original backers saw their investments tripled.

Stout continued to design for Ford and soon had the famous Ford Trimotor flying. The Trimotor represented an attempt to apply automobile production-line methods to the building of aircraft. Ford immediately recognized the limitations in performance caused by excess weight. The first objective of the design was strength; the second was lightness. Passenger comfort came last. However, thanks to Ford's weight consciousness, the Trimotor outperformed all of the world's existing transports in speed, range and economy of operation. Affectionately known as the "Tin Goose," the Ford Trimotors were dependable, easy to fly, and able to operate out of small, unpaved fields.

Though the prestige of the Ford name contributed immeasurably to public confidence in aviation, Henry Ford himself refused to fly. (His only exception was a short ride with Lindbergh.) One day young Harry Brooks, trying for a Detroit–New York nonstop record in a midget plane, overshot his goal and was lost at sea. Deeply grieved, Ford lost interest and gradually withdrew from aviation. (Although production ceased in 1932, one Ford Trimotor is still in scheduled passenger service in this country and several more in out-of-the-way spots around the world.)

The last of the great aviation holding companies was Aviation Corporation, or AVCO. Apparently inspired by the success of United, AVCO was sponsored by some of the proudest names on Wall Street. W. Averell Harriman was chairman of the board, and Robert Lehman of Lehman Brothers was chairman of the executive committee. There were sixty-seven other directors, men of prominence in every phase of American industry. While the management and board of directors represented a cross section of the most impressive financial talent in the United States, there was at no time either a definite plan of operation or a management team of prior experience in the aircraft industry.

Unlike United, which had a vertical, integrated operation, AVCO was a horizontal structure, particularly vulnerable to operation problems. Despite this weakness, 2,000,000 shares were eagerly subscribed at $20 each by an enthusiastic public, and AVCO immediately began buying properties, anything and everything that pertained to aviation. In the airline field AVCO acquired Colonial Airways (fallen on evil days since the departure for Pan American of its original guide, Juan Trippe) serving New York, Cleveland, Boston, and Montreal; Universal Aviation Corporation, operating from Cleveland, Chicago, St. Louis and Louisville; Embry-Riddle, from Chicago to Cincinnati; and Southern Air Transport, wandering across the face of Texas and ranging as far eastward as Birmingham and Atlanta. In addition to these airline operations, there were charter services in Alaska and Cuba, flying schools, a variety of airplane and aircraft engine facilities, a motor busline (apparently misleadingly titled to suggest an aircraft company), a broadcasting station, and an aerial photography organization. At the peak of its mood of acquisition AVCO had about eighty subsidiaries. On the basis of total mileage it represented perhaps the largest air transportation system in the United States, but its 9,000-mile collection of routes was utterly incoherent and patternless.

Meanwhile the boom continued and stock prices kept rising. The acclaim accorded to Lindbergh carried over into public demand for aviation stock, producing jumps in value of several hundred percent. Through the holding companies, concentrations of capital became available for the next step in the airlines' development: consolidations of the existing fragmentary routes into national airline systems.

CHAPTER VII

# Wall Street and Washington

"The business of America is business," said President Calvin Coolidge, "and it wants a business government." In less than a century business had transformed the nation from a rural agricultural economy into intense urban industrialization. As living standards rose the businessman became the leading figure of the country, his influence spreading to broader fields,* culminating in the ultimate responsibility for putting government on a "businesslike basis."

In 1928, Coolidge ("I do not choose to run") was replaced by his Secretary of Commerce, Herbert Hoover, famed and respected as "The Great Engineer." Like his Republican predecessors, Hoover believed in business—but with subtle differences. As

---

* The best-selling book of 1926 was *The Man Nobody Knows* by Bruce Barton, a head of the advertising agency, Batten, Barton, Durstine and Osborn, in which Barton praised Christ as history's greatest businessman, who "took twelve men from the lowest walks of life and built them into the greatest sales organization the world has ever known."

an engineer, his approach was that of a professional man with a standard of responsibility to society as a whole, beyond the salesman's crass commercialism. He saw business, not as business alone, but as an opportunity for service where profit was not the goal, but rather the byproduct.

As President, Hoover dedicated his Administration to mobilizing the economy of the nation to his great purpose: the abolition of poverty. To this end, he sought efficiency, cooperation, and "a rising vision of service which would unite society and business in a new sense of dedication and cooperation." He believed that business organizations which had formerly been controlled by arbitrary individual ownership, now—through the mass distribution of stock ownership—had become rather an association of thousands of partners in a single enterprise. Accordingly, managers of such concerns should develop community, rather than selfish, interests, and business organizations should move toward cooperation and efficiency. Hoover saw the nation, "passing from a period of extremely individualistic action into a period of associational activities." Overall, he urged the business community into collective action against "waste and overreckless competition."

In no other area of the economy were Hoover's principles carried out so expressly as in the airline industry, through the efforts of his Postmaster General, Walter Folger Brown, who singlehandedly shaped the industry from a random assortment of short, unconnected mail routes into the basic transcontinental airline system we know today.

Brown was an Ohio lawyer, long active in Republican politics, and then chairman of the Republican National Committee. Tall, thin, correctly and immaculately dressed, precise in word and action, his hard eyes and steel-rimmed glasses reflecting his earnestness and purpose, Brown was all efficiency. From his role as Assistant Secretary of Commerce under Hoover, Brown had

## Consolidation and the Growth of Government Control [ 71

moved over to function as Hoover's campaign manager. Upon his election, Hoover followed time-honored tradition and appointed his chief political lieutenant Postmaster General. From the Inauguration ceremony, Brown returned to his mahogany desk in the Post Office Department to review his responsibilities and authority. In the black-leather portfolio of a Cabinet officer, he read that it was his duty "to encourage commercial aviation . . . and contract for the Air Mail service."

Like the able lawyer he was, Brown began an intensive study of U.S. commercial aviation, and the various Air Mail contractors lost no time in bombarding the new Postmaster General with their respective arguments and requests for greater privileges. True to the traditions of private enterprise, each company sought a greater share of government business. However, the more Brown learned of the industry, the more offended he became. At the time, the airline industry consisted of forty-four different companies, nearly all of them small, undercapitalized, and solely dependent upon government contracts for survival. As Lindbergh, Boeing, and other prophets had seen long since, there was little incentive for progress either in aircraft design or airline service as long as cheap single-engined planes were adequate for the mail. Passengers imposed great burdens of safety and service, vastly increasing the costs of operation. Per pound, mail was probably ten times as profitable as passengers— and a lot less trouble.

The real question Brown faced was how to relate his statutory duties "to encourage commercial aviation . . . and contract for the Air Mail service." What was the proper role of government Air Mail contracts? If the only purpose was the carriage of mail, then the present system of competitive bids was acceptable. The pressure of competition did generally assure the mails being carried at the lowest cost to the government—and certainly it was the fairest method of allocation. But there was a definite drawback to competitive bids; the effects of this drawback were evident already. Faced with the annual threat of losing mail contracts to lower bidders, operating companies were unwilling to invest in new equipment. Any shoestring company, however marginal its operation, posed a constant threat. As long as this system prevailed, Brown saw the industry tied forever to government support, with short-term investment, small lines, obsolete planes, and poor safety records, all resulting from cost-cutting practices. The only objective for most companies seemed to be to get government mail contracts—understandably so, since a government contract meant the difference between profit and loss. To Brown, the Air Mail business was "like a kennel at feeding time," each operator fighting all others for each morsel of government money. Those without contracts fought for one; those with contracts fought for bigger ones. Where was the "encouragement of commercial aviation"? The more he reflected on the problem, the clearer it seemed to him that the solution lay in eliminating competitive bidding. Mail pay should then be used to support only those companies which were strong enough to contribute to the development of commercial aviation.

In keeping with his President's philosophy, Brown saw business as an opportunity for service. The aviation industry had before it an ideal opportunity to contribute to the welfare of the nation by developing a new system of air transportation. Against this background, Brown could only look with disfavor on those operators who refused to share his vision. As long as competitive bidding prevailed, government support would go, not to the progressive developer, but rather to that operator who cut the most corners, flew the cheapest equipment, and took the greatest risks.

The railroads offered a parallel to the Postmaster's thoughts. Their contribution to economic development was incalculable, but their benefits accrued only after they had reached maturity and stability. The early days of the railroads were chaos; like the

## Consolidation and the Growth of Government Control [ 73

airlines, a jumble of short, uncoordinated routes. Furthermore, the railroads' development was marked with a long series of unsavory episodes: shameful stock manipulations, cutthroat competition, bribed legislatures, tragic accidents caused by cost-cutting operations, etc. Brown determined that it was his destiny to lead the airlines out of chaos into order.

United's transcontinental system had shown what could be done with imagination, effort, and adequate financing. Correspondingly, Brown determined to consolidate the other existing, fragmentary routes into independent, competing national systems. Bigger, safer planes would be built. All aviation would benefit. In time, with the growth of passenger revenues, the airlines' dependence on mail-subsidy requirements would be reduced. To achieve these objectives, Brown proposed new legislation to (1) eliminate competitive bidding and permit contracts to be let either by negotiation, or by extension of existing routes; and (2) compute mail payments on the basis of capacity flown, whether needed for mail or not. Thus airlines and manufacturers would have real incentives to provide large aircraft, with the unused mail space available for sale to passengers. As a further encouragement to progress, additional payments were also provided for multiengine equipment, radio, and other safety measures.

Brown carefully laid the necessary Congressional groundwork for passage of his bill. But for such an experienced politician, he made a serious blunder: he failed to consult Congressman Clyde Kelly, the sponsor of the original Air Mail Act of 1925. Congressmen's egos are notoriously sensitive, and Kelly considered himself the spiritual godfather of all Air Mail legislation. There followed one of those curious contradictions of human nature often manifest in American politics. Although he was previously on record as favoring the new legislation in principle, Kelly now fought it bitterly. Marshaling forces on the floor of Congress, he succeeded in striking the crucial clause authorizing the Postmaster General to contract by negotiation. Brown was furious—but half a loaf was better than none. Other powers were still available; perhaps the authorization for negotiation would not be necessary after all.

Following the passage of the new Air Mail Act in April of 1930, Brown called representatives of the major airlines to Washington. In the imposing office of the Postmaster General he revealed his plans for a new national air transportation system. He began by saying that he had been deeply impressed with the success of United. The only line operating coast to coast, United was, in addition, the only line making money and the only Air Mail line carrying passengers. It was, in short, precisely the kind of operation which the Postmaster General wished to see developed. But as long as United alone offered such service, it constituted a monopoly. Much as Brown disliked reckless competition, he disliked monopoly more. True to his President's principles, Brown sought efficiency and stability in business; but he also sought competition. While open competition was preferable to monopoly, regulated competition would be better than either.

Accordingly, Brown proposed to develop two other transcontinental lines which could provide competition for United, but over different routes. One line would run from New York through Pittsburgh, Saint Louis, and Kansas City, to Los Angeles, paralleling United's New York–Chicago–San Francisco route. Another would run from New York and Washington, south through Atlanta, Dallas, and Oklahoma City, to Los Angeles.

Brown concluded the meeting with the seemingly naïve proposal that the operators themselves work out a plan to integrate the existing companies into the structure he envisioned, compensating the integrated companies for the loss of their routes and identities. His proposals were received with uniform dis-

## Consolidation and the Growth of Government Control [ 75

taste. The small operators feared the larger; the larger disliked being told what to do; and United, the only line which conformed to Brown's plans, saw the Postmaster General's proposals merely as a device to generate competition which would damage its business opportunities. Under these conditions, it is not surprising that the requested proposals for compliance with the Postmaster General's desires were slow in coming.

Annoyed at the delays and lack of cooperation, Brown fell into that great weakness of businessmen in government. He began to confuse the methods of private and public business. Clear in the conviction of his own rectitude, he arbitrarily selected those companies he personally believed most suitable and cooperative and proceeded privately with his plans. In his own mind there was no element of favoritism involved. Brown was convinced that the country needed the new transcontinental airline systems. Such systems would require centralized management and strong financing. Smaller operators could either cooperate or get out. Brown recognized that the smaller companies had performed useful pioneering work—but those days were over. The new, improved equipment required integrated organizations for the full realization of their potential.

The Postmaster made no secret of his plans, nor of his scorn for the non-cooperating smaller companies. He felt they had lived out of the public pocket too long and deserved no further consideration. As he explained it:

> There is no point in taking Federal money and dishing it out to every little fellow who is flying around the map and not doing anything to develop aviation in a broad sense ... the thing to do is to spend that money so that, if possible, we could develop some people who would compete with each other and bring their aeronautical industry up to a point where it could finally sustain itself. Helping some little fellow make good his losses for a few years and having him and the country no further along than when we started—there is nothing in that.

The simultaneous creation of two new transcontinental airlines was hardly a simple task, but Brown was undaunted by the magnitude of the effort. Seeking strength and stability,* he almost inevitably turned to the two other major aviation holding companies, AVCO and North American, as the only existing sources of capital adequate for the task of providing competition for United—and for each other. Although eager for the opportunity, the two groups were deeply distrustful of each other, and Brown was forced to hold their respective hands and keep them in line every step of the way.

As the basis for his proposed central route, Brown picked Transcontinental Air Transport, the combined air-rail passenger service which was then operating without a mail contract. TAT was loosely associated with Western Air Express, through the North American Aviation holding company—and Brown determined that the two should merge. However, Western had already spurned two earlier private proposals from TAT. "Pop" Hanshue of Western had no desire to fly across the country. He felt comfortable with the runs which his pilots had mastered and on which he was making a substantial return. TAT, on the other hand, had lost money from the beginning, and Hanshue saw no future in merging into a losing proposition. Believing himself secure in a mail contract over his old routes, Hanshue turned down all proposals.†

While Hanshue was playing hard to get, another company

* Brown believed that shaky finances would lead to slipshod safety procedures. Many other responsible men in the industry have shared this view. In fact, several recent nonsked crashes have been traced at least in part to cost cutting.

† Hanshue also felt that he and his line would lose their identity and freedom by coming under the dominance of TAT and the parent North American Aviation group. His darkest suspicions seemed confirmed when it was suggested to him that he might wish to order some of the new Curtiss Condor planes, built by the manufacturing affiliate of North American. While it was a safe and comfortable airplane, the Condor had notoriously poor altitude performance, and Eastern pilots had reportedly had some trouble clearing the Alleghenies. Asked when he might like delivery, Hanshue, thinking of the Rockies and the Sierras, burst out: "Not before we have a tunnel through those goddamn mountains."

## Consolidation and the Growth of Government Control [ 77

entered the picture, Pittsburgh Aviation Industries Corporation. The board of directors of PAIC was stocked with the leading figures of Pittsburgh industry, including representatives of the Mellon family. At the time of the incorporation of PAIC, the intention was to undertake a regular airline service across the state of Pennsylvania. Upon being advised by the Department of Commerce that scheduled passenger service over the mountains was impractical until the lighted airway with its attendant radio stations and emergency fields was completed, PAIC had operated a flying school and a charter service out of the Pittsburgh airport. Because of its expense and effort in pioneering aviation in Pennsylvania, PAIC felt that it had an equity in the newly proposed central transcontinental route. There was some justification for this position, since TAT—the major company on the proposed new route—had never flown in Pennsylvania prior to that time. (The operation of TAT involved carrying passengers over the Pennsylvania railroad out of New York, across the Alleghenies, and into Ohio during the night so as to avoid the rugged terrain in eastern Pennsylvania.) Postmaster General Brown recognized certain justification in the PAIC position and agreed to incorporate it in his plans. The management of TAT was not openly hostile, and at this time Hanshue and the Western people had not as yet agreed to any kind of a merger at all.

While discussions on the proposed merger between Western, TAT, and PAIC were proceeding, a complication arose in the form of Pittsburgh Airways, a charter service which had in fact started the first passenger service over the Alleghenies, although on a random and unscheduled basis. Pittsburgh Airways was less generously financed, and its civic backing was of a lesser order of prominence; nevertheless, it had carried passengers over the Alleghenies whereas PAIC had not. Therefore, Pittsburgh Airways felt that any future Air Mail contract awarded in Pennsylvania belonged to it. When it presented its case in Washington, Brown explained that he was interested in a through transcontinental system, not a single intrastate line. Accordingly, he favored PAIC over Pittsburgh Airways, since PAIC was willing to join in the proposed transcontinental system, whereas Pittsburgh Airways wished to stay independent and operate on a local basis only.

Despite the logic of Brown's statements, the management of Pittsburgh Airways felt that it was being discriminated against because of the social prominence of members of the PAIC board of directors. Pittsburgh Airways people made some unpleasant noises to this effect around Pittsburgh and Washington for several months, hoping for a change in Brown's attitude. (There were claims that Secretary of the Treasury Andrew Mellon had made a deal for PAIC with Postmaster General Brown during a Cabinet meeting.) Eventually it became clear that Brown intended to advertise for bids only on a "through" basis. In that case it was hopeless to continue to seek a local route. At the last minute Pittsburgh Airways made an agreement with two other small companies to join together and submit a bid on the "through" route themselves. One of the other lines was United States Airways, operating between Kansas City and Denver; the other was Ohio Transport, which claimed to have carried some passengers between Youngstown and Dayton, Ohio. Combined, the three companies—calling themselves United Avigation—could hardly have claimed to constitute a through system or an integrated operation, but they nevertheless planned to submit a joint bid for a transcontinental route.

The formation of United Avigation forced Brown's hand. He believed it incapable of providing safe, competent service—but it could be very troublesome unless the TAT-Western merger took shape at once. In no mood for further foolishness, Brown told Hanshue that there would be no contract of any kind

## Consolidation and the Growth of Government Control  [ 79

for Western unless the TAT merger went through without delay.

The last stumbling block to the merger was AVCO, which owned a major 20,000-share block of Western stock and could thereby obstruct the merger. Although AVCO's airline subsidiary, American, had been promised the southern transcontinental, AVCO feared that the proposed TWA group might get greedy and try for both. Solemn assurances were given by Brown and TWA—and AVCO grudgingly withdrew its objection to the merger. A new corporation, Transcontinental and Western Air, Inc., was formed, with 47.5 percent of the stock going each to TAT and Western, and the remaining 5 percent to PAIC. Muttering and disgruntled, the colorful Hanshue moved East and took over the presidency of TWA, complaining bitterly about Eastern politics, weather, and women. Despite the transcontinental mail contract, the new company was soon in financial difficulty.

Through its prior participation in North American Aviation, General Motors had a significant interest in TWA and had nominated as its directors two remarkable General Motors vice-presidents, Charles E. Wilson (subsequently chairman of General Motors and Secretary of Defense under President Eisenhower) and Ernest R. Breech (later to become president of Bendix, chairman of Ford, and finally to return to TWA in 1960 as chairman, as well as one of the bank-nominated trustees for Howard Hughes' stock).

Trained as an accountant, incisive and candid in comment, the crisply mustached Breech had risen in General Motors through its bus and motor-coach division and was familiar with transportation accounting and management. Because of his background, he soon became the dominant force at directors' meetings. To executives of the caliber of Breech and Wilson, the management situation in TWA was appalling. Trouble reached a head with the crash of a TWA Fokker, killing Knute Rockne, the famous Notre Dame football coach, and inspiring a Congressional investigation. Breech took over as chairman and installed a complete overhaul of the system.

Even with its management squared away, TWA's political troubles were far from over. To preclude what he termed "wildcatters" (such as United Avigation), whose operational safety and financial stability he distrusted, the Postmaster General had inserted a clause in the request for bids requiring night flying experience. United Avigation had ignored this requirement and had submitted a bid two-thirds that of TWA. Disqualified immediately by Brown, United Avigation filed a formal protest with the Comptroller General, who, after considerable delay, ruled that United Avigation was qualified to bid and should be awarded the contract.

His plans in jeopardy, Brown countered that, apart from their lack of prior experience, United Avigation's bid was unrealistically low, hence incompetent, and a potential safety risk. (It is significant to note that, even with its higher bid, TWA lost more than $1,000,000 during its first year.) With the Comptroller General favorable to the case of United Avigation and Congressional interest increasing over the cause of the "little fellows," it became essential for Brown's plans to eliminate United Avigation at once.

The method Brown chose was quite simple. A key component of the Avigation group was United States Airways, flying (without a mail contract) between Kansas City and Denver. Brown awarded this mail route to American—at the maximum permissible mail rate. American, at Brown's direction, immediately sublet the route to U.S. Airways. The subcontract was far more profitable than any potential gain from participation in the Avigation group. U.S. Airways quickly withdrew—and the opposition of United Avigation collapsed. TWA was secure in possession of the central transcontinental system.*

Turning his attention to the planned award of the southern route to American, Brown ran into more trouble, primarily from Earl Halliburton. A tough Oklahoma oil millionaire and cousin of the famous adventurer and travel author Richard Halliburton, Earl had been experimenting with an air passenger service in the Southwest. While the line lost money, a mail contract might have made it profitable. But Halliburton was not in a position to offer transcontinental service, nor could the economies of the type of flying he had performed fit into the more difficult and demanding system. Brown looked upon Halliburton as one of the "wildcatters" who had no interest in the development of the airline industry as such, but merely wished to take their turns at the public trough. Halliburton was associated with William P. McAdoo, Woodrow Wilson's Secretary of the Treasury, and Brown felt that he was trying to make political trouble. Halliburton in turn charged that Brown was discriminating against him because of his Democratic associations. Carrying his battle to the press, Halliburton offered to carry all first-class mail across the country at half the existing rates. Experienced operators felt that Halliburton's proposal was an impossibility, but his claims began to stir public criticism. Before long the entire industry was in a turmoil. Fearing the effect on his long-range plans, Brown felt himself forced to buy off Halliburton.

The price of Halliburton's cooperation was high—$1,400,000. American paid it in the form of a purchase of Halliburton's airline (which he admitted was not worth half that amount). But American refused to absorb all the hush money itself, demand-

---

* Scandal still dogged TWA's footsteps, in that the President's son, Herbert Hoover, Jr., was a radio engineering consultant to TWA—suggesting that patronage was part of the transaction. Young Hoover resigned and, with United Avigation already out of the running, controversy eventually subsided.

ing that TWA make a contribution. Accordingly, TWA purchased the 20,000 shares of Western owned by AVCO, plus some other property of dubious value, for the identical amount, $1,400,000.*

So at last Brown's master plan was accomplished. Three major airlines now spanned the nation, and the basic structure of the airline industry had taken shape.

* Despite their obvious collusion, American and TWA were, to the end, deeply distrustful of each other. Regardless of the agreements entered into between them, the representatives of the two lines appeared for the formal submission of bids so suspicious of each other that each had prepared a full bid over both routes, in case the other appeared to be deviating from the proposed agreements.

## CHAPTER VIII

## *The New Deal*

The stock market crash shattered America's faith in itself, in business, and businessmen. People who had lost their ideals after World War I, now lost their savings and their jobs as well. The dream of prosperity which had seemed "just around the corner" in 1929, gave way to the harsh reality of poverty. The nation was crushed by a force it had not foreseen and did not understand. Misery and despair sought some explanation for this condition. As frustration mounted, the inevitable search for political scapegoats began.

Obvious targets were businessmen and bankers whose talk of prosperity and sale of now worthless stocks seemed somehow to be behind all the suffering. Hoover and his business government were quickly turned out of office, and Franklin D. Roosevelt's New Deal brought promise of investigation and reform.

There was obviously much that needed reform in the business and banking practices of the twenties. A shocking series of scandals was soon disclosed. The heads of the nation's two greatest banks were involved in disgraceful conduct. Albert H. Wiggin, president of the Chase Bank, was revealed to have used inside information to make a quick killing in the market. The most spectacular of Mr. Wiggin's operations were the successes he enjoyed in selling short the stock of his own bank—after which he smugly announced reduced earnings, or other unfavorable business news about his own institution. Even more galling, the short sales of Mr. Wiggin were financed by loans from the bank itself. And then there was the head of the National City Bank, Charles Mitchell (later to be called "Charley Mitch, the son-of-a-bitch"), who had not only used inside information for his personal profit and grossly misused bank funds in his dealings, but in addition had participated in a scandalous series of tax evasions.

The aristocratic Richard Whitney, head of the New York Stock Exchange, had the poor judgment to gamble with his customers' funds—and lose. Perhaps most disturbing of all were the disclosures of J. P. Morgan, the younger. The Morgan name had been the very symbol of strength and stability in the financial market. Twenty years before, the elder Morgan had been called upon to testify at other hearings on financial practices. Then the stately gentleman had replied with profound dignity: "The first thing is character. Before money or anything else. Money cannot buy it. A man I did not trust could not get money from me for all the bonds in Christendom." Now Morgan's son told a different story—"Preferred lists": a group of friends and "special customers" to whom the House of Morgan sold stock at prices substantially below the public market. Other major Wall Street houses had their preferred lists also, including the names of nearly all the prominent figures of the twenties, Democrats as well as Republicans. Embarrassingly, members of Franklin Roosevelt's Cabinet were involved, including the Secretary of the Treasury. (Other Cabinet members urged the resignation of those so involved, but Roosevelt disagreed, saying that many people had done things in 1929 they would not think of doing in 1930.)

Of all the New Deal investigations, one of the most sensational, linking business wrongdoing with high Republican officials, was Senator Hugo Black's hearings on the Air Mail contracts of former Postmaster General Brown.

Today Hugo Black is a justice of the Supreme Court, widely respected for his liberal philosophy and concern for civil rights. However, in 1932, Black was the junior Senator from Alabama, just beginning his second term in the Senate and ambitious for wider recognition. The son of a country shopkeeper, Black was raised in the red-clay country of Alabama, acquiring the rural prejudices of the poor whites against the wealth and power of the rich cotton areas. He was educated in the local schools, taking a degree in law at the University of Alabama. There followed a rough-and-tumble career as a police court judge and prosecuting attorney, and inevitably, politics. In those days in Alabama, local politics meant the Klan. In the rural areas of the South, the Klan not only stood for white supremacy, but also for local rule in opposition to the dominance of big-city money and politics. With his election to the Senate, Black dropped his Klan affiliations, but he was not always entirely in support of New Deal legislation. Historian Arthur Schlesinger, Jr., in his sympathetic biography of the New Deal, *The Age of Roosevelt,* reported that Black "became hysterical" over the prospect of a Federal relief plan which might feed Negroes as well as whites. But even stronger than his white Southern prejudices was Black's country-bred antagonism toward big business.

Black's committee was formed during the lame-duck session of Congress, before Roosevelt's inauguration, to investigate the mail contracts by which the government subsidized our Merchant Marine. The chairmanship offered a splendid opportunity for publicity to advance a political career, but the prospects for really significant scandals in the Merchant Marine investigation were dim. Shipping subsidies lacked popular appeal, particularly in competition with the truly sensational revelations of those committees investigating business activity in the stock exchanges.

At this point Black was introduced to Fulton Lewis, Jr., then a young Hearst reporter, recently graduated from the University of Virginia. Lewis had a friend who had worked for the Ludington Line, an airline passenger service operating between New York, Philadelphia, and Washington. The Ludington Line had been founded by a pair of prominent Philadelphia brothers, on the concept that passenger service could be profitable, even without a mail contract. In September of 1930, the Ludingtons had introduced a new type of airline service, with planes leaving between New York and Washington every hour on the hour. (This obviously attractive airline service was thereafter ignored by the major airlines from the Ludingtons' time until Eastern's "Shuttle" plan started in 1960.) The Ludingtons flew trimotor Stinson monoplanes, operated on an economy basis. To save gasoline, the Stinsons were taxied to the runway on only one engine. They took off on high-test aviation fuel, but once aloft they cruised on cheaper automobile gasoline. By such economies, the Ludington Line became the first carrier in the history of commercial aviation to show a profit without government assistance or subsidy through mail contracts.

Already marginally profitable without a mail contract, the Ludingtons sought to increase their earning power by the addition of a government mail subsidy, feeling that they had earned the right by virtue of their successful operation. To their surprise and extreme annoyance, the contract they sought between New York and Washington went instead to Eastern Air Transport on a bid three times that of theirs. Curious at this discrepancy, Lewis dug into the files of the Post Office Department and discovered similar cases. Before long he had developed a damning indictment of apparent favoritism by Postmaster General Brown in awarding Air Mail contracts.

At this time Lewis was married to the daughter of an arch political rival of the Postmaster General, and it has been alleged that his curiosity in the Air Mail contracts had a personal, rather than a reporter's, interest behind it. Regardless of personal pique, the evidence gathered by Lewis was sufficiently sensational to arouse any worthwhile reporter's interest, but to Lewis' surprise and annoyance, his exposé of the Air Mail contracts was not approved for publication by his boss, William Randolph Hearst. Frustrated and angry, Lewis was not unwilling to see his material fall into the hands of Senator Black. With Lewis' material, Black had evidence on which to base a personal crusade against the practices of big business and the previous Republican Administration.

The various smaller operators who had been denied contracts by Brown were ardent allies of Lewis and Senator Black. Eager for revenge, the smaller operators presented Black with a picture of sinister monopoly power strangling free enterprise.

Reading the testimony today in the light of history, it seems clear that Black was confused by personal prejudice.* His indignation at some of the organizational and financial practices of the airlines caused him to overlook the companion question of airline progress. In Black's hands the hearings became more of a prosecution than an investigation. With his leading questions concentrated on market manipulations and securities flotation, Black ignored the issue of advances in aircraft development, passenger service, or safety. Opportunities for cross-examination were not available, and witnesses were not given full

---

* Regrettably, Justice Black refused to discuss any aspect of his investigation with the author.

opportunity to develop arguments to refute charges. Black's daily summations (announced just at presstime so that any reply would have to wait for the next edition) made two basic points: first, that small, independent airlines had been forced out by sinister Wall Street interests seeking to monopolize Air Mail subsidies; and that such corruptors of the public treasury made exorbitant profits for themselves in stock manipulations.

Black seemed to make no effort to equate the good with the bad, or to present the alternatives as they existed at the time of the decisions. For instance, in the case of the award of an Air Mail contract between New York and Washington to Eastern Air Transport instead of to the Ludington Line, the facts were as follows: Eastern offered a major route network, north and south along the eastern seaboard; it was doing the kind of job that Postmaster General Brown felt the country needed; on the other hand, the Ludington Line operated only over 200 miles of airway. Ludington was willing to carry mail for 25¢ a mile over this 200-mile segment, only because it was supported by the heavy passenger traffic between the nation's largest city and the Capital. Ludington was not willing to provide service at the same rate over any other segment. In other words, Ludington wanted to pick the choicest section of the system and get it on its own terms. No airline system could be built to span the nation, if that system had to meet the competition of rivals bidding only for the short, most profitable sections. (This identical problem arose twenty years later with the advent of the so-called "nonsked" operators who wanted to skim the cream of the passenger market between the major cities with their war-surplus C-54's.)

Unable to meet the competition of Eastern Air Transport, Ludington might have been forced into bankruptcy and disappeared, for Eastern was clearly under no legal obligation to buy out a defeated competitor. Instead, Eastern paid a substantial price for Ludington, since Brown had made it clear that the

## Consolidation and the Growth of Government Control [ 89

equities of the situation demanded that Eastern buy out Ludington as a condition to receiving the mail contract itself—hardly the act of a sinister monopolist.

But Black ignored such mitigating factors, perhaps himself caught in the wave of public indignation his charges had generated. In the depths of the depression, there was a strong psychological urge to prosecute and punish those who had made money in the market where so many others had seen their lifetime savings and security wiped out. Accordingly, Black turned to the financial backgrounds of the airline companies. The irony of the situation was that Black concentrated his fire on United Aircraft & Transport, without doubt the outstanding company in the industry. Boeing and Rentschler had put United together long before Postmaster General Brown had instituted his plan of mergers and consolidations for a national transportation system, and were in fact substantially damaged by the new competition created. Moreover, it was the example of United that inspired Brown to establish the new systems to provide competition for what he considered United's monopoly. United had been the pioneer in providing better and safer equipment, radio facilities, and whatever else was needed for improved safety and service. On the manufacturing end, the Boeing planes with Pratt & Whitney engines were the finest in the world. By developing Pratt & Whitney, Rentschler had significantly reduced the prices that the government paid for military aircraft engines by instituting a second and competitive source to the Wright factory. Brushing aside these obvious national benefits, Black instead concentrated on the profits made by Boeing and Rentschler.

Rentschler's original cash investment in Pratt & Whitney was less than $1,000. In addition, of course, Rentschler provided his time, engineering and management talent, and risked his future on the outcome. When his engineers built the best engines in aviation, his company prospered. With the company's success, the price of its stock rose rapidly, also pushed along by the general market boom. Black took none of this into consideration. Instead, he computed what Rentschler might have gotten had he sold all his stock at the peak of the market boom—perhaps as much as $35,000,000. The fact that Rentschler had not sold was not deemed relevant. Black's only concern seemed to be that Rentschler could have profited enormously had he sold out. (By the time of the hearings in 1934, Rentschler's shares in United were worth less than 20 percent of their peak value.)

In addition to his stockholdings, Rentschler had an incentive compensation contract with the company whereby he was paid a percentage of the company's profits. Such contracts were then, as now, common business practice, particularly at the advent of a new and untried business. As United became outstandingly successful, Rentschler's contract provided him with a substantial income. Black argued that such an arrangement was immoral and unjust in any company doing business with the government.

Not that the airline industry was blameless—far from it. The error was that Black focused on the wrong targets—and for the wrong reasons. Lobbying activities had been carried on to a disgraceful degree. American had advised its Washington representatives that it was better not to itemize their expense accounts, thereby permitting freer distribution of favors and entertainment for government officials. TWA arranged jobs for relatives and made liberal "loans" to Post Office officials. Senators' relatives were hired for "advice." Clearly, the procedures whereby Brown arranged to break up the United Avigation group to permit the TWA award and to "take care" of Halliburton and free American's routes, do no credit to anyone involved.

But in all such transactions, as in the airline meetings with the Postmaster General, which Black characterized as "Spoils conferences," there was never a shred of evidence that Brown stood to benefit in any way, financially or otherwise, from any of the activities he undertook. Despite every effort to impugn his honesty and intentions, there could be no question but that throughout Brown acted only for what he conceived to be the best interests of the nation.

Out of all the testimony and evidence presented, certain facts were indisputable. The three largest aviation holding companies, United, Aviation Corporation, and North American, ended up holding 24 of the 27 federal Air Mail contracts. In many cases, lower bids by smaller operators over certain routes had been rejected in favor of contracts at a higher price to the major carriers. However, whenever a smaller carrier was deprived of the contract awarded to a larger, Brown made it a condition of the transaction that the larger carrier buy out the smaller at a fair price. Of course the "fairness" of the price is always a matter of dispute, particularly to the smaller carriers, but the fact remains that had the smaller carriers not been bought out by the larger, their properties would have become totally worthless. The really important question, whether such concentrations were necessary or beneficial to the development of aviation, was not considered by Black. Had he made any effort at a constructive inquiry into national aviation policy, Black could have performed an important service.

Instead, in the same manner and tone with which he had conducted the whole investigation, he summed up his case with a blanket, undiscriminating indictment: "The control of American aviation has been ruthlessly taken away from the men who could fly and bestowed upon bankers, brokers, promoters, and politicians, sitting in their inner offices, allotting among themselves the taxpayers' money."

Nevertheless, there was sufficient evidence to make Black's statements plausible. It is likely that he believed them himself. But his sincerity was widely doubted, even among members of his own party, some of whom (including Democratic Postmaster

General Farley) called him a "publicity hound." In any case, Black had worked himself up into a state of righteous indignation during the course of his hearings.

Late in January, 1934, Black was invited to lunch with President Roosevelt at the White House. The usual friendly manner of the President could not daunt the flow of indignation and wrath poured forth by Black. He argued that the Air Mail contracts had been obtained by fraud and conspiracy and urged the President to cancel all contracts immediately. At first Roosevelt was reluctant, but he could not help being impressed by the intensity and bitterness of Black's presentation. The lunch ended and Roosevelt said that he would think it over for a few days.

Meanwhile, Black had turned over his evidence to Carl Crowley, the Solicitor General. Crowley gathered the voluminous data into a hundred-page report and presented it to Farley—with a recommendation for cancellation. Farley thumbed through the pages and looked up. "I can't wade through all that, just tell me about it." It took Crowley some time, for the details were complicated, but eventually the story was presented in sufficient detail to convince Farley that they should go to the President.

Crowley and Farley drove to the White House the following afternoon. It was dusk when they were arranged in a semicircle around the desk of the President. Farley briefly recited what he had been told, with Crowley prompting. From the record and subsequent testimony, it seems clear that neither Roosevelt nor Farley ever actually read the evidence themselves, relying for their judgments entirely upon the presentations of Black and Crowley. Throughout, Farley's approach was moderate. Assuming that Black had a case, Farley still wished to postpone any cancellation until later, using the intervening time to advertise for new bids. By this procedure Farley could avoid interruption in the Air Mail service. The President, egged on by

Black, gradually swung over to a more dogmatic view. Since Black had convinced him that the contracts were crooked, Roosevelt determined upon immediate cancellation.

Even his most sympathetic biographers acknowledge that Roosevelt, particularly in the early days of his Administration, was inclined to be too quick in his decisions, often forming his judgments on brief impressions, rather than on detailed study. Such apparently was the case in the Air Mail situation. In an experimental mood, the only remaining problem for Roosevelt was to determine whether the Army could carry the mail.

The chief of the Army Air Service, Brigadier General Benjamin Foulois, was summoned to the White House. Unsuspecting the magnitude of the decision he was about to make, he was admitted to the President's study. As Foulois approached the President's desk, Roosevelt looked up, smiled disarmingly, and asked whether the Army was qualified to carry the mail. Poor Foulois really had no choice. With the echoes of Mitchell's charges of incompetence and unpreparedness ringing in his ears, he could scarcely admit that his men could not perform the mission the President was about to assign. On the other hand, in the middle of a February winter, Foulois knew that his planes and pilots were not up to the standard of performance that would be expected of them. Benny Foulois set his jaw. "Yes, sir," he said, through tight lips.

The Air Corps assumed responsibility for the mails during the worst weather of the winter. Savage February blizzards, gales, sleet, fog, and intense cold, lashed the nation. Army pilots were not experienced in bad-weather flying; few were even prepared for night flying; none knew the routes they were expected to follow. And the standards they were expected to meet were extremely high. The last private transcontinental mail had set a new speed record.

The cancellation order had been a complete surprise to the airlines and to the nation as a whole. Jack Frye, then vice-president of TWA, was determined to make its last transcontinental flight a memorable one. On the concrete ramp in front of the Douglas hangar in Santa Monica stood a brand new DC-2 transport which had not yet gone into scheduled service. Its silver skin did not even carry airline colors. But Frye knew that it was the fastest and best transport plane flying. Grimly, he strapped himself into the left seat. His copilot, Eddie Rickenbacker, then general manager of Eastern Air Transport, adjusted the radios. Weather reports from the East were threatening—heavy snow expected over the Alleghenies. Under ordinary conditions, Frye would have postponed his take-off, but with the cancellation taking effect at midnight, he felt he had no choice. They were on instruments before Chicago, but with a strong tail wind, decided to go ahead. All other planes had long since been grounded when they touched down on the snow-packed runways of Newark, with the last mail carried by private contractors and a new transcontinental speed record.

The Army pilots had neither the planes, experience nor training to meet this standard. In spite of the odds, they tried. Within a week, 12 pilots were dead and 6 more were seriously injured. The combination of bad weather and inexperience had been too much.

The country was appalled. Eddie Rickenbacker, the leading wartime ace, denounced the decision to have the Army fly the mails as "legalized murder." For the first time since his election, a decision of Franklin Roosevelt's was seriously challenged in the eyes of the public. Most effective of all was the opposition of Lindbergh. With the possible exception of Roosevelt himself, no man in America was more popular. In the years since his dramatic flight, Lindbergh's quiet modesty and hard work had preserved the integrity of his position. The kidnapping and

*Consolidation and the Growth of Government Control* [ 95

murder of his infant son had deepened his place in the nation's affections. Lindbergh sent Roosevelt a sharp telegram:

> YOUR PRESENT ACTION DOES NOT DISCRIMINATE BETWEEN INNOCENCE AND GUILT AND PLACES NO PREMIUM ON HONEST BUSINESS. YOUR ORDER OF CANCELLATION OF ALL AIR MAIL CONTRACTS CONDEMNS THE LARGEST PORTION OF OUR COMMERCIAL AVIATION WITHOUT JUST TRIAL.

Lindbergh was right, and he was the one man in America with the popularity and prestige to take the case to the public. His position was underscored by the fact that the Army experienced more difficulty daily. Lost, off course, wings covered with ice, Army pilots were forced down everywhere along their routes.

Ironically, the burden of responsibility fell, not upon Black or Roosevelt, but on Postmaster General Farley as the man who had signed the cancellation order. One newspaper cartoon depicted him guiltily ignoring the accusing skeletons of dead Army pilots. Farley accepted the public responsibility without complaint, although he subsequently wrote in private: "I was hurt that the President had not seen fit to divert the wrath." (Actually, Roosevelt had little choice, since he could not place the blame on Black without revealing that he himself had acted without full knowledge of the facts; instead Roosevelt later appointed Black to the Supreme Court.)

The cancellation of the Air Mail contracts and the Army Air Mail episode dealt a serious blow to the prestige of the New Deal. The experience also raised serious doubts as to Roosevelt's judgment and the quality of his advisers. In theory, the Army had been called in because the airlines were making exorbitant profits on air mail. But the average cost of flying the mail under the Army was $2.21 per mile, compared with the average figure of 54¢ by the airlines.

For the first time since his inauguration Roosevelt was clearly on the defensive. He had to find a way out as soon and as gracefully as possible. Early in March he told the Secretary of War that: "The continuation of deaths in the Army Air Corps must stop." Thereafter the Army drastically reduced its mail flights until the weather improved. Simultaneously, Roosevelt asked Congress for new legislation permitting private Air Mail contracts.

Roosevelt's request for new legislation to return the Air Mail from the Army to private hands gave Senator Black another opportunity. The resulting Air Mail Act of 1934 forced the separation of airlines from manufacturing operations, banished all executives who had met with Postmaster Brown, and reopened all airline routes to competitive bidding. At a time when all other New Deal legislation was directed toward more centralized planning and price stability, there is a certain irony that Black's legislation should expose a vital industry to the pressures and cost cutting of open bidding in the midst of the depression. The vertical United integration was split into three parts: United Airlines, Boeing, and Pratt & Whitney. North American Aviation sold TWA to the Atlas Corporation and Lehman Brothers, and concentrated on aircraft manufacture. AVCO spun off American Airlines. A good argument can be made that the long-run effect of such split-ups was beneficial, but in the middle of the depression the Black legislation deprived most airlines of their leadership and caused serious financial difficulties.

CHAPTER IX

*Reconciliation, Regulation and Subsidy*

Reconciliation is never easy, particularly if it means admitting mistakes—and there were plenty of mistakes on all sides. After the fiasco of the cancellation, the immediate problem for Roosevelt and Farley was how to give the mail back to the private airlines with as much grace as possible and still save face.

Farley had one group of ardent allies in his corner—the former smaller operators who had been denied mail contracts by Republican Postmaster General Brown. Hungry and eager for revenge, this group had its knives ready to carve up whatever part of the airline system it could get. Had the major airlines been the collusive group they had been accused of being, they could have held out and made things much more difficult for the New Deal. Instead, they were as ravenous for contracts as ever, the large as well as the small. Under these conditions Farley was able to insert a face-saving requirement that no airline represented at meetings with Brown could bid on the new route. Faced with these requirements, the major airlines immediately put into effect superficial reorganizations: Eastern Air Transport became Eastern Airlines; American Airways became American Airlines, and so on. In this way the airlines retained their basic organizations, and at the same time Farley could claim that he had purged the evil elements.

The leader of the independents was Tom Braniff, president of Braniff Airways. Braniff had started in Oklahoma City as a sixteen-year-old fortune hunter in 1900. By 1917 he had entered a variety of businesses successfully—insurance, farm loans and real estate. Tom Braniff's younger brother Paul was one of the early pilots, buying a Stinson airplane and flying it on company business. But since there was not enough company travel to keep the ship busy, Paul Braniff hit upon the idea of a passenger service between Oklahoma City and Tulsa, to occupy his spare time. Three times a day he ferried what passengers he could find between the two cities. Subsequently the Braniffs expanded into Kansas and Missouri, but the operation was not successful and they lost money steadily. Finally Tom Braniff, tired of the losses, sold out to Universal Aviation Corporation, a subsidiary of AVCO; apparently a condition of the deal was that Braniff would thereafter stay out of the airline business.

However, before long, Braniff heard of the possibility of government subsidies and determined to try again. By 1931, he was operating a line between Oklahoma City, Wichita, and Kansas City. This new line competed with a portion of the American Airways system formed from the old Universal group. The larger airline held mail contracts already, and Postmaster General Brown could see no contribution to the national system by giving an additional mail subsidy to Tom Braniff. There was considerable feeling also that Braniff was not a man of his word, having re-entered the aviation business after he had previously

### Consolidation and the Growth of Government Control [ 99

sold out. Some felt that Braniff was merely operating a nuisance line as an attempt to blackmail a subsidy from the government. When the Postmaster General refused to give Braniff a mail contract, Braniff became an implacable enemy of Brown and the Republican Administration.

Under the new administration, Braniff and the other independents, who had not previously held mail contracts, enjoyed a great advantage. They could bid almost as low as they dared, with reasonable assurance that Farley would grant liberal future increases in mail pay, since the New Deal could hardly put them in business and then let them fail. Under such conditions it is really quite surprising that the old airlines won back as many of their former routes as they did. When the smoke had cleared, the only major change was that United had lost its Chicago–Dallas run to Braniff. However, to be sure of getting their old routes back, some airlines' bids were ridiculously low, sometimes less than one cent per mile. Overall, mail pay was reduced nearly 50 percent on a national average.

The Army handed the mail routes back to the private airlines the first week in May, 1934. After its tragic beginnings, the Army had improved its service. Using new Curtiss attack planes and Martin bombers in relays, Army Air Mail pilots brought the last cargo of mail from San Francisco to Newark in 14 hours and 8 minutes. The time was over an hour slower than the record set by Jack Frye in the Douglas DC-2 with the last load of private mail three months earlier, but was an impressive performance nevertheless.

Not to be outdone, Frye himself again set out to carry the first load of private mail for TWA, this time choosing the new Northrop "Gamma" high-altitude research airplane. Flying solo, he brought the mail into Newark 11½ hours after take-off from Los Angeles, another new transcontinental record.

But the airlines needed more than a new record. By the middle of the summer all the major lines were on the point of suspending operations. United Airlines had lost nearly $1,000,000 since the start of the year, and TWA nearly as much. Even though most of the airlines had their old routes back, mail payments were less than half their former amounts, and the depression cut deeply into airline traffic and revenues. The Black committee hearings had been the worst kind of publicity, and the ensuing series of Army crashes seemed to have shaken the confidence of potential passengers.

Hardship shared often unites the bitterest enemies. So it was with the airlines during the depression. Deprived of a comfortable cushion of mail pay, each desperately strove for what little profit lay in the passenger market. Every airline was haunted by the specter of increasing competition. In their struggle for survival, recent rivalries were forgotten and the airlines made common cause.

Although the government was not the only reason for their troubles, most airlines executives chose to regard it as such. "The government got us into this and now it's their responsibility to get us out," was the prevailing attitude. Official Washington felt much the same way. The Roosevelt Administration could not afford to have the entire air transportation system of the nation fail as a result of New Deal action.

A number of drafts of new aviation legislation were introduced to Congress. New Federal regulatory agencies were springing up on every hand, and Washington was a vast struggle for power, with every existing activity seeking to maintain jurisdiction and authority already granted and to gain whatever else might come to hand. The departments of Commerce, State, War, and the Post Office, all wanted a piece of aviation. President Roosevelt himself was said to favor putting the airlines under the control of the Interstate Commerce Commission. On

## Consolidation and the Growth of Government Control [ 101

the other hand, most aviation enthusiasts held out for a new, separate agency.

To resolve the many differences, the President appointed a committee at the assistant-secretary level from each of the competing departments, bureaus and commissions having any claim to commercial aviation. Eventually the members of the committee narrowed down to two primary viewpoints; those who supported control in the Interstate Commerce Commission, and those who sought a new agency. The President was represented on the deliberative commission in the person of his son Jimmy, then serving as his confidential secretary. Jimmy Roosevelt gradually tended to side with those seeking an independent agency, and so convinced his father.

The airlines had meanwhile formed themselves into a powerful and well-financed trade organization, the Air Transport Association, in order to present their case more effectively. Speaking in behalf of the airlines, the president of the ATA argued that they were in a state of crisis, claiming that:

> Of the $120,000,000 of private investment which has been made in American air transport, more than half is gone. This condition of financial starvation not only makes it impossible for these lines to take full advantage of possible technological improvements, but could lead to traffic competition of such intensity that the accident ratio might accelerate instead of decline. Failure to correct the existing situation and to do so promptly, means more than loss to the capital remaining invested in the air transport industry, to the labor employed in it, and to this country's position in civil aviation. It may very well entail a large cost in human life.

A pretty dismal picture—and pretty threatening words. In effect, the airlines of the United States were saying that unless the government provided support and regulation immediately, the airlines could not be responsible for any deaths which might follow. Roosevelt was squarely on the spot. His Supreme Court packing plan had only recently failed—generating considerable public disapproval. Memory of the tragic fiasco of the Army Air Mail episode was still fresh. The New Deal could not afford another setback. Unless favorable legislation was immediately forthcoming, the risk of any airline accident lay on the New Deal. Regardless of the actual cause, public reaction was likely to be that the deaths were caused by the delay of the Congress and Administration. With this gun at their heads, Roosevelt moved swiftly.

The resulting Civil Aeronautics Act of 1938 * gave the airlines almost all that they desired. The routes of the then existing (so-called "Grandfather") airlines were protected, and the threat of outside competition was practically eliminated. Furthermore, a generous subsidy was provided, in effect a blank check. The carriage of Air Mail need no longer be on a contract basis, subject to competitive bids. Instead, government mail pay was to be awarded to a carrier on the basis of "need." Unless a carrier could be shown to be willfully fraudulent or inefficient in his management, he no longer had to fear losses. The government stood ready not only to make up any deficit, but also to insure a return on his investment. All in all, the Civil Aeronautics Act seemed to be a bonanza for the airlines, and the major figures in the industry greeted its passage enthusiastically.

Besides the security of the new Civil Aeronautics Act, the airlines also benefited from significant technical advances, culminating in the great Douglas DC-3. The DC-3 was actually an improved version of the DC-2, which was in part based upon

---

* Under the original Civil Aeronautics Act, both economic and safety regulations were combined under a single Civil Aeronautics Authority. Later reorganizations separated economic regulation into an independent five-man body, the Civil Aeronautics Board. The safety functions were for a time in the Department of Commerce and are now in the Federal Aviation Agency.

## Consolidation and the Growth of Government Control [ 103

the Boeing 247, the first modern, low-wing airliner with retractable landing gear, first introduced in 1931. The great advantages of retractable gear had been apparent for some time, but it was felt that the mechanism and housing requirements would be too complicated and too heavy for general application. Not until Grover Loening produced the first successful amphibian airplane (which had to have its landing gear foldable, to permit landing on water) was it obvious that retractable gear was a practical possibility. Boeing learned the Loening lesson and incorporated it in the Model 247, one of the significant design changes in the history of aeronautics. For all its epochal design characteristics, the career of the 247 suffered from two incurable management decisions. The original Boeing design had called for a 16,000-pound plane, designed around the new and more powerful Pratt & Whitney "Hornet" engine. Seeking support for the new design, Boeing took a poll of the airline pilots, to determine their desires. Pilots are a notoriously conservative group regarding advancement in aircraft design, partially because of inherent caution and partially out of fear that advanced aircraft will lessen their job opportunities. They distrusted the new Pratt & Whitney Hornet engine, preferring the old, reliable Wasps, and feared that the 247 might be too big and too fast. The pilots' poll resulted in the scaling down of the Boeing design until it was far less than the ultimate technical achievement of its time.

Even so, the streamlined Boeing was an obvious step forward from the lumbering, ungainly trimotors. There was nothing else flying which could touch it, and the other airlines rushed to Boeing, seeking the new model. In an effort to preserve a monopoly position for United Airlines, the parent board of directors prevented the sale by Boeing of any of the new models to any other line until United's entire sixty-plane order had been delivered. Boeing protested the decision; the United order would not be completed for three years. If the other lines were not permitted to have at least a token number of the new planes, they would turn to other manufacturers and Boeing might lose the market entirely.

As predicted, TWA turned to the small plant (originally a movie studio) of Donald Douglas, then recently come to Santa Monica. Douglas had previously been shop manager for Glenn Martin, but had gone out on his own after a policy disagreement with chief engineer Larry Bell (who was also soon to start his own company). Douglas had limped along on a series of military orders until TWA's interest brought him the commercial opportunity he had been waiting for. The existing design of the Boeing 247 made Douglas' job easier. The 247 had demonstrated the practicality of all its major design and technological breakthroughs; however, it had been scaled down when it should have been scaled up. In essence, that is what Douglas did. The original pilots' objection to the Boeing 247 had centered on the higher landing speeds inherent in a bigger, more powerful plane. Douglas met this objection with the use of landing flaps—creating an airplane which has been called the "most forgiving" of its type ever to fly, generously tolerating pilots' errors from its first flight to the present. The combination of bigger plane and bigger engines gave the Douglas DC-2 and its improved version, the DC-3, the capacity, speed, and range which changed passenger flying from a marginal operation to a profitable one. No aircraft in history has been so successful so long. By 1938, all major domestic airlines were flying the DC-3.

Protected by the CAB from the threat of outside competition or price cutting in fares, serene in the assurance of subsidy support, and equipped with the efficient and economical DC-3, the airlines passed out of the dark days of depression into a new period of expansion and growth.

PART THREE

# Across the Oceans

CHAPTER X

# Instruments of Empire

Transportation has been the essential instrument of empire from the beginning of recorded time. Carthage ruled the Mediterranean with her triremes; Imperial Rome built her empire on roads; Genghis Khan moved to conquest on horseback. Guided by compass and courage, Portuguese and Spanish sailors found their fortunes beyond the oceans. With the defeat of the Spanish Armada, the tiny island kingdom of England dominated the waters of the world, creating a vast empire. Railroads opened the West and built a great nation in the United States.

The development of the airplane as a vehicle of transport and communication made all prior systems obsolete. Faster than boat or train, conqueror of ocean, mountain, and jungle, the airplane was essential to empires of the future.

The earliest and most rapid development in international air transport logically came from the colonial nations, primarily the French and Dutch. The third great colonial power, England, lagged somewhat behind, complacent in her trust in the British Navy and Merchant Marine.

France had long fancied herself the leading nation in international aviation, from the faltering flight of Louis Blériot across the English Channel in 1909. By 1914, French aircraft design was demonstrably superior to that of any other nation. At the end of the war, Pierre Latecoere, an industrialist from Toulouse who had manufactured military aircraft, began a limited mail service between Toulouse and Barcelona. In 1919, Latecoere flew across the Mediterranean to Rabat in French Morocco, and presented Marshal Louis Lyautey with the morning edition of the Paris *Le Temps*. The great French colonial leader wept with joy and vowed support for Latecoere's airline. Lyautey arranged a formal government subsidy, and Latecoere's biplanes soon crossed the Sahara to Dakar and the rich cocoa and ivory towns of Africa's Gold Coast.

By 1925, service was expanded to South America. From Dakar, on the bulge of Africa, fast express steamers carried the mail across the 1,500 miles of ocean to Natal on the coast of Brazil, where waiting planes carried on over Brazilian jungles, over the pampas country, across the Argentine to Buenos Aires, and later over the awesome Andes themselves.

One of the pioneering French pilots in Africa and South America was Antoine de Saint-Exupéry whose writings in *Night Flight* and *Wind, Sand and Stars* are among the most memorable in aviation literature. Of these early days, Saint-Exupéry wrote:

> He who had flung a bridge over the Sahara was now to do the same over the Andes. They had given him a plane whose absolute ceiling was 16,000 feet and had asked him to fly it over a mountain range that rose more than 20,000 feet into the air. His job was to search for gaps in the Cordilleras. He who had studied the face of the sands was now to learn the contours of the peaks, those crags whose scarves of snow fluttered rest-

lessly in the winds, whose surfaces are bleached white in the storms, whose blustering gusts sweep through the narrow walls of their tricky corridors and force the pilot to a sort of hand-to-hand combat.

Meanwhile, other daring French pilots of a similar company called Air Orient were flying East, across the Balkans and the Middle East toward Saigon and French Indo-China. French airline subsidies were by far the largest in the world at the time, and France was well rewarded. The regional companies, later combined as Air France, operated over more route miles than any other airline, a distinction Air France has maintained over the years.

The Dutch were a nation of seafarers and merchant traders, who had built a colonial empire many times the size of their motherland. Always subordinate to the British on the sea, the Dutch, like the French, turned their hopes to the air. Although the kingdom of the Netherlands is one of the smallest countries in Europe, it rapidly built up one of the largest and most efficient airline systems in the world. By 1927, Royal Dutch Airlines, known everywhere as KLM (for the formal Dutch name which translated literally becomes "The Royal Air Traffic Company for the Netherlands and Colonies, Limited"), had extended service beyond the confines of Europe, across the Middle East and India, down the Malay States to the island of Java and the Dutch East Indies.

The key to KLM's success was Albert Plesman, who until his death in 1953, was the only possible challenger to Juan Trippe as the dominant figure in international aviation. As a Dutch Army lieutenant, Plesman founded KLM in August 1919, as a government-owned airline (some shares have been sold to the public, but the Dutch government still owns 71 percent of KLM today). Its earliest service was operated between Amsterdam and London, using converted British DeHavilland DH-9's, with

British pilots. Before long, the obsolete British DeHavilland (itself an improved model over the DeHavilland DH-4's which continued to dominate Air Mail operations in the United States for nearly another decade) was replaced by the world's first commercial cabin monoplane, designed by the brilliant Dutch engineer Anthony Fokker. Fokker was initially discredited in his native country because of his work for the Germans during the war. But Dutch national pride and his superior designs soon combined to recommend his planes to their national airline.

KLM's equipment and service have always been the finest available. When Fokker moved to the United States, Plesman convinced the Dutch, alone among the great airline powers, to give up any attempt to operate KLM with aircraft of national manufacture. Instead, Plesman bought the best that was available on the world markets. KLM was the first foreign line to operate the Douglas DC-2 and DC-3 in the thirties, and today KLM operates DC-8 jets.

For England, trade with her colonies constitutes her very lifeblood. On every English map, appropriately, the colonies of the Empire are shown in red, connected by red lines marking the trade routes, the storied "Red Routes of Empire." Secure in the supremacy of her Navy and Merchant Marine, England was slow to turn to the airplane. Following the armistice, the British government was reluctant to grant the necessary subsidies. Nevertheless, several private companies undertook air transport operations. Handley-Page, which had produced the best English wartime bomber, instituted service between London and Paris, and later London and Brussels, in converted military models. Several other smaller lines also operated on intermittent bases. None of these operations were profitable, and by 1921 all British civil air transport had gone bankrupt. Parliament then granted a small subsidy to enable Handley-Page to renew London–Paris service. A similar small subsidy was also extended to the Daimler company, but in the face of the heavily subsidized competition from the continent, the British fared badly. In 1923, a committee appointed by the Secretary of the State for Air recommended the merger of all lines then operating into one nationalized company, Imperial Airways. The primary purpose of Imperial was to develop service to the Empire, a matter of economic necessity as well as political prestige.

India was the first goal of Imperial Airways. By 1925, the route was laid out and surveyed. In proper Empire fashion, the passage to India was by way of Egypt and Suez, for the Red Line of Empire sought to cross no more foreign soil than was absolutely necessary. Airports were few in the outer regions, and soon the British turned to the flying boat, for water was the common denominator of the British Empire. England to Bombay took 20 days by the fastest steamer; 33 days to Hong Kong; and 40 to Australia. Imperial Airways soon covered the journey in a week, flying only by day and permitting passengers to sleep in first-class hotels during the night.

Of all the world's early airline powers, the Germans were of most concern to the United States. The French, English and Dutch, occupied with their existing colonial empires, increasingly turned to Africa, India, and the Orient. However, Germany, frustrated in her past colonial efforts in these areas, sought to penetrate South America, and her primary instrument was the airplane.

For a defeated nation, Germany had developed civil aviation in record time. By the Treaty of Versailles, Germany was forbidden to manufacture aircraft, and restrictions were placed upon any German international airline operation. Despite these limitations, German development was rapid. As early as 1921, a German company opened service to Moscow from Berlin. The Junkers Company established an airplane factory near the Russian capital. Fokker supplied a military aviation unit, training at a secret Russian base with fighters from his plant in the Netherlands.

To prepare for the day when Germany might be permitted to operate an international airline under her own name, the Germans began to set up "local" operations in various countries around the world, particularly in South America.

In Brazil the Germans incorporated a "local" line, Sindicado Condor, flying between Rio and Pôrto Alegre. Sindicado Condor was more than a "local" operation, however; it was in fact the base of German airline operations throughout South America. Brazil occupied a strategic position, being the nearest South American country to Europe and also containing a large German population.

Another "local" airline was started in Bolivia: Lloyd Aéreo Boliviano. The mountainous terrain of Bolivia made surface travel particularly difficult, therefore offering air transport an ideal opportunity. German residents in La Paz, the Bolivian capital, were so anxious for airline service that they purchased the first Junkers airplane for LAB and presented it to the airline. The Bolivian government was soon induced to grant a fairly large subsidy.

The master plan for German operations was to develop local operating experience and strong national support for the "local" lines. After an appropriate period of consolidation, the local lines would be connected with a trunk service operating from Germany. Initial efforts in this direction involved a combination airplane and steamship service. Limited at home in her airplane development, Germany had persevered in the lighter-than-air field, producing a remarkable fleet of dirigibles. Soon German dirigibles were making regular air crossings of the South Atlantic. No means of air transport has ever been so luxurious or comfortable. The great craft floated, seemingly motionless, without noise or vibration. Passengers had individual staterooms, as on the finest ocean liners. There were great dining halls and saloons with observation windows. But the dirigible was slow and at the mercy of the winds.

To improve the South Atlantic service, Sindicado Condor bought a giant Dornier flying boat, the DOX. The DOX was an enormous plane, well ahead of its time, powered with twelve Curtiss engines, but apparently pilots were afraid to fly it across the South Atlantic. For nearly two weeks the German officers daily bid their friends good-bye at their African base, boarded the flying boat, and taxied out across the length of the harbor. At the end of the taxi run they would cut the engines, turn around and return to dock, claiming that they were unable to get the heavily loaded boat off the water. The airline management, convinced that skulduggery was afoot, without warning assigned a new captain and chief engineer. During the night the new chief engineer whittled wooden blocks to fit behind the throttle quadrants. When the captain pushed the throttles forward for the take-off run, the flight engineer dropped the wooden blocks in place. The other members of the German crew pulled back so hard on the throttles that the handles were bent sharply. But the flying boat stayed in the air—all the way to Brazil.

The Germans also turned to the use of smaller aircraft catapulted from mother ships, but fuel requirements for the flight were so large that the payload of the aircraft was held down to 100 pounds of mail. The take-offs themselves were from British waters, and it was rumored that the British had granted operating rights to the Germans in order to see that the French had competition on the South American route, since the British could not provide it themselves.

By far the most troublesome of all the German "local" airlines was their SCADTA operation in Colombia. SCADTA had been founded in 1920 by a pioneering Austrian pilot, Dr. Peter Paul von Bauer. The airline was equipped with Junkers aircraft and manned by German pilots. For Colombia, with its rugged terrain and inadequate transportation facilities, SCADTA performed an important service. Before long the company had woven itself deeply into the country's economic life. A particularly important political element was the fact that Germany permitted its nationals to acquire the citizenship of the foreign country in which they might be living at the time. To the intensely proud Latin Americans, this feature was of great significance. Although the entire operation, personnel and aircraft might be German, the Colombians could claim that it was their airline, since all the personnel had also acquired Colombian citizenship. With typical Teutonic efficiency, the Germans took over the post-office system, even to the extent of selling its own postage stamps. More and more, Colombia became dependent upon SCADTA.

Encouraged by his success, von Bauer made plans to extend his airline, and began survey flights throughout the Caribbean area. Lindbergh had warned that foreign airlines were far ahead of those in this country, and SCADTA's plans proved his point. The Navy became increasingly concerned over the security of the Panama Canal. The stage was set for the entrance of Pan American.

CHAPTER XI

## Juan Trippe in the Caribbean Laboratory

Pan American is today the most famous airline in the world; its giant jets a familiar sight at almost every major airport. Its home office, the Pan Am Building, towers above the skyline of midtown Manhattan—the world's biggest office building, symbolically rising out of a railroad station.

This remarkable growth is the product of the dynamic dream of one man—Juan Terry Trippe. Deceptively diffident and mild-mannered, Trippe looks more like a banker than a visionary airline prophet and pioneer. His career has been marked by constant controversy and criticism. His achievement is a tribute to the fundamental accuracy of his vision. Revered and reviled, praised and criticized, he stands alone in the field of international air commerce—an empire builder in the classic sense.

Using the Caribbean as a laboratory, Trippe worked out the techniques which were to make Pan American the model and envy of the world. What was immediately available concerned him not at all. His reach always exceeded his grasp. Firm in vision and faith, he looked beyond the present. When the future became the present, he alone seemed prepared for it. To others less farsighted and prepared, Trippe's anticipation appeared uncanny—and even suspicious. His opponents often charged that Trippe had seduced the government. In reality, more often than not, he was successful because the government could find no one else prepared to perform the same services.

Trippe was born in New Jersey in 1899, the son of descendants of English settlers who had come to Maryland two centuries before. His mother, in a moment of fancy, named him for a favorite aunt, Juanita Terry. The resulting Juan was an invaluable entree in Latin America during the pioneering days, when it was assumed that some dark Spanish blood flowed through his veins.

The Trippe name was already a distinguished one. A schooner named the *John C. Trippe* fought in the battle of Lake Erie in 1813, and since that time there have been several ships in the United States Navy bearing the name. Trippe's father spent his life on Wall Street, heading his own investment firm. Young Juan was educated at the Hill School in Pennsylvania. Entering Yale in 1916, his prewar career was undistinguished. Reserved in manner, solid in physique, he played guard on the football team. But in the company of his brilliant classmates, such as articulate Henry Luce, founder of *Time,* and the dashing "Sonny" Whitney, Juan Trippe was not readily noticed.

In December, 1917, he left college to enlist in the Naval Reserve Flying Corps, soon winning his wings and an ensign's commission. The war ended before Trippe could go into combat, and he returned to Yale in the Sheffield Scientific School, where his postwar college career as a glamorous Naval officer and pilot was somewhat more colorful.

In 1921, Trippe organized the Yale Flying Club with friends

who were later to be his associates in Pan American for many years, Cornelius Vanderbilt Whitney and William H. Vanderbilt of New York—along with Harvardman John Hambleton of Baltimore. The Yale Flying Club prospered, and Trippe and his friends made a name for themselves in various meets throughout New England. Upon graduation in 1922, Trippe joined the investment firm of Lee Higginson & Company as a salesman, preparatory to following his father (who had died the previous year) in a Wall Street career. But the job held little attraction; aviation was in his blood. Within a year he felt stifled by the routine and paper work.

In the summer of 1923, Trippe learned that the Navy was selling some of its surplus seaplanes. His bid of $500 each was accepted for nine of these planes. With them he organized the Long Island Airways, of which he was president, sales manager, pilot, and mechanic. The company was what is now known as a fixed-base operation, ferrying people around New York and Long Island, with an occasional charter flight perhaps to Florida or Canadian fishing grounds. At its peak, Long Island Airways employed six pilots, but the operation was not successful. Trippe had trouble with the dependability of his pilots, complaining that they would run off to give exhibitions at fairs, returning late, and perhaps hungover. Nor was the equipment satisfactory, requiring constant maintenance. The overhead mounted, and Long Island Airways was forced to suspend operations.

The failure of his company was a hard blow for Trippe, not only financially, but also emotionally. He now had to endure the jibes and criticisms of his family and friends, who looked askance on the airline venture and felt that he was jeopardizing a secure Wall Street future. Fortunately for Trippe, within a short time the Post Office Department announced its intention of turning the Air Mail over to private operators. Trippe located his old Yale Flying Club friends and persuaded them to join him in a new airline venture to carry mail from Boston to New York. Putting up $25,000, which remained from his father's estate, he received similar amounts from John Hambleton, Sonny Whitney, and Bill Vanderbilt, thus capitalizing the new company, which they called Eastern Air Transport (not to be confused with the present Eastern Airlines) at $100,000.

Meanwhile, in Boston another group, Colonial Airways, had similarly bid on the Boston–New York route. Rather than fight a competitive struggle (and early revealing a characteristic approach to the problem of competition) Trippe persuaded the Colonial Airways group to join forces. Since Colonial had a paid-in capital of $200,000 and was a somewhat more seasoned prestige group, Trippe agreed to the condition that its nominee, a middle-aged war hero named General John F. O'Ryan, be placed as a figurehead president, but soon no one could question the fact that Juan Trippe was the real head of the enterprise.

It is a matter of considerable pride to Trippe to this day that he won the first Air Mail contract let to private operators in the United States. Colonial Airways began flights over Civil Air Mail Route 1, between Boston and New York, in December, 1925, at first carrying mail, with the idea that passengers might be added sometime in the future if there was a demand. Busy days followed for Trippe and Colonial; eager and ambitious, he handled both operations and management. When the New York–Chicago route was opened for bids in 1926, Trippe fought his board for authority to enter a bid, eventually gaining permission, but losing out to the National Air Transport group organized by Clement Keys.

Difficulties with the older, more conservative, directors of his company continued. When Anthony Fokker, the designer of the famous German fighter planes, came to this country to sell his then advanced trimotor design, Trippe was struck immediately with the possibility of the airplane. He felt that the large, multiengine plane, with its safety and comfort, was what was needed to introduce air transportation to the traveling public. Always alert to the possibilities of publicity, Trippe had his press agents stress the advantages of the airplane. (On one occasion a high tea was served with great elegance to selected passengers on a flight over New York.) But the $37,000 price tag on the Fokker was far greater in the eyes of Trippe's board of directors than any advantages accruing from it. His order for two of the machines caused the dissension to become acute. In a bitter boardroom battle, he and his friends were outvoted. Frustrated and angry, they sold their stock to the other directors and withdrew the cash to start a new company. Without Trippe, Colonial limped along for a time, eventually being absorbed into what is now American Airlines.

Trippe's new company was somewhat grandiosely named The Aviation Corporation of the Americas. The first operation was a charter service from New York to Atlantic City for summer bathers. Late in that summer of 1927, Trippe learned that the Post Office was considering an Air Mail contract between Key West and Havana. He and Hambleton hastened to Florida to look over the situation. Two outfits were already in residence: Florida Airways, headed by the famous war ace Reed Chambers; and another group, Pan American, Inc.

Pan American owed its inception to Major Hap Arnold, later to command the Army Air Corps during World War II. Disturbed at reports from our military attaché in Colombia of German plans to extend airline activity through Central America and the Caribbean, Arnold turned to his friends, Major Carl Spaatz and Captain John Montgomery, and drew up plans for a U.S. airline to head off the Germans, with Arnold as president. Montgomery arranged some financial backing, and Arnold was about to resign his commission, when the Billy Mitchell controversy reached its climax. As a supporter of Mitchell's drive for a separate air force, Arnold told Montgomery he could not "quit under fire." Spaatz stayed with Arnold, and Montgomery went on alone. Pan American had already acquired a contract from the Cuban government to fly mail from Cuba to the United States, but was increasingly short of funds and without planes. Florida Airways also ran into a seige of bad luck. Two of its three planes had crashed, forcing the company into receivership.

When Trippe arrived on the scene with cash in hand, it was logical (and perhaps inevitable) that the three groups should join forces. However, the initial negotiations were far from harmonious. When the talks bogged down, Trippe and Hambleton left their Florida hotel, flew to Havana, met President Machado and came back with an exclusive flying permit between Cuba and the United States. The permit changed the bargaining positions considerably. Now Pan American held a mail contract, but no flying rights. There was little choice but to yield. Thus Trippe came to control Pan American—a moment of destiny in the history of international airlines.

The Caribbean became the laboratory in which Trippe tested the techniques for Pan American's future growth. The first route was 90 miles, from Miami to Havana. In competition with crack express steamers, the short flight was of little importance. But Havana was the gateway to South America. Already, European lines were working their way upward from South America toward the United States. Aéropostale, the predecessor of Air France, and various German lines were operating in Brazil, Argentina, Chile, and Colombia. These lines were heavily subsidized and supported by their governments. Similarly, Trippe saw Pan American as the expression of United States foreign economic policy. Almost from the first, he conceived of the line as the "chosen instrument" of the United States, thus infusing his private business with a sense of national purpose.

Trippe worked without salary in those days, under an agreement to be paid in stock. On occasion he advanced rent or other expenses out of his own pocket. Sometimes when funds were short he or his wealthy associates signed personal notes to tide things over. Probably the fact that Trippe could carry on without an immediate profit enabled him to take the long-range view which was the key to his eventual success. Although a small company with paid-in capital of only $200,000, the seventeen directors of Pan American represented a combined wealth of nearly $1,000,000,000. Relieved of the nagging necessity for an immediate return, Trippe and his board of directors could permit themselves the luxury of building for the future.

It was apparent to Trippe that the vast resources of the South American continent must be developed. The airplane was the ideal vehicle for transportation, because of the nature of the terrain. If the United States did not provide air transport in those countries, foreign nations would assume control. As a matter of national policy the United States could not permit potentially unfriendly foreign powers to dominate the air so near the vital Panama Canal. Thus, as a matter of national defense, the United States government must encourage and support a U.S. airline throughout the length of South America. Trippe determined that that line should be Pan American.

The first step was to develop and demonstrate technical competence. Ocean flying presented problems of a totally different character from those faced by domestic airlines. Engines were far from the reliable power sources we know today. In most parts of this country a forced landing was not too serious a problem, because most of the countryside was relatively flat and rescue could be expected almost at once. A forced landing at sea was an entirely different matter—and far more serious. From the beginning, Trippe insisted on multiengine aircraft to reduce the risk of engine failure. The early Florida–Cuba flights were flown in Fokker trimotors. Although the Fokkers were land planes, it was believed that their wooden construction would keep them afloat if forced down at sea. (Andre Priester, Pan American's meticulous Dutch chief engineer, at first refused to fly the improved Ford Trimotors, because their metal construction would sink.)

As Pan Am ventured beyond Cuba, Trippe turned to flying boats, for two reasons. First, airports were scarce but water was plentiful, and it was far easier and cheaper for Pan American to find a sheltered body of water and provide buoys and a launch than to carve a runway out of the jungle; second, the flying boat seemed to provide a measure of safety if forced down at sea.

This safety argument was so strongly held that at that time most people in aviation believed that ocean flying would always require flying boats. Lindbergh alone did not agree. He had chosen a land plane for his historic Atlantic flight, and argued that it was far more important to design airplanes that would stay in the air than airplanes that would float if they stopped flying. Time has demonstrated his logic on the safety question, but lack of airports forced Pan Am to stick with flying boats until the military necessity of World War II provided good airports around the world.

Trippe chose the gifted Russian émigré Igor Sikorsky to design his aircraft. The Sikorsky company was already one of the components of Boeing and Rentschler's United group. To encourage their interest and insure his aircraft supply, Trippe offered them stock in Pan American on very favorable terms, below the current market. He saw Pan American not only as the expression of national policy, but as the voice of the total aviation community of the United States. Trippe did not consider his view monopolistic. He visualized competition on a national level, where each country would support its international airline with the totality of its available aviation equipment and techniques.

It is important to understand the differences between domestic and international airline operations. In this country, airports, radio and navigational facilities generally were provided by the government. Flights could be made in short stages, requiring less fuel and permitting higher payloads. Navigation was much simpler. Pilots frequently followed railroads, or when lost, circled local water towers to read the town's name. Pan American had none of these advantages. By foot, muleback, and dugout canoes, Pan Am engineers (many of them young men just graduated from Yale; the company has consistently reflected the college loyalty of its chief executive) climbed the mountains and penetrated the jungles to provide their own radio and weather-reporting facilities. Pan Am devised new navigational techniques and developed long-range radio direction-finding instruments. The magnitude of these difficulties discouraged U.S. domestic airlines, accustomed to simpler and more economical operations, from venturing into overseas flying.

Even the climate seemed adverse. Tropical rains were so heavy that one pilot reported "... three inches of fresh water on the surface of the ocean." Planes coming down from higher altitudes to the warm surface air became coated with moisture which stalled engines and fouled electrical circuits. During the early days of their operations Pan American copilots all carried ladies' electric hair dryers to keep their equipment free of moisture (a trick which the author was pleased to pass along to some pilots of the Royal Air Force Auxiliary Squadron in Hong Kong more than twenty years later).

While Pan American personnel were mastering the techniques of long-range overwater flight, Trippe was preparing himself on the economic and political level. The development of international aeronautical law, following World War I, had deviated sharply from the maritime "Freedom of the Seas" concept, in that every nation insisted upon the sovereignty of its own airspace, requiring permission for landing and transit. Like all international law, this divergence had a very practical basis underlying its grandiose verbiage. The British Navy had long dominated the world's oceans, and no other nation could exercise effective control. A free-trade policy was in England's economic interest, and "Freedom of the Seas" came into being. Compared to ocean vessels, early airplanes were far less self-sufficient. Refueling stops were a necessity, and transit restrictions were relatively easy to enforce.* The doctrine of national air sovereignty was accepted legal theory when Pan American began its expansion.

Accordingly, as he was to do so often and so ably, Trippe accommodated himself to the existing realities of world politics. From the beginning he had conceived of Cuba as a funnel which, for the short-ranged planes of the period, would control all air traffic to South America. From Cuba, Trippe could see two paths: one leading eastward toward Brazil by short hops over the West Indian island chain to the South American coast; the other west to the Yucatan Peninsula of Mexico and then down along the coast of the Central American republics of Honduras, Guatemala and Costa Rica to Panama.

With his position in Cuba secure, Trippe began a series of delicate and artful negotiations to obtain similar exclusive flying permits from the governments of the other Latin-American nations throughout the Caribbean area. Meanwhile, our Navy, deeply concerned with canal security and troubled by the increasing German activity nearby, brought pressure on Congress to subsidize a U.S. airline to preempt service in the Caribbean. The contracts were duly awarded to Pan American, when it was discovered that no competitor could fly into the areas of Trippe's exclusive franchises.

* The sovereignty of national airspace doctrine extends only as far as effective control. Satellites pass unhindered beyond the range of interception, whereas our U-2's are considered an invasion of Soviet airspace—now that their antiaircraft rockets can reach the U-2's altitude.

Trippe thought ahead, planning the next step and leaving the consolidation of the present to others. He himself piloted many of the exploration flights, sometimes with others and sometimes alone. Lindbergh was a technical consultant of Pan American almost from the beginning. His knowledge and personal popularity were invaluable. When Trippe and Lindbergh flew together, Trippe tactfully played a secondary role, and thus Pan American's commercial activities were overshadowed by the popularity and acclaim of the world's greatest aeronautical figure. Occasionally their wives accompanied them. Mrs. Lindbergh was the daughter of Dwight Morrow, a Morgan partner and our former ambassador to Mexico; Mrs. Trippe was the former Elizabeth Stettinius, daughter of another Morgan partner and sister of Edward Stettinius, later to become chairman of U.S. Steel, director of the Lend-Lease Administration, and Undersecretary of State. Obviously the presence of the handsome, charming young couples contributed much to the ease and spirit of friendliness in which Trippe's negotiations were conducted.

Progress southward from Panama was not as easy as in the Caribbean. Colombia, encouraged by the German-dominated line, SCADTA, barred all operations by Pan American along its 600-mile Pacific coastline. In the face of this opposition Trippe moved to out-flank Colombia and anchor down the southern terminus. He bought out a small charter and crop-dusting service in Peru and reorganized it as Peruvian Airways. Shortly thereafter he set up a similar operation in Chile. Within Colombia itself he organized a small airline primarily designed to harass the entrenched German SCADTA.

Now, for the first time, Trippe also met significant political and economic opposition from a United States corporation, the great American trading firm of W. R. Grace & Company, which ran ships, banks, warehouses, and stores, and generally dominated the entire economy on the west coast of South America. Grace, with its own strong sense of mission, believed that passenger trade was its historic prerogative. And it was in a position to back up its position, since radio weather service from Grace Line steamers would be necessary for any air operation in that part of the world. In addition to local economic opposition, Grace threatened to run an airline of its own to the United States, in competition with Pan American. This latter threat might be countered by Trippe through his control of the Panama bottleneck; however, the prospects were dim for a near-term solution. Rather than risk a war of attrition with so powerful a rival as Grace, Trippe characteristically proposed a compromise: a new subsidiary, Pan American-Grace Airways, to be owned jointly (and allegedly with the solemn agreement not to poach on each other's preserve in the future).

A shotgun marriage at best, the union of Pan American and Grace has not proved a happy one.* But at the time it seemed an expedient move. Grace, with all of its entrenched connections together with its radio communication, provided an essential ingredient in Trippe's expansion down the west coast of South America.

The only remaining obstacle was the vital link along the coast of Colombia. In vain Trippe exhausted his repertoire of diplomatic and business blandishments. Dominated by SCADTA, the Colombian government held firm, defiantly claiming that Colombia would never "succumb to Yankee imperialism in the air." With his South American west coast Air Mail service scheduled to start in a few weeks and in the face of the failure of all negotiations, Trippe was forced to play his last card. In a secret meeting, he paid von Bauer $1,100,000 for his controlling stock interest in SCADTA. The transaction

---

* Over the years, Pan American has used its 50 percent ownership to block Panagra's plans for expansion to the United States. The Department of Justice has recently challenged Pan Am's position on antitrust grounds.

was never revealed to the public, in order to appease sensitive Colombian national pride. The handsome, bearded von Bauer remained as president of SCADTA, operating with the same German personnel and voting the stock owned by Pan American at directors' meetings. It was generally understood that Pan American had come to some kind of agreement with SCADTA, but the terms were deliberately vague. The State Department immediately concluded a special air treaty between the United States and Colombia, the Kellogg-Olaya Pact, providing for full reciprocity of flying rights between Colombia and the United States. By a gentleman's agreement, the Colombians flew one of their planes over the Canal Zone to appease public opinion, but no further attempts were made by the Colombian government to fly any of its aircraft to the Canal Zone or to the United States. SCADTA immediately withdrew its objections to the passage of Pan American planes along the coast of Colombia. The deal seemed to please everyone. The Colombian government was able to save face and national pride. Dr. von Bauer pocketed $1,100,000 and remained as president of his airline. Our Navy and State departments were satisfied that the only foreign airline operating within striking range of the Panama Canal was under secret American control.

Pan American air and ground crews rapidly extended their operations, surveying routes, and building landing fields. They reached Lima in May; Santiago in July; and by the end of September had crossed the Andes and inaugurated regular flights to Buenos Aires. Less than 250 miles long at the start of the year, Pan American totaled 13,000 miles by the close of 1929. In one year Trippe had overcome the long head start enjoyed by the European airlines.

Pan American next instituted a series of public relations activities and "good neighborliness," to win local support among the Latin Americans. Pan Am planes were available to make honorary flights on any suitable occasion and to provide humanitarian services during hurricanes and earthquakes. A series of inaugural flights by Lindbergh was extremely popular. In the summer of 1929, the Trippes and the Lindberghs made a goodwill tour of the system, with Lindbergh piloting one of the new Sikorsky amphibians. They drew crowds at every stop, with flowers, cheers, banquets, and speeches. It was a triumphal trip, celebrating simultaneously the linking of two continents and the growth of Pan American.

But a new threat of U.S. competition was developing elsewhere in South America. At the conclusion of the Lindbergh goodwill flight, Trippe learned that a group of American investors had raised $5,000,000 to run a line down the east coast. Already the new line, New York, Rio, and Buenos Aires, or NYRBA ("Near-Beer," the Pan Am pilots called it), had made surveys in preparation of a passenger and mail service.

The president of NYRBA was Ralph O'Neill, a World War I pilot. He had been in charge of aviation training for the Mexican government for five years following the war. After that he traveled in South America for Boeing, selling military aircraft, and became well acquainted with the various governments of South America. His major competition was Jimmy Doolittle, then selling for Curtiss. From his experience and observation in South America, O'Neill hit upon the idea of an airline service. He persuaded Consolidated * to provide fourteen of its new Commodore flying boats, predecessors of the famous Navy Catalinas. O'Neill was fortunate to be seeking financial support at the peak of the boom; money was easy, particularly when it combined the glamour of aviation and foreign trade. His major financial backing was secured from James Rand of the Remington Rand Company, as well as from several other prominent financiers. O'Neill was soon joined by the Bevier brothers, Princeton graduates and wartime Navy pilots who had helped start the

* Later to merge with Vultee to form Convair.

original Pan American, Inc. out of Key West. When their company was taken over by Trippe, the Bevier brothers had been forced out. NYRBA gave them an opportunity to get back into aviation—and to get back at Juan Trippe.

With his many connections in South American governments, O'Neill was able to arrange Air Mail contracts from those countries to the United States, charging rates substantially below those of Pan American. The only remaining problem was to provide revenue for the southbound flights. He was confident that, once he had demonstrated the efficiency of his operation, the United States Post Office would award him the Air Mail contract for the east coast of South America.

Marine stations, hangars, radio communications, repair depots, ramps, floats, mooring buoys, and a vast store of equipment facilities were set up over a 10,000-mile route. The pioneering work was not easy. The new airline was harassed by a series of annoyances ranging from minor bribery and blackmail by petty officials to more substantial and sophisticated attempts at thievery. Knowing that NYRBA must maintain its schedules in order to keep its mail contracts with the South American countries, enterprising citizens would trump up fictitious claims and attempt to seize its planes as they landed. Although the suits had no substance, NYRBA could not afford delays and was often forced to pay off. Such shakedown operations may have been merely a little spontaneous larceny on the part of a few local businessmen, but NYRBA regarded them as part of a devious plot by Pan American.

At a particularly crucial moment, NYRBA was warned that the sheriff in Rio was waiting to attach the northbound plane when it landed. To avoid detection, the mail was flown to a small cove just south of the main harbor. Mail pouches were transferred to a launch, taken ashore, loaded into an automobile and driven over a mountain pass to the Rio waterfront. The NYRBA flying boat from the north was already enroute and could not be warned. O'Neill placed the mail in a fast speed boat and raced to the landing area before daybreak. Precisely on schedule, the NYRBA flying boat arrived with the dawn, touching down at the far side of the harbor. Brazilian police boats converged from all sides, but the launch was quicker. O'Neill pulled alongside and transferred the mail while the launch was at full throttle. With the plane's hatches still open, he shouted for the pilot to take off. Vainly, the police watched their quarry fade in the sky.

In spite of such efforts, the NYRBA mail schedules could not always be performed on time. Pan American put increasing pressure upon the South American governments to cancel the NYRBA contract for inadequate performance. Desperate to keep his contracts, O'Neill bought two small, single-engined racing planes. They would leave Buenos Aires a day following the slower Commodore flying boat and chase it northward, hoping to catch it at Rio where the late mails could be transferred for the final stages to the United States in time to make the scheduled guarantees. Meanwhile in the U.S. the crash in the stock market had seriously disturbed NYRBA's backers. Of the original group only Jim Rand continued his support, making up deficits out of his own pocket.

Without a mail subsidy from the Post Office, NYRBA's future was hopeless, and Postmaster General Brown could see no point in subsidizing competitive U.S. airlines, believing it a waste of public funds to encourage the duplication of facilities and services. The inevitable sale to Pan American was a bitter disappointment to O'Neill, but his primary antagonism was directed toward the bankers who had withdrawn their support and forced him to capitulate. Bitterly, O'Neill charged that "our line was just a plaything to them." Under the circumstances, in the middle of the depression and with the serious losses incurred by his line, O'Neill felt fortunate to have received any settlement at all from Pan American. Explaining the sale, he said, "We would never have managed it if the Postmaster General hadn't stuck by us. He knew we pioneered that line and took all the hard knocks. All he had to do was let Pan American know that he approved the merger." *

The day after the transaction was concluded, Brown advertised for bids on a new Air Mail route extension, the one NYRBA could not obtain, down the east coast from Paramaribo to Rio, Montevideo and Buenos Aires—nearly 7,500 miles. Pan American took over the planes and personnel of NYRBA and began flying the route immediately. By 1930 Trippe's position in South America was supreme.

* O'Neill returned to South America to seek new opportunities. Quite by accident, the author met him in the spring of 1960. O'Neill held an exclusive franchise from the Bolivian government to operate a gold dredge on three rivers deep in the interior, on the back side of the Andes. For centuries, the Indians had panned gold from the top gravel on the river bottoms, dating from before the days of the Incas. O'Neill proposed to fly in a modern dredge. He had approached a group in this country, seeking backing, and I was retained by them to negotiate with him. Not until the end of the discussions did I realize that I was talking with the former president of NYRBA. There were too many obstacles for my clients to accept the risk. But somewhere, someday, I hope that South America does provide Ralph O'Neill with the gold mine he has sought for so long.

CHAPTER XII

## From the China Clippers to the North Atlantic

Oceans always held a fascination for Juan Trippe. Perhaps the sea was in his blood; his Maryland ancestors had operated clipper ships out of Baltimore generations before. From his earliest days in aviation, Trippe dreamed of his airline circling the world. The operations in the Caribbean and South America were merely initial steps in that great purpose. No suitable aircraft were available at the time.* But, as always, Trippe looked to the future; in his silent, subtle way he began the necessary negotiations.

In December, 1929, in the midst of his expansion in South America, Trippe approached the British. Preliminary agreements were reached to cooperate in future transatlantic service

\* Obviously the farther an aircraft flies, the more fuel it must carry, thereby reducing its payload. For comparison purposes, the most efficient land transport of the 1930's, the Douglas DC-3, required about 30 percent of its useful capacity in fuel over its normal routes. On the other hand, the Pan American Clippers carried as much as 80 percent of their capacity in fuel—and they were the most efficient and economical long-range airplanes in the world at the time.

through a jointly owned subsidiary, Pan American-Imperial Airways Corporation. Then, investigating a southerly route to Europe via the Azores and Lisbon, Trippe discovered that the French company, Aéropostale, held an exclusive concession. After some discussion, the head of the French line suggested that perhaps Trippe would care to share with the French in an exclusive transatlantic traffic agreement, utilizing the Lisbon–Azores route, then generally considered the most desirable for year-round flying. (The northern route was somewhat shorter, but ice in the harbors would prevent flying-boat operations during the winter.) Trippe revealed his agreement with the British and suggested cooperation, but the French would not tolerate English intrusion.

Trippe's refusal to join the French without the British was not entirely philanthropic. England controlled all the refueling stops along the northern route, Ireland, Canada and Newfoundland, as well as Bermuda in the south. The U.S. had no such intervening islands in the Atlantic, and Trippe did not wish to alienate the British on the North Atlantic for the sake of half of a deal with the French on the southern route. If possible, he hoped to gain both alternatives. Searching for some means of accord, he delayed the French representative in New York for three weeks until the head of Imperial Airways could arrive by boat from England. With his consummate ability as a negotiator, Trippe at last achieved an unbelievably favorable secret agreement under which the British and French were to divide 50 percent of the service on the southerly route and Pan American was to have the other 50 percent for itself, with the further understanding that service was to be inaugurated simultaneously by all three parties.

The following summer, 1931, Trippe asked Sikorsky for a new, long-range flying boat. He also sent out two Arctic expeditions; one to Greenland, and the other to Iceland, to determine flying conditions in those areas. In 1932 he arranged for the Lindberghs to fly a specially equipped Lockheed Sirius on a Great Circle route along the Arctic steppingstones to Denmark. (The story of this flight is vividly described by Anne Morrow Lindbergh in her book *Listen, the Wind*.) By 1933, Trippe's routes were well surveyed, and the new Sikorsky Clippers were performing better than expectations in their flight tests.

Neither the British nor the French, for all their route pioneering, had made similar strides in long-range aircraft development. Without comparable equipment of their own, they refused to permit Pan Am to inaugurate service alone. But with the superior performance of his new Clippers, Trippe could outflank the British, flying over the northern route to Scandinavia and thence into Europe. With the threat of being bypassed entirely, England would be obliged to accept American transatlantic service, even though her own was not ready. But just when Trippe was preparing to start, a series of riots and civil disorders overthrew the friendly government of Newfoundland and precluded operations through that area.

Almost simultaneously, difficulties developed on the southern route. Because of their inability to fly the route in 1933, the French had lost their exclusive franchise with Portugal via Lisbon and the Azores. Despite his best efforts, Trippe was unable to work out any kind of a private agreement, Portugal having by this time returned to her historic alliance with England.

Fruitless negotiations dragged on through 1934. The new Clippers were ready, but they had nowhere to go. The national pride of both the British and French would not permit them to accept service by Pan American until they were similarly prepared. At this point the State Department stepped in, preferring to handle the crucial questions of transatlantic air rights by direct diplomatic negotiation with the foreign countries, instead of leaving such affairs to a single private company. With the matter now in the hands of governments, Trippe felt that a solution would be a long time in coming.

Although the European powers did not have aircraft capable of making the Atlantic flight, the shorter-staged land route to their colonies in the Orient had been mastered. KLM Royal Dutch Airlines extended scheduled service to Batavia, Dutch East Indies, in 1930. Air France followed in 1931, reaching out as far as Saigon, Indochina. Imperial Airways crossed Europe and North Africa to Cairo by 1930, thence via Baghdad through India and down the Malay Peninsula to Singapore. Germany's Lufthansa organized a "national" subsidiary inside China called Eurasia, which was to be joined with Lufthansa's trunkline moving from Europe across Asia. By 1934, the rich Far Eastern market was less than 8 days from Europe's capitals by air, while the only American service was by steamer from San Francisco, taking more than 21 days. The Orient was the historic route of the Yankee clipper ships, and it was unthinkable to Trippe that foreign airlines should gain the upper hand in this rich trading area previously captured by tough New England sailors.

Flying the Pacific was considered far more difficult than the Atlantic because of the greater distances involved. However, the technical disadvantages were more than offset by the political advantages. The island steppingstones in the Pacific were open to an American airline.

Even while he was most deeply engaged in negotiations for the Atlantic route, Trippe had been surveying the Pacific. In 1931, the Lindberghs had made a survey flight along the Great Circle route from Alaska out the Aleutian chain, across the Bering Straits, to Siberia, Japan, and China (reported by Anne Lindbergh in *North to the Orient*). The Lindberghs' flight showed this route to be feasible—and nearly 1,500 miles shorter than the mid-Pacific crossing via Hawaii.

Following the Lindberghs' flight, Trippe purchased two small Alaskan carriers, to develop operational experience in Arctic flying. In 1935, he applied to Soviet Russia for landing permissions for exploratory flights across the Bering Straits in Siberia. At that time the Russians appeared reasonably receptive to transit rights; however, the State Department put its foot down on such negotiations, on the grounds that a reciprocal exchange of service would ultimately be required. With diplomatic tensions also increasing between the United States and Japan, Trippe temporarily abandoned thought of the northern Great Circle route (which the CAB awarded to Northwest after the war—over Trippe's violent protests).

As early as 1932, Pan American had made inroads on the Asian continent when it bought out a nearly bankrupt American airline system established in China three years before by a Curtiss-Wright group. The company was reorganized as the China National Aviation Company, with nominal stock control being held by the Nationalist Government of China. However, Pan American controlled finances and operations. Thus Trippe hoped to "anchor down" the opposite end of his future transpacific line, as well as gain a foothold against the local German-operated company, Eurasia.

While domestic carriers were suffering from the Black investigations and the Air Mail cancellation period, Trippe was relatively unhampered. Critics claimed that his monopoly of U.S. international air transport was considerably more dangerous than the centralization of control in three domestic holding companies. But Trippe escaped interference, primarily because of the critical national interest in maintaining our pre-eminent international airline, and also because there was no other means of performing the service; the Navy had no comparable aircraft and no private competitors remained. The effect, however, was that the government took an increasing interest in Trippe's activities and our State Department began to insist upon its

Across the Oceans [ 135

right to handle negotiations with foreign governments, rather than leaving the matter to Trippe's private discretion.

The interference of the State Department was not too damaging in the Pacific. True, the State Department did preclude operations over the northern Great Circle route via Russia and Japan, but on the Central Pacific route the crucial fueling stops were all American possessions, and Trippe had little need for tedious foreign negotiations. The mid-Pacific airway was set up to run from San Francisco via Hawaii, Midway, Wake, and Guam, to Manila. From Manila alternate routes led northwest to Shanghai, connecting with CNAC, or due west to Hong Kong and Singapore, connecting with the long overland routes of the European airlines.

During the summer of 1935, routes were surveyed with a specially equipped Sikorsky Clipper, and flying stations and radio navigation facilities were set up on island bases across the Pacific. Manila was the nominal outpost at the end of the transpacific airway, but Trippe's real objective was the great harbor at Hong Kong, the gateway to Asia.

The Chinese had never granted any foreigners, as such, the right to fly into their territory, primarily to prevent Japan from seeking the same rights. Of course, Pan American was already entrenched inside China by means of its investment in CNAC, but technically CNAC was a Chinese airline. The parent Pan American system was prohibited from using any Chinese port as a terminal. The only apparent point of entry was the British-owned island of Hong Kong on the Chinese coast. But here again, as in the Atlantic, the British blocked Trippe's path.

Trippe then turned to the tiny Portuguese colony of Macao, a few miles from Hong Kong on the Chinese mainland and less than seventy miles down the estuary from the major Chinese port of Canton. In the Atlantic the Portuguese were happy to cooperate with the British, but it was a different story in the Pacific. In competition with Hong Kong, Macao had steadily lost business as a port. Therefore the Portuguese were eager to have the economic advantage of transpacific air communication with America. Through Macao, Trippe could have the access to his Chinese affiliate, without stopping at Hong Kong.

Outflanked, the British and Chinese merchants demanded air service to America, lest they lose business to the Portuguese in Macao. Opposition collapsed. Once again, the agile Trippe had overcome all obstacles by artful personal diplomacy and achieved his purposes without giving up any reciprocal flying privileges to airlines of other nations. (Trippe's chief objection to government negotiation, aside from delays, had always been that reciprocal rights may be required, thereby creating unnecessary competition.)

Having penetrated China, Trippe turned his attention to Australia. This British colony, already served by Imperial Airways from Europe, was extremely reluctant to grant concessions to an American line. But Australia is substantially closer to the United States than it is to England, and once again local businessmen were quick to recognize the advantages of markets in the United States. Before long, Trippe was granted the exclusive franchise he sought.

At last, preparations were complete. Enroute radio facilities were installed, and the magnificent new Martin *China Clipper* was loaded and ready. Along the waterfront of San Francisco Bay, 150,000 people had assembled to watch the take-off. Over Pan American's radio network came the distant call: "Honolulu calling San Francisco." Governor Poindexter of Hawaii spoke: "Hawaii is no longer isolated by twenty-four hundred miles of sea."

And then, Manila calling San Francisco: "From the other side of the world to you, Postmaster General Farley, and to you, Mr. Trippe, the people of the East send greetings—across the breadth of the ocean which, since the beginning, has been a barrier separating the peoples of the East and of the West. Today the arrival of the *China Clipper* will finally sweep away that barrier of time and space forever." So spoke President Quezon of the Philippines.

To the waiting *Clipper*, Trippe radioed: "*China Clipper*, are you ready?"

"*China Clipper*, standing by."

Turning to the man beside him, Trippe said, "Postmaster General Farley, I have the honor to report that the Trans-Pacific Airway is ready to carry the first Air Mail for the United States Post Office across the Pacific to the Philippines." Into the microphone Trippe commanded: "Captain Musick, you have your sailing orders. Cast off and depart for Manila in accordance therewith."

The bands began to play, and with thousands of people cheering, the *China Clipper* taxied slowly out into San Francisco Bay. Then, her engines racing and a great wake of spray widening behind her, the majestic flying boat lifted off the Bay, climbed slowly across the magnificent harbor, banked over the unfinished Golden Gate Bridge and pointed her nose toward China.

While building the Pacific air route, Trippe had never halted his efforts on the North Atlantic. The blue-ribbon run was not only a matter of prestige, but was also the world's richest international passenger market. In the spring of 1935, when the government had indicated its desire to take over negotiations on the North Atlantic question, Trippe had advised the Secretary of Commerce that Pan American stood ready to cross the Atlantic at any time. In the light of the Black hearings and the domestic Air Mail cancellation, the government moved slowly. Eventually a general invitation was issued to all American airline operators who might be interested in the transatlantic tour. Discussions dragged on, but no other carrier was in a position to equal the equipment or service of Pan American on this route. The State Department finally reached an agreement with England, calling for a twice-weekly service between the United States and England, to be shared equally by American and British airlines for fifteen years. But again the British insisted upon inserting the requirement that service was not to be undertaken by an American company unless a reciprocal British service began simultaneously.

In the spring of 1937, Pan American ran a survey flight across the Atlantic, and Imperial Airways flew a similar one to this country. But the Imperial Airways aircraft was not a commercial plane, since no English aircraft at the time had adequate range and capacity. England, therefore, decided to delay service until it could develop multiengine flying boats with performance more nearly equal that of the American planes. Desperate to catch up with American transport design, the English resorted to bold and imaginative experiments: first mid-air refueling, and then the remarkable Mayo Composite aircraft. The Mayo technique involved a piggyback arrangement where a smaller, four-engine float plane, too overloaded with fuel to take off by itself, was mounted on the back of a large Short flying boat. With the power of all eight engines, the two attached aircraft could stagger into the air, where the float plane could be released and fly on alone.

Trippe had formerly been willing to accommodate himself to British delays for two reasons: first of all, "The sun never sets" on the British Empire—nor on potential British air bases; and he had no desire to alienate a country that might provide him with future necessary bases elsewhere in the world; secondly, surveys showed that at that time 47 percent of all North Atlantic traffic originated in England. Thus both politically and economically, Trippe hoped to have England on his side, but his patience wore thin as the years dragged by. Once again he undertook secret negotiations with the Portuguese, as he had for rights to Macao on the other side of the world. With his sorcerer's skill at the bargaining table, he was able to secure an exclusive twenty-five year franchise for landing rights in the Azores and Lisbon, excluding all other American companies, and without requiring any Portuguese reciprocal rights to the United States.

Even with Portuguese agreement, Pan American service was hampered for a time by the fact that the English refused to permit landing at Bermuda for a fuel stop. Pan American planes could handle the eastward flight comfortably on a nonstop basis, but the western return flight was against prevailing winds, making it a marginal operation. Late in 1938, Pan American received delivery of new Boeing 314 Clippers, the ultimate in flying-boat design. These magnificent and luxurious aircraft had a flying range of 3,500 miles, enabling Pan American to ignore Bermuda on nonstop flights.

By this time the English were more concerned with the approach of war on the continent than with maintaining national prestige in competition with Pan American in the North Atlantic. With the Nazi threat increasing daily, rapid transatlantic service became a necessity. Prestige was put aside, and Pan American was finally permitted entry into England. On May 20, 1939, the Boeing *Yankee Clipper* took off from Port Washington on the first scheduled commercial flight to Southampton, England.

Even in this moment of triumph, mutiny broke out on the flagship itself. Secretive by nature, Trippe had always kept his plans to himself, much to the annoyance of fellow members of his board of directors. In spite of his achievements, many within the company were frustrated and annoyed at such one-man control.

Ironically, the leader of the internal opposition was Trippe's old friend and early associate, Sonny Whitney (the most active of the original founders, Hambleton, had been killed in a plane accident several years before). A slim, handsome young man with curly blond hair, Whitney had inherited more than $20,000,000 while a Groton schoolboy and was often regarded as a playboy of limited and superficial interests. But whereas Trippe had only one interest in life—Pan American—Whitney's interests were many and varied. He took over his family's racing stable, played international polo, entered the movie business, and had mining interests in Canada. He was also an active director of the American Museum of Natural History and the Whitney Museum of American Art, as well as the Metropolitan Opera Company. Often married, he was attracted to women and they to him. For a time his interest turned to politics, and he ran for Congress in 1932 as a Democrat from Long Island (one of the very few Democratic candidates in the country not to be elected in the Roosevelt landslide).

Whitney often said that he liked the Pan American venture because it was an "outdoor" business. He took much pride in the part he had played in helping to finance it and he bitterly resented the fact that Trippe did not seem to value his judgment or take him into confidence on plans. Whitney, the largest single stockholder in Pan American, claimed that he deserved more consideration, both because of his stockholdings and because of his support in the early days. Feeling rebuffed and ignored, Whitney organized other disgruntled directors and succeeded in having himself elected chairman of the board and "chief executive officer."

The fierce financial duel left Trippe holding the empty title of president. An icy chill settled upon the Pan American offices; Trippe and Whitney refused to speak. The other executives were forced to take sides, and the future of Pan American was in serious jeopardy. Without Trippe, it was perfectly clear that Pan American was a hollow shell.

World War II was threatening; new problems and emergencies were occurring daily. Trippe had kept all of his knowledge in his head, and there was no time to try to educate Whitney in the affairs of Pan American. Thoroughly chastened, the board of directors stripped Whitney of his powers and titles and returned them to the man who, almost single-handedly in one decade, had circled South America and spanned the world's two mightiest oceans.

*PART FOUR*

# World War II:
# Air Transport Comes of Age

*CHAPTER XIII*

# Achievements of the
# Air Transport Command

The war changed all that had gone before. This country found itself fighting on remote battlefields across vast oceans. Transportation was the key. Men and arms were desperately needed—in England, Africa, the Philippines, Alaska. Time was of the essence, and the airplane was the only answer.

Germany and Japan held strategically advantageous positions, known to military theorists as "interior lines of communication"; that is, their battlefronts formed an arc around their homelands, facilitating the problem of supply. We, on the other hand, were forced to transport our men and weapons across great distances. China, then our ally in Asia, was nearly sealed off from us already. A sea voyage of more than 13,000 miles, nearly 50 days, would be required to bring our supplies to ports behind the Himalayas. China's one remaining source of supply, the Burma Road, would soon be cut off. Without the airplane, China's case was hopeless.

In the Middle East, Germans and Italians threatened Egypt and Suez, Britain's life line to Australia and the key to Africa. From their bases in Italy and Greece, German and Italian aircraft controlled the Mediterranean. British forces in Egypt could be supplied only by going all the way around Africa. Similar logistic problems presented themselves in India and Australia. Our European ally Russia was almost totally cut off. The one remaining supply route was the frozen, hazardous, bloody ocean route across the Arctic above Norway. Alaska and the Aleutian islands were vulnerable to the Japanese. We had no land supply line to these areas, and our garrisons were thinly manned. Perhaps the simplest problem was that of supplying England across the North Atlantic. And this route, too, had its problems; although the weather was perhaps better than in other areas, it was still a formidable obstacle, not to mention the threats of German submarines and bombers.

For all of these desperate supply problems, the airplane alone seemed to offer potential solution. But faced with the magnitude of the task, equipment and preparations were pitifully small. The Atlantic had been flown commercially only two years before, and Pan American operated only two flights a week between England and the United States. In those days ocean flying was still a great event. Crowds would gather in San Francisco or New York to watch the take-off of the Pan American Clippers for England or for China, but before long ocean flying would become a commonplace, repeated not only daily, but hundreds of times per day.

Where to begin? The fine network of domestic airlines within this country were equipped with short-range transports (primarily the Douglas DC-3) which were not capable of carrying a significant load over the distances now required. (So few and so desperately needed were our long-range transports in the early days of the war that the progress of each individual plane was important enough to require immediate reporting to General H. H. (Hap) Arnold, Chief of the Army Air Corps.) Despite its obvious military significance, long-range aircraft development in this country had been severely delayed by the old interservice rivalries. In the early 1930's, Boeing tried to sell a four-engine bomber design to the Army—but the Navy protested. Arguing that long-range Army bombers would intrude on the Navy's role as defender of our coasts, the aggressively effective Navy lobby quickly convinced Congress to limit Air Corps appropriations to short-ranged, twin-engined aircraft and to restrict the Air Corps' strategic role to a 100-mile radius of the coastline. Fortunately, despite the obstacles, Boeing continued with a limited, privately financed development program which was to produce the famous B-17 "Flying Fortress."

Boeing had looked for commercial customers, but in the middle of the depression the only airline really interested in long-range flight was Pan American—and Pan Am demanded flying boats to permit landings in those parts of the world where airports did not yet exist. To meet Trippe's requirements, Boeing embarked on the design of Model 314. It was a regrettable decision. Pan Am's needs were relatively small, and only twelve Boeing Clippers were sold, yet the 314 flying boats occupied nearly all of the working capital and engineering force that Boeing had available for commercial four-engine development—costing the Boeing Company several million dollars, and more important, its leading position in commercial air transportation.

Douglas also recognized the need for a four-engined transport, but despite the success of the DC-3, Douglas lacked the capital to finance the DC-4 development program alone. In late 1936, United, TWA, American, Eastern and Pan Am, all agreed to help underwrite the project. However, by the time the DC-4 had reached the prototype stage, development costs were more than double those originally anticipated. Furthermore, its operational capability was somewhat limited. To take full advantage of the plane's speed and range, high-altitude flight was desirable, but the DC-4 lacked the necessary cabin pressurization.

Meanwhile, by 1938, Boeing had recognized the error of the flying-boat project. Using the wing and much of the engineering data from the Flying Fortress designs (resistance in Congress by the Navy had been gradually overcome as the importance of airpower became ever clearer), Boeing brought out the first pressurized four-engined airliner, the Model 307 "Stratoliner." While the airline underwriting group behind the DC-4 had mutually agreed not to buy another aircraft in the 50,000-pound category, the new Boeing 307 weighed precisely 49,500 pounds. Taking advantage of this loophole, TWA and Pan American pulled out of the DC-4 deal and bought the new Boeings, receiving delivery in 1940. However, neither company had much opportunity to exploit the new aircraft in commercial operation. Military necessity soon demanded the services of all the four-engined transports this country could produce.

A typical power struggle rapidly developed between the military services over who would get what. The Army and Navy each wanted its own air transport operation, and obviously the Army Air Corps felt that it alone was the proper unit to operate such a service. President Roosevelt had granted the Secretary of War the power to take over all U.S. airlines, but the airlines' lobby, the Air Transport Association, argued that it could perform better in private hands. Final decision on this point was up to General Arnold. The Navy had continued its independent efforts to build up its own Naval Air Transport Service, and Arnold envisioned endless arguments over each individual plane and pilot if the airlines' crews and equipment were commandeered. Instead, Arnold set up the Air Trans-

## World War II: Air Transport Comes of Age [ 147

port Command, a quasi-military organization for which the various airlines would fly under contract.

With the Japanese threatening the Aleutians, an air route to Alaska was an immediate necessity. The operation was contracted to Northwest Airlines, because of its experience in sub-zero weather conditions along its mountainous routes across the western states bordering Canada. Under the guidance of George Gardner, a Northwest vice-president, the company began its route in Minneapolis, flying across Canada by way of Edmonton and White Horse to Fairbanks. Soon an outside route was added, running up the coast to Anchorage, which route Northwest shared with United. Of the two, the inside route was far more important. Across it flowed the major portion of the airborne supplies for our forces in Alaska. It also became the American half of the famous Alaskan–Siberian, "Alsib," delivery route over which more than 6,000 U.S. bombers and fighters were flown to the Russians under the lend-lease program.

The subcontract services of the other U.S. airlines expanded rapidly. Before long, ten commercial airlines, including all the major ones, were flying under contract for the ATC: American and TWA across the North Atlantic; Pan American and American Export in the Central Atlantic to Africa. In the Pacific, United and Pan Am ran to Guam, New Guinea and Australia; Panagra and Eastern flew to Central and South America. Together, these lines carried nearly half the total ATC traffic.

The "Hump" was by all odds the Air Transport Command's greatest achievement. From India to China across the Himalayas, the ATC moved 1,000,000 tons of cargo a year. Aviation gasoline and military supplies to China were brought to Assam, Burma, from Calcutta, on barges up the Brahma Putra River, or up the ancient and tired Bengal and Assam railway. Other supplies of high-priority freight were flown all the way from the United States across Central Africa into Assam. While the Japanese held Burma, ATC pilots took off from Assam and flew north over the "Angel's Playground," a series of ridges 20,000 feet high. Even more than the Japs and their "Zero" fighters, pilots dreaded the Himalayan weather. On one night alone the ATC lost 9 planes in a storm over the Himalayas, as well as the lives of 50 flyers.

As the only prewar international airline, Pan American played a special part, particularly prior to the actual outbreak of hostilities. In South America, German penetration in air transportation had persisted. Ten years earlier, Juan Trippe had eliminated commercial rivalry by secretly buying control of SCADTA in Columbia. However, actual operational control remained in the hands of Peter Paul von Bauer, and all his aircraft, pilots and ground personnel were German. In 1938, on his return from a visit to Berlin, von Bauer came to New York and offered to buy back SCADTA's majority stock from Trippe. At the time Trippe needed the cash, but War and State department officials urged him to delay negotiations and agreed to underwrite whatever additional costs might be incurred. Eventually a deal was worked out between our State Department, the Colombian government and Trippe, whereby control of SCADTA was to pass into the hands of the Colombian government. Under the pretense of setting up a new nonstop Caribbean route, a large contingent of Pan American personnel arrived in Colombia. At dawn the next day SCADTA's principal airfields were invaded by Colombian soldiers, accompanied by Pan Am air and ground crews. The German pilots and ground crews were given their discharge and the Americans took over. The name SCADTA was changed to Avianca. Similar "delousing" of Nazi-dominated airlines took place in Peru, Ecuador, Brazil and Bolivia, where German regional airways had penetrated the local economies.

Prior to our entry into the war in July, 1941, President Roosevelt had asked Trippe to build an airway across Africa

## World War II: Air Transport Comes of Age [ 149

from the Atlantic to the Nile, as a communication and transportation support to the beleaguered British Army in Egypt. Pan American was selected for this enterprise because the United States was not yet at war and it seemed more appropriate to have the operation in the hands of a private company, rather than a function of our own military. Perhaps even more important, Pan American had the organizational and management skills to provide the needed services. The War Department backed the company in every respect, providing reserve airmen for flight crews and granting draft deferments to Pan American personnel, as well as high priorities for matériel and shipping space. By the end of 1941, Pan American had completed the route to Cairo and had established long-range communications.

But for all Pan American's achievements, there were some bitter critics. In their view, the company was far too concerned with entrenching itself as a commercial operator. Following his usual practice, Trippe endeavored to negotiate exclusive landing rights wherever his organization built airfields.

Tensions developed, particularly on the African route. In order to minimize the friction between the high rates in civilian pay and the lower military pay scales for men working side by side on the African route, as well as to consolidate military discipline and control, the Army offered commissions to all Pan American employees operating on the African route. Pan American executives, on the other hand, advised their African employees to reject the proposal. To many this action seemed one more example of Trippe's commercial motivations. On the other hand, as one Pan American executive put it: "We were fighting to hold our organization together because we felt that we could serve our country best in that fashion."

The British objected strenuously to Pan American's commercial operations in Africa. Trippe argued in reply that our government gave "too little thought to the commercial future of

American aviation." So great had the tensions become, that an executive order was prepared, calling for the War Department to take over all of Pan American. Confronted with this alternative, Trippe at last capitulated in the military acquisition of the African route. However, despite the minor disagreements, Pan Am's many wartime services were recognized in the award of the Harmon Trophy by Harry Truman in 1947.

From its meagre beginnings, the Air Transport Command grew at an unprecedented rate. Considering the conditions prevalent at its introduction, its achievements were amazing.* By 1944, twenty-six scheduled flights of the Air Transport Command crossed the Atlantic Ocean daily in each direction. Thirty-eight round trip flights took place daily across the Pacific. In India, 71,000 tons of cargo were flown into China over the Himalayas in one month. After the victory in Europe and in preparation for the final moves against Japan, the Air Transport Command brought 160,000 passengers from Europe across the Atlantic to the United States during the summer of 1945. At its peak, the Air Transport Command operated over 1,000 four-engined transports. On a few days' notice, it flew the first wave of occupation troops into Japan, including two fully equipped divisions, carrying with them their jeeps, tractors, bulldozers, and trucks.

Whereas, before the war, an ocean crossing was a newsworthy event, under the ATC, air transport had come of age. Transportation was now thought of in terms of thousands of passengers and thousands of tons of cargo. Well-equipped routes,

---

* Fearing Army dominance in the ATC, the Navy had refused to participate, choosing instead to build up its own Naval Air Transport Service. By the end of the war, NATS operated 226 four-engined transports over similar routes, causing unfortunate duplications where planes of one service flew empty while supplies were desperately needed by the other. This condition has, hopefully, been remedied, and today all military air transport is carried by MATS, the Military Air Transport Service, operated by the Air Force for the use of all of the services.

radio facilities, and convenient airfields ringed the world. Military necessity had brought into being new airplanes and airports, which in a space of three years had brought about a complete international air highway system. Aviation had developed from a daring adventure to a routine means of transportation.

PART FIVE

*Postwar Politics*

CHAPTER XIV

*The "Chosen Instrument":*
*Pan American vs. the World*

The end of the shooting in World War II merely marked the beginning of new battles in the airline industry. Although air transport had expanded and improved almost incredibly, the basic problem, as always, was competition. Arguments involved two areas, international and domestic; internationally, the domestic trunklines all wanted hunting licenses on what Juan Trippe considered his private preserve. Meanwhile, back in this country, a number of ex-G.I.'s with wartime savings and surplus planes wanted a chance to enter the airline business on their own—much to the annoyance of the established domestic operators.

The first battle broke out in the international area, in the summer of 1943. The U.S. Air Force was still bombing Germany and Japan when General "Hap" Arnold called the top airline executives of the country together for a conference in Washington, saying that the time had come for U.S. operators to agree on postwar international aviation policy. The meeting then adjourned to the office of the Air Transport Association where the feud broke in earnest. Of all the operators present, only Patterson of United expressed his reluctance to carve up the empire of Juan Trippe. Patterson's studies had convinced him that the market was not big enough to support more than one carrier at that time. Not so, the others present. The issue was clearly drawn: only Patterson and United stood with Trippe and Pan American. From the conference room of the Air Transport Association, the battle moved on to countless bars, hotel lobbies, government corridors, and the halls of Congress.

Pan American had taken the risks of overseas pioneering, and had made money at it. It had originated the techniques of overwater flight. It had developed long-range radio and directional finding equipment; cruise control procedures to minimize gas consumption; and numberless other trade secrets—secrets which Pan American shared with the other carriers in the war effort of the Air Transport Command. During the war, Pan American had also greatly expanded its operations. With government assistance, it had built a system of bases through Central and South America and across Africa. Its Chinese affiliate, CNAC, had kept open a life line across the Hump to China, after the closing of the Burma Road. But despite its expansion, Pan American's preferred position also came to an end. The other operators of the Air Transport Command had acquired a free schooling in overseas operations. The war-built chain of airports across the North Atlantic, particularly Gander and Greenland, simplified operations considerably. The route could be flown easily with the newer and more economical four-engined land transports, the DC-4's and Constellations. Prior to the airports, flying boats had been required, and as the only airline so equipped, Pan Am had the oceans to itself. With the ready availability of the new airplanes and airports, those days were over.

The glamour and potential profitability of the international market held great appeal—and that market seemed wide open. The devastation of the war had destroyed effectively the commercial aviation activities of the other nations of the world, and the United States was the only country at the time technically or economically capable of offering international airline service. Therefore, it was argued, additional United States airlines should be permitted to compete with Pan American as the only immediate source of effective competition. To Trippe, such a view was dangerously shortsighted. Looking into the future, he saw that the altruistic policy of our State Department would be to foster the development of many foreign international airlines, all of which would compete with Pan American. Additional competition from other United States airlines would only intensify the inevitably ensuing overcapacity on international routes. Steadfastly Trippe maintained his earlier arguments for Pan American as the "chosen instrument" of United States international aviation.

But the deck was stacked against him. In spite of his success (or perhaps because of it), Trippe's chosen instrument theory seemed to have few friends in Washington. The opposition had the backing of President Roosevelt himself. Prior to our entry into the war, Roosevelt and Churchill had agreed that the United States would supply England's needs for transport aircraft, freeing all English production for combat planes. At the Quebec Conference in 1943, Churchill required F.D.R.'s promise that he would not use our technical superiority in transport planes to England's postwar disadvantage. (In all things national, Churchill was guided by his famous declaration, "I have not become Prime Minister to preside over the dissolution of the British Empire.")

Upon his return from Quebec, Roosevelt called a meeting at the White House to discuss postwar aviation policy. Present were Undersecretary of State Edward R. Stettinius, Jr.; Assistant Secretary of War for Air Robert A. Lovett; Assistant Secretary of State Adolf A. Berle, Jr.; Harry Hopkins; and L. Welsh Pogue, chairman of the Civil Aeronautics Board. Berle recalls that when Roosevelt began to discuss international aviation an embarrassed hush fell over the room, for everyone realized that Pan American's president, Juan Trippe, was married to Edward Stettinius' sister. As Roosevelt began to discuss Pan American specifically, Stettinius gracefully got up and left the room, to permit the President greater freedom of expression. Roosevelt stated his considered judgment that all U.S. international traffic should not be handled by a single line; in his opinion the scope of responsibility was too great to be entrusted to any one man or company. "Speaking frankly," he said, "Trippe thinks Pan American should get all the business. Perhaps Pan American is entitled to the senior place and the lion's share, but competition whenever possible is a better system."

Despite the massive odds against him, Trippe fought with every means at his disposal in his personal crusade to prevent what he believed to be a national mistake. In the bitterness of the ensuing struggle, many people questioned his motives and tactics. However, history has demonstrated the accuracy of his predictions.

Four years previously, in 1939, the American Export shipping steamship company had set up a subsidiary airline to fly the North Atlantic in competition with Pan American. Export claimed that it was seeking to "save American aviation from being strangled by the Pan American monopoly." Trippe argued that the existence of two competing American lines would be an invitation to European governments to play off the Americans against each other, resulting in losses for everyone.

The Civil Aeronautics Board took the position that a competing airline to Europe would provide the stimulus of competition to improve service and would serve as a yardstick for comparison of costs. At hearings before Congress, representatives of the War and State departments testified to the need for an added ocean service by a new, independent company. The international counselor of the CAB, Samuel P. Gates, entered a brief in which he stated that: "Whereas Juan T. Trippe, president of Pan American, and several other high executives had not visited South America in six or seven years preceding 1942, at least five of the persons whose salaries are included in the executive group spent 20 percent or more of their time in Washington, and yet no clear explanation of the manner in which their time was spent in the nation's Capital is contained in the record." The implication was that Trippe and his executives were more interested in lobbying in Washington than they were in paying attention to the efficiencies of flying over their routes. Adolf Berle, speaking for the State Department as well as the War Department, testified to Congress that any additional expense incurred by the government to introduce a second airline on the North Atlantic was considered worthwhile in the interests of national defense. Such arguments were persuasive and eventually prevailed. The CAB handed down a formal decision, authorizing Export to fly an experimental service in 1940.

Undaunted, Trippe determined to carry his fight to Congress, where he hoped to prevent the appropriation of funds for the subsidy requested by American Export. Senator Carter Glass, introducing Trippe to the Senate committee, stated: "Mr. Trippe, we have under consideration the very simple question of whether your company is a monopolist or whether the other company is a monopolist and to which monopolist we must give the most money." Ignoring any attempts at levity on his cherished subject, Trippe pointed out that England, France,

Germany, Japan, and the Netherlands had all tried having several competing, or "zoned" airlines. After much trouble and loss, each country had ended by combining them into one government-subsidized monopoly. Thus it was not a question of competition between carriers of one country, but rather competition between the "chosen instruments" of each nation for the air routes of the world. For this reason both the Republican and Democratic administrations in the previous years had encouraged, through mail subsidies, the development of Pan American along monopolistic lines, until world leadership had been won by America's semiofficial international airline. Trippe argued for setting up Pan American as a regulated monopoly, like the telephone industry. In conclusion, he made the surprising offer that he sell the government 49 percent of his company's stock and thus create a semisocialized company along the lines of the British.

Trippe's appearance and persuasion were successful. In a late night session the appropriation for American Export was defeated by a narrow margin. Thwarted, Export management announced that it would go ahead preparing for a transatlantic service without benefit of government subsidy. But here again Trippe had them blocked, for his exclusive franchise with the Portuguese precluded any other American commercial company from refueling in the Azores or in Lisbon. When the State Department requested a modification from the Portuguese government to permit American Export to land, Portugal asked for a reciprocal permission to run a Portuguese line to New York. Alarmingly, the proposed Portuguese airline was to be managed by a group of suspected Nazis. Our State Department, embarrassed, broke off negotiations for commercial privileges for American Export.

Nevertheless, the new company began military contract operations for the ATC. Expansion was rapid during the war. It was clear that Pan Am could expect more trouble when the shooting stopped.

Trippe's lawyers, hoping to head off more competition, pressed upon the CAB the theory that it was illegal for a surface carrier to control an air carrier. American Export Airlines must be separated from its parent, American Export Steamship Company. The apparent objective was to weaken American Export so substantially that it would either go out of business or sell out to Pan American. For the first time it appeared that wily Juan Trippe had outsmarted himself, and his tactic backfired. With surface transportation companies prevented from controlling an airline, the only logical alternative was another airline, and only a prosperous and powerful airline could afford to buy Amex.

Except for Pan American, there were only three other airlines capable of taking over. United had already expressed its disinclination to compete in international traffic, leaving only TWA and American. Because of their significant contributions to the ATC, TWA executives believed that they had a substantial opportunity to win an international operation for themselves without tying themselves up in a merger with Amex. American Airlines, however, did not wish to take a chance on losing out on the North Atlantic. Confident that Amex was certain to receive renewed CAB authorization, American jumped at the opportunity to have access to what was considered the most lucrative route.

American's merger with Amex also benefited TWA. The CAB reasoned that it was unfair to permit American Airlines to become an international operator by the indirect avenue of a purchase of Amex; TWA, it was thought, ought to be granted an equal opportunity. Thus Pan American's attempts to weaken Amex into a subordinate and ineffective competitor actually brought onto the North Atlantic the two strongest possible competitors. While Pan American lawyers claimed "foul" and sought rehearings before the CAB and in the courts, Trippe was active on Capitol Hill.

With the aid of Senator Patrick McCarran, coauthor of the Civil Aeronautics Act of 1938, Trippe was able to introduce into the United States Congress a bill calling for the creation of the "All American Flag Line"—Trippe's chosen instrument theory in a new package. The basic argument is best expressed in Trippe's own words.

> Our position has been that in international air transport, as in international telecommunications, our nation's best interests would be served by concentrating the effort of the United States behind a single American international operation, strong enough to compete on even terms with the great foreign flag air transport monopolies created by other principal trading nations. This operation would take the form of a community company in which all American transportation interests able to contribute would be permitted to participate under an organization plan approved by the government.

The bill eventually died in committee, but in any event it served the purpose of gaining time and delaying the inauguration of competitive service. In delaying tactics, Trippe was aided by an unexpected ally. The city of Baltimore had spent millions of dollars preparing its brand new Friendship Airport.* When it was learned that the CAB decision in the North Atlantic case did not specify Baltimore as a coterminal with New York, Maryland Senators flew into action. A petition was presented to the President, signed by 13 of the 20 members of the Senate Commerce Committee, denouncing the CAB decision and requesting that, if domestic airlines were to be allowed to compete with Pan American internationally, it was only fair to permit Pan

---

* Squeezed between the more active terminals of Washington and New York, Friendship has always been in difficulty. Prospects brightened briefly when Washington-bound jets had to land on Friendship's long runways, but politics returned to ruin this opportunity, and the vast new Dulles Airport in Virginia (almost as far from Washington as Friendship) has been built to serve our nation's Capital.

The airlines began with the Air Mail—and the Air Mail began with war-surplus DeHavilland DH-4's. Inefficient and unsafe, the DH-4 was known as the "Flaming Coffin," but its low price recommended it to most of the early companies. Lindbergh flew the first Air Mail from St. Louis to Chicago in a DH-4 on April 15, 1926. (*American*)

Eddie Rickenbacker, the leading U.S. ace in World War I, later to head Eastern Airlines, with his SPAD pursuit plane. (*Eastern*)

Bill Boeing (*right*) flew the first international mail from Vancouver, British Columbia, to Seattle, Washington, on March 3, 1919. (*Boeing*)

Boeing later started an airline to demonstrate the advantage of his B-40 over the old DH-4's. Its success led to the formation of United Airlines. (*United*)

Inspired by United, Hoover's Postmaster General, Walter Folger Brown (*left*), used his position to force the consolidation of small companies into national systems. Brown's plans were attacked by Senator Hugo Black (*right*), now a Supreme Court Justice, whose investigation brought about the cancellation of all private airline contracts and led to the tragic Army Air Mail experiment. (*Harris & Ewing*)

Franklin Roosevelt and C. R. Smith, president of American Airlines, during his wartime service with the Air Transport Command. (*American*)

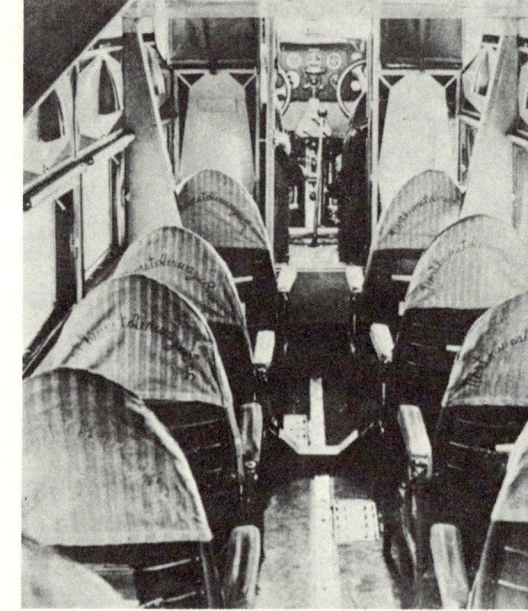

Transcontinental Air Transport, a predecessor of TWA, was a combined air-rail service. Passengers slept in Pullmans at night and were transferred in special trailers to Ford Trimotors for daytime flights. Note the simple Ford instrument panel. (*TWA*)

American Airlines rose to the top of the domestic airline industry through C. R. Smith's aggressive salesmanship. The lumbering Curtiss Condor (*top*) offered the first sleeper service. Then Smith got together with Donald Douglas (*left*) to introduce the world famous DC-3. (*American*)

Howard Hughes' unconventional business habits tend to obscure his significant technical contributions to aviation. Here he stands beside the F-1 which he personally designed and flew to a transcontinental speed record in 1938. (*TWA*)

Under Hughes, TWA pioneered "over-weather" flying in the first pressurized transport, the Boeing 307 (*top*). TWA's Boeings became the nucleus of the Air Transport Command at the start of World War II. Hughes also played a major part in the design of the Lockheed Constellation. The "Connie" was a great advance in transport design but the war delayed its commercial debut. (*TWA*)

The China Clipper outward bound over the Golden Gate. (*Pan American*)

American Pioneers: (*Top left*): The Sikorsky S-38 used in the
 days in Latin America. (*Top right*): The Lindberghs in the
heed Sirius which they flew on surveys of the northern Atlantic
 Pacific Great Circle routes. (*Middle*): Juan Trippe plotting on
ffice globe. (*Bottom*): Lindbergh and John Hambleton loading
-38 for their inaugural flight from Havana to Barranquilla.
nbleton was later killed in a crash but his son carries on in the
pany today.) (*Pan American*)

An Imperial Airways flying boat on the Thames. (*BOAC*)

(*Above left*): An Argosy enroute from London to Paris in 1925 for Imperial Airways, the predecessor of BOAC. (*BOAC*)

(*Above right*): Antoine Saint-Exupéry (*left*), pioneering pilot for France, wrote poetically of the early days in Africa and South America. (*Air France*)

(*Left*): The "piggy-back" combination used by Imperial Airways for long range on the North Atlantic. (*BOAC*)

(*Below left*): Germany originally used Zeppelins to connect with her "local" airlines in South America. (*Below right*): The giant twelve-engine Dornier DOX was also used by the Germans on the South Atlantic. (*Lufthansa*)

(*Above*): The replica of Lindbergh's *Spirit of St. Louis* in flight, trailed by a Boeing 707. (*TWA*)

(*Middle*): A Sikorsky S-42 which Pan American used on survey flights on both the Atlantic and Pacific. Some romance went out of aviation with the passing of the flying boats. (*Pan American*)

(*Below*): The loading and take-off of the Boeing 314 Clipper on the first commercial flight across the North Atlantic in the spring of 1939. (*Pan American*)

The Douglas DC-4 called the C-54 by the Army, was the mainstay of the wartime ATC. In the postwar days, it was no match for the Constellation, but Douglas caught up quickly with the DC-6, the most economical and efficient of all piston-powered transports. (*Eastern and American*)

The Boeing Stratocruiser, based on the wartime B-29, was a passenger favorite because of its double-deck fuselage with a bar on the lower level. (*Northwest*)

Turboprops were an interim step between piston power and pure jets. Rapidly overtaken by jet development, turboprops were not an economic success. Capitol went broke trying to meet the payments on its Vickers Viscounts. (*Capitol*)

The Lockheed Electra was plagued by a series of tragic crashes.

The British led the world into the Jet Age with the graceful De-Havilland Comet. Early models revealed structural defects and came apart in flight—a blow from which British aviation has not yet fully recovered. (*BOAC*)

The first practical jet transport was the Boeing 707, originally ordered by Pan American. Note the engine placement on pods under the wing, instead of in the wing roots as on the Comet. (*Pan American*)

The Douglas DC-8, despite its late start, gave the Boeing 707 severe competition in early orders, largely because of the airlines' respect for Douglas's reputation. (*Eastern*)

The Convair 990, like the DC-8, followed the same general design of the Boeing 707. Offering little improvement in performance, the Convair was a costly failure for its manufacturer. The bulges on the wing behind the engines were an unsuccessful attempt to improve efficiency. (*American*)

The French Caravelle (*above*) was the first jet to recognize the aerodynamic advantages of placing its engines at the rear of the fuselage. (*United*)

Boeing learned its lesson from the Caravelle and designed its new 727 (*below*) with three jets mounted at the tail. (*Boeing*)

American to enter the domestic field. But before the argument could receive serious consideration, the Senators' fickle interests were distracted and the excitement subsided.

There was yet another string to Pan American's bow. Even if American and TWA had authorization from the CAB and had the equipment, pilots, and personnel ready to inaugurate service, there remained the final question of diplomatic clearance. The two primary powers, the United States and Great Britain, were still far apart on their theories of postwar air transport. The United States stood for competition and a minimum of restrictions. (Congresswoman Clare Boothe Luce, wife of the powerful publisher of *Life, Time* and *Fortune,* had declared in her famous "Globaloney" speech: "American postwar aviation policy is simple: we want to fly everywhere. Period!") Great Britain stood for the principle of distribution of traffic by quota, with strict regulation of fares, flight frequencies, and subsidies. No new competitive international U.S. airline operations could be undertaken until these questions were resolved. Since Pan American was already authorized to provide service to England under its prewar contracts, it was greatly to Pan American's advantage to have the disagreements between the United States and Britain drag out as long as possible.

The British, still crippled from the war, feared that American superiority in equipment and experience would completely dominate postwar international air traffic if unlimited freedom of competition were permitted. Similarly, the French, Dutch and Belgians favored the British position. On the other hand, nations which had little opportunity to become important airline powers, but which might gain by efficient air transportation service—such as in Latin America—tended to side with the U.S. position.

The conflict of interest gave third parties an ideal opportunity to play off the two great powers against each other. For instance, in Egypt, State Department officials pointed out the desirability of having Cairo become a great aerial crossroads. At the same time British agents suggested that the Americans would ruin local airlines, such as Egypt's little Misr Airwork. The United States countered, arguing that as a feeder to a U.S. trunkline, Misr would gain more tourist traffic than ever before. An additional inducement on the American side was the presence of Payne Field, just outside Cairo, which had been built during the war by Americans and now held thousands of dollars worth of equipment, as well as its hangars and other facilities. The Americans suggested that the entire facility might then be available to the Egyptians, if the Egyptians offered a U.S. line permission to use the field. Similar inducements were offered in the various Arab states, and a favorable decision seemed near. However, at this juncture the United States strongly began to support the Zionist movement for the formation of the State of Israel, seriously impairing relations with the nearby Arab nations.

While the United States and Britain were engaged in such petty skirmishes, opportunities for reconciliation increased with the formation of the International Air Transport Association, a voluntary organization of representatives from all the world's air transport systems, intended to stabilize air transportation on world routes. The British sought regulation of routes and rates, and IATA seemed to be a suitable means. Although IATA had no absolute power to enforce its regulations (since all of its decisions had to be unanimous, permitting any disgruntled operator to block action), it was a sufficiently workable tool to permit the British and Americans to come to accord.

With agreement seemingly at hand, Pan American suddenly announced that it planned to reduce its one-way fares on the North Atlantic from $375 to $275. Such action was precisely what the British had feared: evidence of the outbreak of cutthroat competition and fare reductions by the Americans which would wreck the international aviation economic structure. The reason for the timing of Pan American's announcement of the fare reduction is unclear. Critics suggest that it was anxious to prevent the United States and Great Britain from coming to agreement, hoping to delay the introduction of more competition. (Pan American subsequently had difficulty demonstrating the basis for its proposed reductions when ordered to do so by the CAB.)

At the time of Trippe's announcement Pan American and American operated 5 flights a week each to London, but this frequency was simply by sufferance of the British, in the absence of any formal contract between the two countries. The British could break the agreement at a moment's notice, but they could not shut out Pan American entirely because of the old private prewar agreement allowing 2 flights a week. Instead, the British tried to retaliate against Pan American by cutting it back from 5 flights to 2 and permitting American to continue on a 5-flight basis. In this action the British were blocked by the CAB, which refused to permit such manipulation.

Finally Pan American agreed to give in and restore the former fare, provided it got half the new London frequencies plus the two to which it was entitled under the old prewar agreement. There are those who suggest that this was Trippe's intention all along and that he would have lost his shirt had he actually instituted the lower fare. But by threatening to reduce rates, knowing that he would not in fact be permitted to do so, Trippe put himself in a position where he could claim that Pan American alone sought to reduce fares on the North Atlantic. The new competitors,* who had boasted that the threat of competi-

* The original CAB plan called for a system of "area" competition whereby American would serve England, Scandinavia, and Russia; Pan Am would have London and Northern Europe; and TWA would have the Southern route through Spain and France to Rome and Cairo. When American soon sold out to Pan American in 1949, TWA was permitted access to England, and Pan Am overlapped on TWA's Southern route.

tion would bring lower fares to the public, now seemed to have ganged up under the protection of the IATA cartel to force Pan American to raise fares.

With Trippe back in line, negotiations were resumed between the United States and Great Britain. An additional factor influencing the British toward reconciliation was a large American loan presently under consideration in the Senate. The loan request was humiliating to the British and they had no desire to see American Congressmen set off air rights against the loan terms. Final agreement was reached in Bermuda in 1946. The Americans gained access to routes they sought, and the British won the stabilization they desired by "consultation" on routes and rates through the medium of IATA.

Recognizing that the cartellike restrictions might not be popular in this country, the points of the Bermuda Agreement were grandiosely described as "The Five Freedoms of Flight" by the State Department (in accordance with Harry Hopkins' famous dictum that the American people would accept anything with the word "freedom" in it). The Five Freedoms were: the rights of transit and landing; and the carriage of passengers to; from; and beyond. It was the basic understanding in Bermuda that each country should provide service in proportion to the total traffic generated from one country to the other. In other words, "beyond" service should not exceed the "to" and "from." This approach was reasonably workable between Britain and the U.S., since the primary traffic flow was New York–London. As the smaller nations introduced international service, they naturally demanded the same terms as the British, as a matter of national prestige, if not economics. In such cases, the "beyond" service was far more significant than the "to–from." For instance, what about the Rome–New York passenger who flies KLM via The Hague? Just which "freedom" is he: to whom; where; and when? (If you know, write the State Department at

*Postwar Politics* [ 165

once; because several high-ranking officials have been trying to figure it out unsuccessfully for nearly fifteen years.)

Despite its inadequacies, the Bermuda Agreement seemed at the time an amicable adjustment of the differing national viewpoints. Thus, Bermuda became the steppingstone for international airline service—and in addition opened the gates to Juan Trippe's private preserve for other U.S. companies.

While U.S. competition on the North Atlantic was gall and wormwood to Trippe, worse was yet to come. In the Latin-American decision the CAB put Braniff down the west coast of South America.

Once again Pan American might not have been faced with this new competition if it had mended its fences earlier. Prior to the award to Braniff, the only U.S. competition for Pan American in South America was Panagra, jointly owned with W. R. Grace & Company. Grace had always hoped to connect a line to the United States gateway, but Pan American used its half interest to prevent Panagra from providing through service to this country. However, had Pan Am not blocked Panagra, it is entirely possible that Braniff might never have been designated as a second South American carrier, since Panagra could have qualified as desired competition over these routes.

From Pan American's point of view, the CAB's Pacific decision was the unkindest cut of all. Northwest Airlines was awarded the Great Circle route from Seattle, through the Aleutians, Japan to the Philippines. Ever since the days of the China Clippers, Pan Am had regarded the Pacific as its private pond.

Before the war, Northwest had been merely a regional carrier, operating from Chicago to Minneapolis and out to Seattle. Its major contribution to the war effort was the opening of a route across Canada to Alaska and the Aleutians—a route which became particularly crucial during the Japanese invasion of Kiska and Attu. Because of its pioneering efforts in this part of the world, Northwest was picked to provide competition for Pan Am in the Pacific.

As was to be expected, Trippe denounced the CAB decisions as national folly—and proceeded to fight the newcomers at every turn (wounds from those wars are still fresh). Northwest's Great Circle route in the Pacific is nearly 1,500 miles shorter than Pan Am's Central Pacific run via Hawaii—a significant advantage, particularly today with nonstop jets. However, in South America, Braniff enjoyed no such advantage, and Pan Am was able to make considerable trouble, some of it most unpleasant.

There are numerous stories of assaults, intrigue, and even sabotage—all disputed—but a Congressional report states that Pan Am airport employees were guilty of serious safety violations, such as turning off runway lights during night landings of Braniff planes and refusing necessary refueling. Critics charge such acts to Trippe himself, but more likely they were the spontaneous expressions of overeager employees. In any case, Braniff's South American routes have never been profitable. It appears unlikely that the CAB will continue subsidies to Braniff, and the company can hardly operate at a loss indefinitely. A possible solution may involve a Braniff merger with Panagra, since a recent antitrust decision has ordered divestment of Pan Am's 50-percent interest.

In the Pacific the situation is equally difficult but somewhat less immediate, since Northwest's Great Circle route is presently profitable. Actually, the Great Circle route from Japan and the Orient to the U.S. is much the shortest and best route for nonstop jets. (Pan Am's Hawaii route was more desirable in the earlier piston days when stops were required and passengers understandably preferred Honolulu to Alaska.) In addition to Northwest, Pan Am's chief Pacific foreign competitors, BOAC, Japan, and the Australian Qantas, have access to the Great Circle run, leaving our foremost international carrier at a serious disadvantage. On the other hand, Northwest would be badly hurt if Pan Am came on the Great Circle. Here again, perhaps the only long-term way to maintain competition among U.S. carriers is merger, probably Northwest and TWA for an around-the-world service competitive with Pan Am. But is there enough traffic to fill the big jets of two U.S. carriers against the competition of several strong foreign lines? Sooner or later, U.S. international airline policy is going to have to face up to the hard logic of Juan Trippe's cherished chosen instrument argument.

CHAPTER XV

*The Challenge of New Competition*

The remarkable wartime achievements of the Air Transport Command produced almost unlimited optimism and enthusiasm for the future of air travel. Wartime growth had been so great as to render meaningless any prewar judgments. Typical of the prevailing mood was the opinion of C. R. Smith as he returned from his duties as a major general in the Air Transport Command. In a speech to his fellow executives at American, C. R. said: "Anybody who can't see the day when we will fly a thousand planes, damn well better get out right now." (Today American flies substantially less than 200.) The expansion mood was not limited to the existing airlines alone. Even as the major domestic lines were eagerly entering the international market, newcomers were knocking on the domestic door. Now, for the first time, political pressure began to be brought to bear for the introduction of new airlines, beyond those certified as "grandfathers" by the Civil Aeronautics Board in 1938. This conflict between the "ins" and the "outs" was to continue to plague the industry for fully a decade.

As outside political pressures increased, the technical transition from twin-engined transports was changing the character of the industry (just as the transition to jets is doing today). While the DC-3 was a remarkable airplane, it was overshadowed by the new four-engined transports, the Douglas DC-4's and the even more impressive Lockheed Constellations.

Lockheed was founded in San Francisco by the Loughead brothers who chose a simplified spelling for the company name. Their first aircraft, the Model G (so called to create the presumption that it was not their first effort), was flown from the foot of Laguna Street in San Francisco Bay in 1913. Lockheed experienced the common difficulties of all native American aircraft designers during World War I; however, its design talents finally led it to the Lockheed Vega, a high-winged, all-metal cabin monoplane. The Vega was fast and forgiving, and pilots loved it. In the Vega *Winnie May*, Wiley Post flew around the world in eight days. Amelia Earhart, Kingsford-Smith, the English explorer Sir Hubert Wilkins, were all Lockheed pilots. The "Stellar Series" of single-engined Lockheeds became world famous—Vega, Altair, Orion, Sirius—particularly the Sirius the Lindberghs used on their survey trips in the early thirties for Pan American over the Great Circle routes to the Orient and across the North Atlantic. But the depression halted Lockheed development and the company went bankrupt.

Robert Gross gathered a group together and paid $40,000 for the Lockheed name and assets. Gross had been captain of his hockey team at Harvard, and after graduation started in the investment banking business in New York with Lee, Higginson & Company, whose offices Juan Trippe also graced briefly. Like

Trippe, Gross soon became fascinated with flying and left the banking business behind. At Lockheed he built the first Electra, a twin-engined, low-winged transport. A fine, fast airplane, the Electra was limited to half the passenger capacity of the DC-3 and was not a financial success,* either for its operators or its builders (ignoring the omen, Lockheed was to use the Electra name again thirty years later in its jinxed turboprop design).

In 1938, Lockheed had embarked on the development of the Constellation as competition for the Douglas DC-4. A prime mover behind the Constellation development was Howard Hughes, who had just bought TWA and believed that the Constellation would make TWA the greatest airline in the world. However, the war prevented the Connie from proving her superiority in commercial operations, and all production went directly into military service. Though delayed three years, the Connie was the most advanced transport flying in 1945.

But the war had given Douglas time to catch up—with the improved DC-6. Powered by the reliable and economical Pratt & Whitney R-2800 engines, the DC-6 was to offer the lowest seat-mile cost of any piston-powered transport plane.

Boeing's postwar entry was the Model 377 Stratocruiser, based on the design of the B-29, but with a double-deck fuselage. The fastest and longest ranged of any of the aircraft then flying, the Stratocruiser was also by far the most comfortable from the passenger point of view. Its big hull was roomy and quiet, with a bar on the lower deck entered by a circular stairway. Passengers loved the Stratocruiser, but a series of engine and propeller problems made it an expensive aircraft to operate.

Another major market was a replacement for the venerable DC-3 on shorter trunk routes. Douglas itself brought out the abortive DC-5, which never went into airline service, but the

---

* Actually Lockheed more than recovered its costs later through a military version, the "Hudson," which was sold to the British in great numbers for antisubmarine patrol.

chief contenders were the Convair 240 and the Martin 202. Neither of these companies had been a major factor in the commercial market, and both were anxious to establish themselves commercially as a hedge against declines in military orders. Early orders were fairly evenly split, but improved versions of the Convair came to dominate the short-haul market.

With the prospect of the new postwar airplanes, particularly the large DC-6's and Constellations, the major airlines tended to concentrate their services between the larger cities, where traffic was available to fill the big planes. But the smaller cities in this country also wanted air transportation. A number of new companies argued that they could provide "feeder" service more economically than the large carriers could. Surplus DC-3's were available at remarkably low prices, $20,000 or less. For a comparatively few thousand dollars it seemed probable that a new company could finance such equipment and carve out a place for itself in the anticipated postwar airline boom. Every town had its Congressman, ever ready to proclaim the growth and glory of his community—and the absolute necessity for airline service. Of course subsidies would be required at first—just to get the feeder lines on their feet. But future growth would soon make all airlines profitable—at least that was the theory.

The prospect of new airline companies filled the grandfather carriers with horror—particularly the thought of subsidy. They well knew that once government money was invested in a company great forces came into play to keep that company in business. (To permit a subsidized company to fail would indicate poor judgment in putting it in business in the first place, and bureaucrats fear a mistake more than a deficit.) The grandfather carriers, quite correctly, foresaw that the local market would not support full airline service. If new feeder carriers were authorized, inevitably the egos of their executives and the economies of the business would impel them to try to cash in on the richer runs between the major cities—precisely as the grandfather carriers themselves had done. Rather than admit the failure of the experiment, the CAB would follow the line of least resistance and authorize expansion of the "locals" into larger markets in an effort to reduce subsidy costs. (We will return to the accuracy of this prediction later.)

Against the feeder concept, the grandfathers argued in the alternative: that no more service was necessary, but that if more service was required, they should provide it. A conservative argument in an expansive time, the grandfathers' position was disregarded and the CAB lavished approval, and subsidies, on the new feeder lines—which promised that they would never try to cut into the grandfather carriers' routes, but would always serve as feeders to the major systems. So came into being Allegheny, Mohawk, Piedmont, North Central, Frontier, Bonanza, Ozark, Pacific, etc.

Despite their pessimistic (but accurate) predictions regarding the local service markets, the major airlines themselves embarked on a reckless race for expansion, deluging the CAB with requests for new routes and ordering new aircraft as if the entire expansion of air travel would accrue to each company alone. In their CAB presentations, some airlines' supposedly careful surveys of future markets were overly optimistic by more than 500 percent. (New aircraft orders were almost exactly as excessive and erroneous as were to occur in the jet-buying programs ten years later—the same mistakes made by the same men for the same reasons.) There was no attempt to combine or correlate market research. Each line made its plans and submitted data most favorable to its own position. Without any independent standard of comparison or basis of judgment, the CAB was incapable of effective control of overexpansion.

In theory, the CAB is qualified for policy determination by the *expertise* of its members—but in fact, such *expertise* is generally lacking,* particularly in the postwar period, when wartime growth of air transport had rendered invalid any prewar precedents.

The problems caused by the introduction of local service feeder companies, and the overexpansion of the existing airlines was compounded by the appearance of new coach and cargo companies, or "nonskeds." Both the prewar grandfather carriers and the new feeder lines had been granted certificates from the CAB requiring scheduled service and entitling them to subsidy, if needed. The coach and cargo companies were operated under an exemption from the certificate and schedule requirements (which denied them subsidy) and gave rise to their informal nickname. †

An outstanding example was the Flying Tigers Line founded by Bob Prescott, one of the original Flying Tigers from the American Volunteer Group in China. Financed out of the savings of this heroic fighter squadron, most of its personnel were former Tiger pilots. Wishing to keep their group intact and to stay in aviation, these men formed an airline to develop low-cost passenger and freight transportation. Similar groups were springing up all over the country. The scheduled airlines protested loudly, claiming that the nonsked carriers could not be counted on; that their maintenance would be affected by their need to economize, producing substantial safety risks. Finally, the grandfather lines charged that the irregulars would skim off the profitable cream of the traffic, forcing the scheduled carriers into a subsidy status.

* Critics charge that most CAB members are political hangers-on, whose aviation backgrounds or qualifications are negligible or nonexistent, such as Congressmen rejected by their constituents or ambitious attorneys who regard the CAB as a steppingstone enroute to the lifetime sinecure of a federal judgeship.

† More formal terms of address, such as noncertificated or large irregular carriers, have been tried, but the nonsked nickname persists. The nonsked airlines hate the name and claim that it was thought up by the scheduled airlines to imply undependability.

In the prevailing spirit of optimism, the CAB was inclined to grant most of the requests that came before it. The old arguments in favor of competition were as strong as ever. To these were added the fact that the grandfather carriers had not moved too quickly toward low-cost coach air transportation, nor had they seemingly pursued the development of air cargo. Many critics believed that the major lines were content to rest on their oars, safe in the protective custody of the CAB. If new blood wished to risk its own money without subsidy to bring about low-cost passenger or cargo transportation, so much the better. Within the halls of Congress it was easy to generate support for more competition. "The little man" is always favored, particularly when such groups were composed of authentic war heroes like the Flying Tigers. To almost everyone it seemed that the postwar market would be large enough to support the various applicants.

Almost overnight, optimism was replaced by despair. During the first eighteen months following the war, the scheduled domestic airlines lost more than $36,000,000. The causes were reasonably complex; overexpansion of routes, overcapacity in equipment, increasing labor costs, integration problems with new aircraft, inadequate financing programs—and plain poor judgment. Rather than recognize the real reasons, all of the parties chose to blame the CAB. The major airlines took the position that it had authorized too much competition, but from the CAB's point of view, the airlines had brought it on themselves. They had applied for new routes and new competitive services which the Board had granted, and to the CAB it was unfair of the carriers to complain now about the expansion they had sought so ardently.

The primary point of controversy soon became the air coach question. The scheduled grandfather airlines chose to blame their financial difficulties on the diversion of traffic flowing to the nonskeds' coach flights. Arguing that coach flights were economically unsound and constituted potentially dangerous price cutting, the scheduled airlines demanded that the CAB put the nonskeds out of business. The nonskeds naturally fought back, claiming that air coach flights were an obvious public benefit and that the scheduled airlines were a bunch of incompetent "fat cats," safe in the CAB subsidy, which stood in the way of progress.

Just to compound the confusion even more, several of the scheduled airlines soon began to offer air coach flights themselves, thereby weakening the earlier arguments. Capital was the first of the domestic airlines to offer this service. Faced with the overwhelming competition of United, TWA, and American between Chicago and New York, Capital felt it had nothing to lose by offering coach flights. Its immediate success was deeply galling to its bigger competitors, particularly as it tended to bear out the charges of the nonskeds by demonstrating the desirability of coach services.

National quickly followed Capital's example. Over its major New York–Miami route, National was faced with the dominant and entrenched position of Eastern. From his personal evaluation of the particular characteristics of the New York–Miami market, George Baker, National's president, believed a major segment of the traffic to be especially price conscious—and therefore susceptible to coach service. Baker's estimate was accurate—and his competitors were forced to follow.

The nonsked carriers claimed, with considerable justification, that their competition had brought about the introduction of air coach services. The lower fares might have contributed to the losses of the major carriers, but lower fares were clearly a substantial public benefit. Congress was eager to see the nonskeds continue, and yet, at the same time, it could not politically justify the continuation of an annual subsidy of more than

$36,000,000 to the scheduled airlines. While no one offered an agreeable solution, all combined to criticize.

As criticisms mounted, the point of attack shifted to the subsidy situation. But as long as the subsidy was buried within the general classification of Air Mail pay, the full degree to which the Federal Treasury was underwriting the airlines' losses was not immediately apparent. Therefore within Congress various political pressure groups began to agitate for clarification. Here the nonskeds had a strong ally in the Association of American Railroads, the trade association which serves as spokesman for the railroad industry. The railroads had begun to feel sharply the effects of competition from the airlines and wished to demonstrate the degree to which Federal funds were underwriting this competition. The railroads felt then, as they feel today, that it is folly to subsidize airlines to take traffic, particularly local traffic, away from the railroads, thereby causing a further loss of rail service and profitability, combining to create a spiral of ever-decreasing transportation services to the nation as a whole. The railroads argue, with considerable logic, that the only remedy is to place the regulation of all transportation agencies under one regulatory body.

The position of the airlines was immediately upheld by their lobby group, the Air Transport Association, which loudly asserted that the airlines had received less money in the form of subsidy than the railroads had received in their earlier years—an argument perhaps not precisely on point. Secretary of Commerce W. Averell Harriman began to criticize the Civil Aeronautics Board for overselling aviation. Historically, the Commerce Department had maintained a strong interest in civil aviation, and the CAB dreaded the thought of coming under the dominance of the Secretary of Commerce, whom they felt wanted to become a transportation czar. Another active antisubsidy group was the shipping lobby—an anomalous position, since shipping companies have long enjoyed a quietly profitable relation with the various Commerce committees of the Congress, silently siphoning off substantial subsidy for years without any significant outcry.

In 1948, the Post Office Committee of the House issued a strong report, severely criticizing both the airlines and the Civil Aeronautics Board, emphasizing the high cost of local service lines, the high salaries of airline officials, the poor management of some of the airlines, and the CAB's freedom to make experiments without direct action of Congress. Spurred on by the complaints and pressures of the certificated airlines and alarmed by the mounting Congressional criticism of the subsidy burden, the CAB began to crack down on the operations of nonsked carriers, on the grounds that their activities deprived the certificated lines of potential traffic. The nonskeds immediately carried their case to Congress, claiming that they were risking their own money and deserved the right to operate, while their competition, the major carriers, were trying to drive them out of business with Federal subsidy support. With charges of "monopoly control," the nonskeds demanded to know the full amount of public subsidy being used against them.

Up until this point (early 1950) the major airlines and the CAB had stood together in their opposition to separating subsidy payments, claiming that the administrative and accounting difficulties were too great. However, critics maintained that their real reason was a desire to conceal the true amounts. At this point the influential Hoover Commission submitted its report, containing a strong recommendation for separation of subsidy from mail pay and for the separate appropriation by Congress of airline subsidies. The appeal of the Hoover Commission was strong throughout the country, and its recommendations tended to focus even greater public attention on the issue.

Foremost in the fray was the handsome young Congressman

from Massachusetts John F. Kennedy, who introduced the first legislation calling for separation of subsidy from mail pay. Before long the issue was strongly overlaid with personality conflicts. At a Democratic testimonial dinner, chairman O'Connell of the Civil Aeronautics Board was reported to have made strongly critical remarks concerning the character and competence of the New York City delegation in Congress, particularly the perennially cantankerous Congressman Rooney from Brooklyn—then, and still, chairman of the House Appropriations Committee. O'Connell's remarks were quickly carried back to Representative Rooney, who vowed that he would have O'Connell's scalp. Relations between the CAB and Congress deteriorated rapidly.

President Truman called a conference of top officials, including Congressional leaders, the Postmaster General, and CAB chairman O'Connell. Just what was said at that conference is not recorded, but immediately thereafter chairman O'Connell publicly reversed his earlier position completely and came out squarely for the principle of subsidy separation. A prominent Senator stated bluntly in a nationwide radio interview that he suspected certain very large airlines had too great an influence with certain CAB members. The threat was clear, and the opposition of the airline industry began to weaken.

Just as tensions reached the boiling point, the advent of the Korean War rendered the subsidy question moot. The need for military airlift in the Pacific was suddenly so acute that almost all of the nonskeds were quickly absorbed into military contract operations. Increasing military and business activity also restored the profitability of the scheduled airlines.

At this writing the major carriers have all been off subsidy for several years, except for Pan Am's African Division, which is supported as a matter of national interest, and the CAB has indicated that it does not intend to return any major carrier to subsidy. On the other hand, the current feeder, or local, service subsidy bill will run well over $85,000,000 and goes higher every year. In dollar amount the current local service subsidy represents a far greater drain on the public treasury than the amounts which caused such turmoil during the height of the nonsked controversy. Yet so far there has been no significant outcry. The explanation is simple. There is no other interest group in a position to benefit from calling public and Congressional attention to the situation. The most articulate nonskeds have disappeared, and the railroads are too busy seeking subsidy themselves.

CHAPTER XVI

*The Fateful Climax
of the Air Coach Controversy*

The Korean War provided a strong stimulus to the economy generally and to the airlines in particular. Nevertheless, the battle between the "ins" and the "outs" continued unabated. By the early 1950's, all of the scheduled airlines were offering air coach service, led by TWA. Recognizing that its Constellations would soon be outclassed in passenger appeal by the faster DC-7's of American and United, TWA felt that it had no choice but to turn to greatly expanded air coach operations. Confronted with TWA's decision, American soon followed, and then grudgingly, United.

Since the major airlines were now all offering coach service, they took the position that the nonskeds were making no public contribution and constituted a drain and diversion of needed revenue from the scheduled carriers. The CAB responded with new restrictions on the nonskeds, limiting permissible coach frequency to ten flights per month between any two cities.

Faced with such limitations, some of the nonskeds (such as Slick, Seaboard and Tigers) turned to cargo and military charter operations exclusively. However, several others, with strong support in Congress, persisted in air coach activities, most notably the North American complex (trade-name litigation by the manufacturing company later forced a name change to Trans American). North American was owned by an enterprising group of entrepreneurs, Messrs. Weiss, Fischgrund, Lewin, and Hart, but it owed its success to the ingenuity of its attorney, Hardy Maclay. To get around the CAB restrictions permitting only ten flights per month, Maclay set up several shell corporations —in effect, the Monday Company, Tuesday Company, and so forth. In addition, there was a sales company which served as ticket agent for all of the operating companies, and an equipment holding company which owned the airplanes. In practice, the sales company offered the public daily DC-6B air coach service coast to coast (including the first nonstop flights eastbound). The Monday Company would lease its airplane, fly its schedule, turn the plane over to the Tuesday Company— and go out of business for a week. By this strategem, daily schedules were maintained. To complaints that it was offering scheduled service in direct violation of the CAB regulations, North American blandly replied that no single company was flying more than four or five flights per month, well within the CAB ten-flight restriction. To its great discredit, the CAB permitted this transparent subterfuge to continue, to the mounting frustration and fury of the certificated trunklines, as well as the considerable personal profit of the individual members of the North American combine, who happily took down nearly $150,000 apiece every year of their existence (an estimated annual return on investment of over 500 percent).

To counter the "diversion" argument, the nonskeds agitated for a fare investigation by the CAB to determine whether the scheduled airlines were making too much money as it was. The threat of a fare investigation was the lowest blow imaginable to the scheduled airlines. Crying "foul," the scheduled airlines drew back to their corners and mounted a savage counterattack and publicity campaign. Airline spokesmen accused the CAB of a "lack of guts" for submitting to political pressure and permitting the nonskeds to fly at all. To marshal public opinion in their behalf, the Air Transport Association embarked on a massive campaign to present their position in public periodicals. Before a Congressional committee investigating these practices, an ATA official admitted that material prepared by it had been placed verbatim in such influential prestige journals as *Life*, *Time*, and the *Saturday Evening Post*, as well as through syndicated columnists, including Eleanor Roosevelt. The nonskeds claimed that such editorial support was a pay-off in return for the huge airline advertising budgets.

Embarrassingly, the scheduled airlines were in truth enjoying record profits at the time (approximately 15 percent on invested capital). The airlines took several positions regarding such profits: first, the condition was only temporary, resulting from the Korean War; second, such profits were necessary to finance new aircraft; third, it was high time for some profits, after the lean postwar years.

At this moment in time there was a vacancy on the CAB, and the remaining four members split two-to-two over whether to investigate the fare levels and profits of the airlines. The appointment of the new member, Harmar Denny, became the crucial element. When the fare question was presented for vote, Denny cast his ballot in favor of the investigation. Immediately thereafter he was privately visited by Stuart Tipton, then general counsel (now president) of the Air Transport Association, which represented all of the scheduled airlines and was vigorously opposed to any fare investigation. What transpired between Denny and Tipton is of course unknown, but Denny changed his vote—thus quashing any inquiry into the airlines' profits.

Obviously such behavior left the parties open to criticism and raised serious doubts as to the competence and character of CAB proceedings. Against this compromising background the scene was set for the fateful climax of the air coach controversy.

The pivotal figure was the new CAB chairman, Ross Rizley, a former Republican Congressman from Oklahoma, who was appointed in 1954, to "clean up the mess in the CAB." In January of 1954, the CAB had sent its recommendation to the White House regarding the Seattle–Hawaii route. Both Pan American and Northwest had been flying the route on temporary authorizations. At the conclusion of the temporary certificates, CAB had evaluated the route and concluded that the potential traffic could not support two carriers. Seeking to maintain competition in the Pacific area, the CAB had recommended Northwest as the sole carrier. Never one to let CAB decisions deter its efforts, Pan American quickly rounded up support, including Commerce Secretary Sinclair Weeks, and Sherman Adams, assistant to the President. After discussion at the White House,* Eisenhower reversed the CAB's recommendations and gave the route to Pan American. Northwest fought back, with strong Congressional support. So vigorous was the Congressional interest that President Eisenhower admitted publicly that he had "made an error," and instructed the CAB to recertify both carriers on the run on a temporary basis, to determine whether sufficient traffic to justify competitive carriers could be developed in the near future. The confusion in this case clearly pointed up the lack of airline policy or planning, and Congress threatened a thorough investigation and overhaul of the CAB.

* Under the Civil Aeronautics Act, all international route awards of the CAB are subject to Presidential approval. While Hawaii was still a territory, its air routes were considered international.

Seeking to smooth things over, Eisenhower appointed Rizley, known in Congress for energy, ambition and tact, but totally innocent of any airline background or qualification. Rizley made no secret of his eagerness to leave the CAB for the security of a lifetime appointment as a federal judge; nevertheless, he promised action before he left.

The greatest vulnerability of the airlines and the CAB seemed to be in the monopoly charge, one to which Congress is always sensitive. The chief proponents of the monopoly·argument were naturally the nonsked airlines. At the same time, the nonskeds could hardly claim that their own hands were clean, since those still operating were in open and flagrant violation of CAB restrictions. The heart of the monopoly argument lay in the dominance of the so-called Big Four—American, United, TWA, and Eastern—who between them controlled more than three-fourths of all domestic airline traffic. Furthermore, the earnings of the Big Four were at an all-time peak, despite the alleged diversion of the air coach operators.

Out of this confused and controversial situation Rizley evolved a compromise solution. First, he would exclude the nonskeds on the grounds of their violations of CAB regulations, thereby placating the scheduled airlines. To counter the inevitable monopoly arguments, Rizley determined to cut the smaller scheduled airlines into the Big Four markets, thereby greatly increasing internal competition among the grandfather carriers themselves.

Compromises are seldom satisfactory, and Rizley's was no exception. The best rationalization for his theory of expanded internal competition was that the carriers already in each market were not providing sufficient service. Anticipating this approach, each carrier ordered more than enough new jet transports to meet all foreseeable traffic demands, thereby hoping to preclude additional carriers. At the same time the smaller airlines, eager for access to richer routes, similarly ordered excessive numbers of new jets, to demonstrate their capabilities.

The obvious result was orders for an impoverishing number of new jets, creating capacity beyond any possible future traffic demand. The magnitude of the folly was readily apparent to objective observers (*Fortune* Magazine carried an article at the time outlining in detail the inevitable consequences), but the various airline executives, seemingly blinded by their competitive antagonisms and infatuated with the glamour of the new jet transports, plunged heedlessly ahead into the Jet Age.

PART SIX

## Advent of the Jets

CHAPTER XVII

## The Equipment Race

The jet engine represented a radical advance in aircraft propulsion. Invented by the Englishman Sir Frank Whittle, in 1930, the jet was first used in operations by the Germans during the last days of World War II. So great was its superiority that all postwar military combat aircraft were designed around the new power source. It was inevitable that the jet would eventually be applied to commercial transports. But the early jets had a prodigious thirst for fuel, and U.S. airline executives doubted that they would prove as economical in commercial operations as the highly refined piston-powered transports already flying.

The British, however, approached the problem differently. During the war their aircraft industry had been entirely devoted to the production of combat aircraft and lagged far behind America in commercial design. Forced by circumstances to fly American transports in the early postwar period, the British tried a bold gamble: they determined to leapfrog the entire developmental cycle of four-engined piston-powered aircraft. It was quite clear that the long lead of experience acquired in the United States gave this country an almost insurmountable advantage. On the other hand, the jet engine was an English invention. How much more appropriate, and potentially lucrative, was the prospect of proceeding with jet transport development while America concentrated on perfecting her lead in piston-powered aircraft. Accordingly, they undertook design studies which led to culmination in the DeHavilland "Comet."

The Comet was far ahead of its time. Introduced on Empire routes in 1952, it offered a combination of speed and comfort heretofore unknown in commercial aviation. However, the original Comet I's were not economical aircraft. Their fuel requirements were too high to permit nonstop transatlantic flights, and they were limited to the London–Rome–Johannesburg and Far Eastern routes of BOAC.

By the standards of its time the Comet was a thoroughly tested aircraft, but a tragic and unforeseen development lay in store. A Comet inexplicably came apart in flight—and then another—each time in areas where the wreckage could not be examined. The crashes became a matter of unusual national concern, for the Comet was more than an airplane to the British people; it represented England's technical and commercial abilities rising from the ashes of war.

One clear summer day, shortly following the first accidents, another Comet thundered down the runway at Rome, lifted smoothly into its soaring climb, and dissolved in a flash of flame over the Mediterranean. A few simple Sicilian fishermen, quietly hauling their nets, were appalled as bodies and pieces of wreckage hurtled down around them from the cloudless sky. All England was horrified. The vaunted Comet became a national disgrace.

An explanation was demanded, but the evidence lay scattered

600 feet down at the bottom of the sea—beyond the reach of divers. Yet England determined to recover the wreckage, regardless of difficulty or cost. The Royal Navy brought in the latest submarine-detection devices; television cameras and floodlights were lowered to scan the bottom; with careful, heartbreaking effort, substantial portions of the plane were eventually recovered.

From these pieces came telltale clues. The distribution of wreckage on the ocean bottom and the examination of the pieces themselves clearly indicated an explosion from within. Yet nowhere in the wreckage or on the bodies of the victims was there evidence of an internal fire. Then came the breakthrough. The explosion had been caused by the Comet's own altitude cabin pressurization. Unexpected stresses in cabin pressure differential during altitude flight had weakened the metal skin at the corner of a cabin window. The window gave way and the cabin pressure had exploded like a bomb—a blow from which British aviation has not fully recovered to this day.

In this country, jet development was slower and far less spectacular. With the early jet engines available after World War II, the costs of jet operation were much too high for all but military operations. The only possibility seemed to be a very large plane, so that the high operating costs per mile could be spread over a sufficient number of paying passengers. However, most airlines in this country were not interested in really big transports carrying more than 100 passengers. The 60 to 70 seats on the economical DC-6's seemed just about right; each airline wants to operate a full pattern of daily schedules. Very few cities generate enough traffic to permit frequent full flights for 150-passenger planes—as the airlines are finding out today.

The Boeing company was dominant in the construction of large military aircraft. Following the success of its wartime

Flying Fortresses and B-29's, Boeing moved into jets with the swept-wing B-47. Recognizing the passenger appeal of the speed and smoothness of jet flight, Boeing tried to interest the airlines in a design proposal of a jet-powered Stratocruiser in 1949. Only Pan Am showed real interest and, recalling its experience with Pan Am on the 314 flying boat, Boeing decided that a commercial jet design was too big a risk to take for one airline's order.

Nevertheless, Bill Allen, Boeing's lawyer-trained president, believed in the inevitability of the jet transport and felt that a flying prototype was the only way to convince the reluctant airlines. But a prototype would require an investment of at least $15,000,000—more than Boeing could risk after several profitless postwar years. Its previous commercial venture, the Stratocruiser, had lost nearly $14,000,000, and opinion in the company was sharply divided over the desirability of re-entering the commercial field at all.

However, the Stratocruiser losses had been recouped from military sales of a tanker version—the KC-97. Allen thought he saw a chance to reverse the sequence by a jet-tanker proposal for the Air Force. At the time, the Strategic Air Command was refueling its B-47 jet bombers from slower, piston-powered Boeing KC-97 tankers. SAC officers were enthusiastic about Allen's idea for a jet tanker, but the Pentagon was dubious. A paper proposal was inadequate. Here again, a flying prototype seemed to be the only way to persuade doubtful buyers. At the same time, a jet tanker prototype could also demonstrate passenger potential—and so Allen decided to gamble.

The Boeing prototype decision was a shock to the rest of the industry. Most airline executives, as well as most manufacturers, thought that jets were many years away and that a generation of turboprops would intervene. The turboprop was a hybrid, utilizing power from a jet engine to turn a propeller, exchanging speed for economy. The English Viscount turboprop was already flying for Capital and such prominent figures as American's C. R. Smith and Eastern's Eddie Rickenbacker had committed themselves to large orders for the Lockheed Electra turboprop.

The Boeing jet prototype was flying in 1954, and it was immediately apparent that the Air Force would need jet tankers. Harold Talbott, Secretary of the Air Force, announced a jet-tanker competition to give a chance to other builders before Boeing's lead was insurmountable. Douglas and Lockheed quickly entered, but Boeing's head start was already too great.

Despite Boeing's military lead, the commercial jet market was tempting. Lockheed, already committed to the turboprop Electra, finally elected to stay out. But Douglas, long dominant in the commercial transport market, really had little choice if it wanted to retain its position. Although Boeing had substantially greater jet experience and had a prototype flying, Douglas enjoyed a superb reputation and could benefit, as it had in the past, from Boeing's pioneering. Douglas' great DC-3 followed and was to a large extent based upon the design of Boeing's earlier Model 247. The bigger Douglas soon drove the Boeing from the sky.

The same thing almost happened in jet transports. The fact that the Boeing 707 prototype was already flying meant that its design was already several years old—and engines had improved. The first 707 was designed around the Pratt & Whitney J-57 engine, giving the 707 a range of less than 3,000 miles. When Douglas entered the picture, the more powerful J-75 engine was in prospect. Boeing did not want to increase its costs by redesigning the 707, but Douglas could start from scratch to accommodate the bigger engine, giving the DC-8 a 1,000-mile range advantage.

Despite the activity at Douglas and Boeing, the airlines still did not seem too excited over jets. Most companies planned to let the DC-8 come along, compare prototypes, and make decisions at their leisure. Secure in large orders for the turboprop Electra from American and Eastern, Bob Gross of Lockheed was giving a speech in Chicago to the effect that jet transports were many years away when news reached him that Juan Trippe had placed an order.

Turboprops never had any real attraction for Trippe, who saw pure jets as the really significant aircraft. Moreover, the English had redesigned the Comet, and Trippe could not stand the thought of BOAC beating him on the Atlantic with jets. With characteristic secrecy, he went to the Coast and personally ordered twenty-five DC-8's from Douglas and twenty 707's from Boeing. The Boeing 707 was too short ranged to suit Trippe, but clearly it would be the first available. So Trippe bought it—with the understanding that he could convert the order to a larger version if Boeing were to build one. To cover himself, Trippe also ordered the DC-8, which had the range he wanted. Buying both, Trippe guaranteed that Pan American would be in a position to operate the first jets on the North Atlantic prestige route.* But the Pan American order was not nearly big enough for either manufacturer to break even. Competition for more orders grew intense.

United was the next to fall. Boeing felt the order was secure, with its promise of rapid delivery of the 707, but the cautious Patterson took his time. United engineers had built a mock-up of a jet cabin—half DC-8 on one side and half 707 on the other—to study the advantages of each. After such preparations Patterson knew exactly what improvements he wanted: first and

---

* Although his first Boeing 707's were ready in the fall of 1958, Trippe held up service for a few weeks, permitting BOAC to fly the first commercial jet across the Atlantic. There are two schools of thought regarding Trippe's motives for the delays. Pan American holds that, in his inherent philanthropy, Trippe wanted to buoy British pride after the earlier Comet disasters. A more practical view is that Trippe feared the British might make a fuss on landing rights over the noise level of the 707 (the Comet is slightly quieter). However, if they themselves started jet service, the British opposition would be minimized.

*Advent of the Jets*  [  193

foremost, a wider fuselage to accommodate more seats. Douglas, working only from a paper proposal, readily agreed to any change requested. Still confident that Patterson needed early delivery to compete with American's Electra turboprops, Boeing refused to make any changes whatever. Patterson chose Douglas.

The decision was a deep shock. Boeing's adamant refusal to make changes had been based upon an effort to keep its break-even point relatively low (50 planes was an early estimate) by avoiding any additional tooling costs. Suddenly Boeing realized that despite its lead, Douglas was well on the way to capturing the market from under its nose. Eastern was already known to favor the DC-8. Unless Boeing was willing to make some changes, it was entirely possible that no more orders would be forthcoming—leaving Boeing with a sizable loss on the investment already made, not to mention the blow to its prestige and morale.

American then became the crucial customer, and the Boeing sales team approached this in a different frame of mind. C. R. Smith liked speed, and the Boeing was clearly faster than the Douglas. When Boeing agreed to widen the fuselage to Smith's specification, American ordered the 707—and put Boeing back into contention.

Once committed to some changes, Boeing reconsidered its earlier engine decision—and came up with a bigger "Intercontinental" model incorporating the J-75 engine. With the J-75 engines the Boeing 707 was competitive in range and somewhat faster than the DC-8—but international sales still presented problems, particularly British pride, still stinging from the Comet crashes. "Buy-British" sentiment ran high, and BOAC was very reluctant to make a decision on an American plane. Some progress toward saving national "face" was achieved by agreement to use Rolls-Royce engines, but BOAC officials indicated that they would defer decision until the Commonwealth nations had bought American jets, thereby reducing criticism of BOAC at home.

Douglas was still very much in the race.* Earlier international orders were split; SAS bought the DC-8, while Air France bought Boeing. The first round of the Empire competition went to Douglas, with Trans-Canada Airlines. Air India favored Boeing, so the Australian Qantas became the decisive order. Douglas was heavily favored, having enjoyed long-established relationships with Qantas on DC-4's, DC-6's, and DC-7's. The Qantas and Douglas people knew each other well, but Boeing knew nobody, and so asked BOAC to make appointments for them. Some Qantas people interpreted the BOAC requests as an indication that BOAC favored Boeing. How much influence this factor had in the decision is not clear—but Boeing won. With Qantas came BOAC.

With several versions of the 707 already committed, Boeing proceeded to design a smaller, shorter-ranged model known as the 720, thus offering a far wider model selection than Douglas—and scoring heavily in the intermediate-range domestic market. The final count is not in, but present orders favor Boeing nearly 3 to 1.

That the stakes were high and the risks great in the jet transport game is proven by the case of Convair. It wanted to play—but not to take too big a risk. By hedging, Convair lost a great opportunity, as well as nearly $500,000,000, an all-time record for corporate bad judgment.

With a position already secure in the short-haul market with its twin-engined 340 series, Convair began to look into the possibilities of commercial jets. Despite its prior bad experiences on 340 orders (an agreement reached at midnight in a

---

* Considering that Boeing had a proven airplane already flying and could offer far earlier deliveries, the many DC-8 orders must be recognized as a remarkable personal tribute to Donald Douglas. There is also a note of coincidence in that the Douglas vice-president for sales, Nat Paschall, was Bill Boeing's stepson.

rented car parked in the Las Vegas municipal dump was repudiated in daylight), the first person Convair talked to was Howard Hughes. Dizzied by another ride on the merry-go-round of Hughes' indecision, Convair was left behind when Boeing and Douglas came out with their preliminary designs for the 707 and DC-8.

With Boeing and Douglas already in the field, it seems perfectly clear that there was no practical possibility for the long-range market to absorb another similar model. The only really logical alternative was the short-range field. Here the market was wide open. Convair was already established and enjoyed worldwide prominence. Both Boeing and Douglas acknowledged that, had Convair moved quickly into the short-haul market, nobody could have caught it. Fully committed in their own race for the long-range market, neither Boeing nor Douglas could afford the engineering time or talent to compete simultaneously in both the short- and long-haul areas.

But Convair backed away from the opportunity, as being too big a risk—and instead tried for the far riskier intermediate-range jet. Two factors apparently influenced Convair's decision. First of all, Convair feared that the piston-powered DC-6's and 7's forced off the long-haul routes by jets would dominate the short-haul market. There was some validity in this position, except that it failed to consider the enormous public appeal of jet travel which was bound to make itself felt soon. Secondly, Convair was worried that no really suitable jet engine was then available for a short-range transport. One was bound to come in time, as it always had, but Convair was afraid to wait. In entering the intermediate area, Convair thought it had the opportunity to do to Boeing and Douglas what Douglas had almost done to Boeing—ride on the prior design and engineering experience of its competitors and come in behind them with a better engine. All along, Boeing had recognized that the real danger in being first was that somebody might come out with a design that was really new and better. Instead, Douglas, and then Convair, were apparently content to follow the same general design concepts as Boeing, thereby forfeiting their best opportunity.

Boeing engineers, naturally enough, had incorporated their prior piston experience into their jet designs. Piston engines had to be spread over the wing surface to provide clearance for the propellers. Obviously jet engines did not need propeller clearance, yet our designers were so accustomed to having engines in the wing that, when the jet came along, they were placed almost in the same positions that propeller engines would have been. (Reminding one of the old story of the automobile designer, who when asked why he had placed the motor in front of his horseless carriage, replied, "That's where the horse used to be.")

True, there were certain advantages in hanging the engines beneath the wings, particularly from the point of view of weight distribution. At the same time, the low-hanging engines were constantly endangered by loose dirt and gravel from the runway. The outboard engines are so low that a tire or wheel failure on one side might well rip off the engine and lead to more serious trouble. Most important, the wide spread of centers of thrust produces a condition of asymmetrical trim during engine-out procedures.

European designers, freed from the habits and limitations of prior 4-engined piston experience of this country, approached the jet differently. The DeHavilland designers of the original Comet buried their engines in the wing roots, close to the fuselage. This design had two advantages: the thrust was concentrated near the center of the aircraft, thereby reducing control problems, and the general aerodynamics of the wing were undisturbed by engine placement. Our designers criticized the Comet on the grounds that an engine failure would damage the structure of the fuselage, whereas our pylon-mounted engines would not. It remained for the French to find the logical conclusion. In designing the Caravelle, the engineers of the semi-nationalized Sud-Aviation Company mounted the engines at the tail of the fuselage, combining the advantages of safety, centralized thrust, and improved aerodynamics over the wing itself.

The quietest and easiest to handle of all jet aircraft, the logic of the Caravelle design was at once apparent. Several American airlines expressed strong interest. United ordered 20, with an option for 20 more. TWA was at the point of a big Caravelle order, limited only by its shaky financial condition. Rather than attempt the engineering costs involved in producing its own short-range model, Douglas entered into an agreement with the Caravelle manufacturers to market and service the airplane in this country.

Boeing, however, embarked on a design of its own, the 727. The new Boeing will be the first trimotor aircraft to fly in this country since the late 1920's—and this time all three engines will be mounted in the tail, following the design concept of the Caravelle. With its 707 four-jet series dominant on the long-haul market and its trijet 727 showing great promise for the short-range field, Boeing is once again the leading air transport manufacturer of the world.

With their present jets, the airlines' equipment race seems to be over, at least for the time being. The existing aircraft can do everything the airlines need to achieve their dream of low cost, mass air transportation. The next step, supersonic transports, seem to be at least a decade away. Quite apart from the problems of technical development, there are substantial additional difficulties in noise, passenger protection, and air traffic control. The relative speed advantage would make only slight differences except on the longest transcontinental or international runs. However, the major factor delaying the supersonic transport is its enormous development cost, considering its relatively small market. It is most unlikely that any private manufacturer could risk it alone. The costly example of Convair's recent experience with its jet program is all too familiar. All in all, there is no one whom I have talked with in the airline industry who is in any hurry to see the supersonic transport come along.

However, their hands may be forced by foreign development. The prestige factor is a significant element, particularly to the French. Her aircraft manufacturers are nationalized.. Hence, it is much easier for the government to sponsor supersonic development, without charges of favoritism of one company over another. Sud-Aviation, manufacturer of the Caravelle, is already well under way with a Mach 2 airplane. Our designers hope to wait and move directly to a Mach 3 or 4 aircraft, which they believe would be far more economical. But they may not have the time if Air France puts a Super-Caravelle into service on the Blue Ribbon run between New York and Paris.

Our domestic airlines are having plenty of problems putting their present jets to economical use as it is. The fact is that the technical capabilities of the jets have outrun the market for their service. It seems almost inevitable that economic pressure will force consolidations in the industry, to which question we will return later. Meanwhile, it seems appropriate to take a closer look at some of the individual companies which make up the airline industry today.

PART SEVEN

# Jet Age Giants

CHAPTER XVIII

## The Example of United

Over the years, between 70 and 80 percent of all domestic air travel had been carried by the Big Four: United, American, Eastern and TWA. Such dominance is almost inevitable in that those carriers fly between our largest cities, obviously the richest airline markets. At the same time, the dominance of the Big Four carriers, despite their internal rivalries, also provided a certain security.

For the part quarter century, each of the Big Four has been under the policy guidance of a single individual, whose personality and philosophy are inevitably reflected in his company. Patterson's United resembles a well-run public utility; Smith's American is aggressively sales-minded; under Eddie Rickenbacker, Eastern was the most cost-conscious; and in the hands of Howard Hughes, TWA had varied from boldly venturesome to weakly hesitant. (Juan Trippe's Pan American is in a class by itself. Always the proponent of a benign public-utility approach,

Trippe has simultaneously shown himself to be a most savage competitor.)

In the face of the size and strength of these major carriers, the smaller have of necessity been forced into more innovations and promotions in their efforts to gain recognition and acceptance, particularly George Baker of National and Bob Six of Continental. Among the other trunklines, Northwest, Braniff, Delta, and Western have faced somewhat less direct Big Four competition on their major routes, hence their struggles have been less intense—and somewhat less colorful. (Capital, of course, has already succumbed to United, and Northeast's days are apparently numbered.)

The dominant domestic airline today, United has always been the steady cornerstone of the industry. Begun by Bill Boeing, expanded by Frederick Rentschler of Pratt & Whitney, United was the first transcontinental carrier. As the airline outlet for the leading aircraft and engine manufacturers of its time, United's equipment and techniques were the example around which our national air transport system was shaped. In the New Deal investigations of the prior Republican Administration's relations with the airlines, United, as the outstanding company, became the easy target and innocent victim of political vindictiveness. Boeing Aircraft and Pratt & Whitney were split off from the United operation. Its leaders banished, its financial structure impaired, a badly crippled company was handed over to William A. Patterson, then thirty-four years old.

Careful and cautious by nature, the banker-trained Patterson became even more conservative in his policies for the airline. As a conservative company in a dynamic industry, United's record in the late 1930's was disappointing, and it was rapidly overtaken by the hard-driving and aggressively sales-minded C. R. Smith of American. Yet over the years most of Patterson's policies have proven out in practice. With the Capital merger in

1960, Patterson's United once again became the largest domestic airline.

Patterson was born in Honolulu. His father, a sugar plantation superintendent, died while he was still a boy. As soon as he was old enough, his mother enrolled him in a military school outside Honolulu and returned to the mainland to live with her relatives and try to find work to support the family. Patterson hated the school and ran away. He was caught and returned to school, but a second effort was successful. He made it to the waterfront and signed on as a cabin boy on a sailing ship returning to San Francisco. The crossing took twenty-four days, and Patterson was seasick every one of them. But he reached the mainland, joined his mother, and went to work as an office boy in the Wells, Fargo Bank. Working by day at the bank and going to school at night, he managed to finish three years of college.

One noon hour, Vernon Gorst, president of Pacific Air Transport, a marginal mail carrier, came into the bank to borrow a few hundred dollars for a new airplane engine. The unusual part of the transaction was that the engine lay at the bottom of San Francisco Bay in the wreck of an ill-fated plane which had crashed on take-off, attempting a nonstop flight to Hawaii. Gorst thought the engine could be salvaged, but Patterson was dubious. Nevertheless, Patterson was fascinated at the story Gorst presented and agreed to look over the operation of Pacific Air Transport. After investigation, Patterson decided to take a chance and loaned Gorst $5,000 to overhaul his equipment. It was Patterson's first loan on his own responsibility. After reading Patterson's report, the bank's president called him to his office and pointed out the substantial risks in the airline business. Patterson replied that the best way to get new business for the bank was to help new companies get started. The bank president agreed but added a further caution: "If this loan turns out badly, you might lose confidence in yourself. Stay close to this loan and see that we get our money back."

Patterson followed the older banker's advice, spending most of his spare time at Crissey Field, going over the operation of Pacific Air Transport, talking with the pilots, learning their problems and helping to put the airline on what approached a businesslike basis. The loan was repaid in full and on time, and Patterson's interest in the company continued.

Competition was increasingly bearing down on Pacific Air Transport. Gorst needed new planes to keep Pacific going, but he couldn't finance the purchase. Pacific's major asset was its Air Mail contract, and to get it, Harris Hanshue of Western Air Express offered to buy Gorst's controlling stock. Gorst brought the offer to Patterson at the bank, seeking his advice. Under the terms offered by Western, Gorst would receive $250 per share for his voting stock, but there was no provision for the hundreds of holders of nonvoting stock. For Patterson, the problem was delicate. Gorst's company was in too much trouble for the bank to grant another loan, and the terms offered by Western were generous, as far as Gorst was concerned. However, Patterson felt a responsibility to all of the stockholders of Pacific Air Transport as a group, and in seeking an alternative solution, suggested to Boeing that Boeing Air Transport buy all of PAT's stock, voting and nonvoting alike, and merge the two airlines. Bill Boeing counteroffered $200 a share for Gorst's stock with a provision that Boeing would keep all of PAT's employees on the payroll and would buy all of the stock held by other PAT shareholders on the same or better terms. Patterson urged Gorst to accept, and to his credit, Gorst did so, although he personally benefited less in the transaction than he would have by a sale to Western.*

* When Boeing handed Gorst a check to close the deal, Gorst looked at it and said, "Well, a fool and his money are soon parted. I want to spend this on a Boeing flying boat to open a Seattle–Alaska airline." Gorst started his company and ran it for five years, hoping the Post Office would accept his offer to fly mail

After his part in the negotiations for the sale of Pacific Air Transport, Patterson returned to his job at the Wells, Fargo Bank in San Francisco. Before long he received a call from Boeing, asking him to come to Seattle. He arrived on a Saturday afternoon and went directly to Boeing's home for dinner, where the conversation was limited to general topics. The next morning Phil Johnson, president of Boeing, took Patterson to the plant, leading him through the workshops, the rows of unfinished airplanes, through Johnson's own office to a brand-new office next door. "I need an assistant," said Johnson. "This is your office."

Patterson's first job was to round up all of the remaining outstanding stock of Pacific Air Transport. It was not an easy job. Gorst had paid off his employees and suppliers for years with stock certificates. The word that Boeing was buying started prices rising. Dog-eared stock certificates began to turn up from improbable places. An enterprising Portland attorney organized a syndicate to bid up the price. The market skyrocketed to $666 a share for the once worthless certificates. Patterson claims he picked up the last two shares from an Oregon prostitute who held out for the highest price.

Patterson had scarcely settled in his new job when the Black Air Mail Act of 1934 banished Boeing and Johnson, leaving United Airlines to Patterson. His first decision as president was a crucial one. The Air Mail routes were again to be placed up for public bid. The major airlines knew that the smaller operators were going to bid low on the new contracts, accepting short-term losses in hopes of an upward adjustment as soon as politics permitted. In the case of this competition, some of the older carriers similarly decided to bid below costs in an effort

---

to Alaska. When the Air Mail service to Alaska was finally authorized, the contract went to Pan American instead. Gorst ended his days operating a busline in Oregon.

to recapture their old routes, hoping for later upward adjustments when the political skies had cleared. Patterson, on the other hand, believed that the only honorable and businesslike approach was to figure costs closely and bid on that basis. Using this approach, United was successful in winning back its transcontinental run, but lost the Dallas–Chicago route to Braniff.

Most of the other former operators also recaptured their former routes. Although angry at the treatment they had received, they were willing to forget the injustice to try to regain the goodwill of the administration. Such politicking was not for Patterson, and he counterattacked vigorously. United's treatment by Senator Black and the New Deal was shameful. To clear his company and former colleagues, Patterson sued for $2,842,000 damages. Naturally the suit was bitterly fought by both sides—for the principle was even more important politically than the money involved. The district court determined that the government's cancellation of United's contracts was arbitrary and without due process of law since United had no opportunity to defend itself. However, the court also held that proper redress lay in the court of claims, where after many delays a token settlement was finally awarded. The verdict was a moral victory for United, but the existence of the suit severely prejudiced relations with the New Deal during the intervening period.

With mail pay reduced by the lower rate in the new government contracts, the airlines turned increasing attention to passengers. In the battle for passenger revenues, United was handicapped by two problems: equipment and competition. TWA was awarded the Chicago–Pittsburgh–Newark route, and American won the Chicago–Detroit–Newark run. Both new routes were slightly longer than United's "Main Line" via Cleveland, but they brought intense competition into a market which had been virtually a United monopoly. TWA launched its route with Douglas DC-2's, twenty-five miles an hour faster than United's Boeing 247's. American followed. With their improved DC-3's, both could soon offer five-hour nonstop services between Chicago and New York. United's Boeings were clearly outclassed. In competition for the new passenger market, the airlines were selling speed. United, for the first time in its history, was at a disadvantage.

In spite of United's best efforts with the 247, before long TWA and American skimmed off the cream of the Chicago and New York markets. The more economic Douglases made money for their owners, while the half-filled Boeings lost it. In 1936, Patterson bowed to the inevitable and bought ten DC-3's from Douglas. United was no longer the leader.

With the advent of the Civil Aeronautics Board in 1938, there was a scramble among the air carriers to provide themselves with bigger slices of potential business. In 1934, United's revenues were three times that of American; by 1938, United's revenues were less than half. Believing that CAB prejudice precluded favorable new route awards to United, Patterson began looking for potential acquisitions, in an effort to recapture his former position. Pennsylvania Central Airlines (a successor to the old Pittsburgh Aviation Industries group) then operated between Washington, Pittsburgh, Cleveland, Detroit, Chicago, Milwaukee, and intermediate points. The company was losing money, but its network complemented United's "Main Line," and Patterson believed that a combined system might be profitable. However, he was unable to reach an agreement on price with Pennsylvania's operators, and the deal fell through. (By the end of the war Pennsylvania had changed its name to Capital Airlines. Its profits did not increase, and Patterson kept his eye on its possibilities for a potential acquisition.)

At this point, Patterson's attention was diverted by another opportunity—Western.* Over half of Western's passenger revenue came from its connection with United at Salt Lake. But both companies were losing the growing Los Angeles, Chicago, New York traffic to TWA and American which offered through service, whereas Western-United passengers had to change planes in Salt Lake. United offered to buy Western on attractive terms, and Western stockholders accepted. The case was the CAB's first merger controversy with opposition from major sources—TWA and American, as well as Western executives who felt their jobs in jeopardy. The Board appointed a distinguished lawyer, Roscoe Pound, then Dean of Harvard Law School, to hear the case as trial examiner. After listening to the evidence on both sides, Pound recommended approval of the merger. To the amazement of United and Western stockholders, the CAB reversed Pound's findings and denied the merger.

With the advent of the war, United, along with the other airlines, soon had more work than it could handle. Its maintenance depots were converted to modification centers for B-17's and B-29's. Its training schools trained Army Air Force navigators, and its own pilots operated a contract transport service across the Pacific to New Guinea.

Prior to the end of the war, Patterson, with his banker's caution, had had his staff study the prospects of the international market, particularly the so-called blue-ribbon route over the North Atlantic. United statisticians calculated that if all first-class passengers on ocean liners were persuaded to switch to airplanes, a fleet of only fifty planes could carry them all. Patterson concluded that it was impracticable for United, or other U.S. carriers, to compete with the inevitable group of government-backed foreign airlines for this relatively small volume

* When Western Air Express merged its primary route with TAT to form TWA in 1930, a few other routes remained independent, and have grown over the years as Western Airlines, Inc.

of business. Therefore he publicly endorsed Juan Trippe's stand on the chosen instrument. To the other domestic airlines, Patterson's position was regarded as a sellout. He recalls that, "At the time, everyone thought I had had one of Juan's treatments." Patterson's reluctance to compete in the North Atlantic, however, was not carried over to the Pacific. Here he attempted to acquire routes from the CAB similar to those United had operated during the war. Awarded the Hawaiian route in the first group of postwar CAB decisions, United quickly captured more than half of the market.

Relations between United and the CAB improved steadily. In 1947, a Board member called Patterson from Washington to say that Western was in such financial difficulty that the airline would probably go into the hands of receivers within thirty days unless something could be worked out. The Board member suggested that Terrell C. Drinkwater, newly elected president of Western, might be willing to sell its Denver–Los Angeles route to United—the asset for which United had sought to acquire Western before the war.

Patterson called Drinkwater and arranged a meeting in Santa Barbara to see if a deal could be worked out. Drinkwater needed fast action to meet his next payroll, and Patterson was agreeable, in order to get the route without having to bid against rival airlines. Since a route certificate had never been sold before, the question of value was a complex one. Drinkwater needed $3,750,000 to save his airline. He and Patterson listed all the tangible assets (airplanes and equipment) Western had for sale in connection with the Denver–Los Angeles route. The total fell $1,128,000 short of the sum Drinkwater needed to keep Western afloat. Patterson and Drinkwater agreed on that figure, $1,128,000, as representing the intangible value of the route.

As a postwar replacement for the DC-3 on United's shorter hauls, Patterson turned to Martin for fifty of his model 303's, intended as an improved version of the 202 which Martin had sold to TWA and Northwest. A series of crashes by the 202's on Northwest gave Patterson's engineers second thoughts about the airplane. It also became evident that Martin was going to lose money selling the plane for the contract price of $320,000. By 1947, United was running some $3,000,000 in the red, and Patterson began to have serious misgivings about his $16,000,000 commitment. With the facts in hand, Patterson went to see Glenn Martin. "I told him that he'd lose his shirt if he sold fifty planes at that price. So we broke the agreement and canceled our order." The cancellation was a release of liability for Patterson, but he had lost more than two years waiting for the Martin. American had the equipment lead and was determined to keep it, moving on with each speed advantage. Reluctantly, Patterson followed—protesting every step.

All along, Patterson had hoped to move from the economical DC-6 directly into jets in one jump. Nevertheless, he was forced into the DC-7 for competitive reasons. The DC-7 itself cost more than the DC-6 and was far more expensive to operate, yet it contributed only a 65-mile-an-hour speed advantage—not an economic bargain. Although the DC-7's range permitted the first transcontinental nonstop service, Patterson still sticks to his guns, claiming that "The industry would have been better off without the DC-7."

As far back as 1945, engineers at United had studied the relative merits of jet engines. By 1952, United's planning staffs had set up an elaborate study of the operating and scheduling problems that jet aircraft would encounter. A "paper jet" operation was set up to simulate actual jet operations over United's routes. Each day two coast-to-coast round trips were simulated, with dispatchers and meteorologists tracking each trip to see how it might be affected by the day's traffic and weather. With two years' experience with the "paper jet" program, Patterson was reasonably sure of what he wanted. Meanwhile, American had moved on to the Lockheed Electra, a turboprop aircraft powered by Allison's turbine engine hooked to propeller blades. As in the case of the DC-7, Patterson saw the Electra as offering only a relatively slight advantage in speed over existing aircraft— an advantage insufficient to cover its costs. This time Patterson determined to let the opposition have a temporary speed advantage. The decision made good sense—so long as United got early jet deliveries.

Under the circumstances, the logical jet selection seemed to be the Boeing 707, since it would be available almost two years ahead of the Douglas DC-8. Despite the time factor, Patterson insisted on a number of design changes, primarily widening the fuselage to permit six-abreast coach seating. Boeing, believing Patterson could not afford to wait for the Douglas deliveries, refused the requested changes. The order went to Douglas.

Boeing's surprise was widely shared. Patterson's insistence on six-abreast coach seating was in direct contradiction to his longstanding opposition to coach flights. Not only had he opposed coach service on economic grounds, he had also suggested that six-abreast seating constituted a safety hazard, preventing rapid evacuation (a charge he has recently repeated). In view of these prior public positions, it was most perplexing that Patterson would willingly wait for delivery of the DC-8, thereby giving American an enormous competitive advantage.

Predictably, United's revenues declined in relation to its competitors. Criticisms of Patterson's policies increased, when suddenly a new opportunity presented itself.

By 1958, Capital Airlines, with whom United had talked merger before the war, was again in trouble. Capital's system was composed of many short, unprofitable hops and a few highly competitive major routes, such as New York–Chicago. In an effort to draw passengers, Capital's "Slim" Carmichael had introduced the first coach service on scheduled airlines in 1949, but the experiment was not sufficiently profitable over Capital's short routes.

In 1955, Carmichael made a crucial decision and went deeply in debt to order the new English Vickers Viscount turboprop airliner, becoming the first U.S. airline to fly with turbine power. The Viscount was a fine plane; fast, quiet, and smooth—but seriously limited in range. In airline operations, the Viscount had no more capacity than the older Convairs, and over Capital's short routes, the Viscount's speed advantage was hardly noticeable.

Capital lost money steadily. Carmichael was replaced by David Baker, a Harvard Business School graduate and Air Force major general. But the interest charges on the Viscount debt were too burdensome for Capital to continue in operation. When Vickers brought action for foreclosure on its loan, Patterson, who had watched developments at Capital closely, stepped in with a take-it-or-leave-it offer for the whole Capital system. United's competitors immediately protested to the CAB, claiming that the merger would benefit United unduly. But the complaining companies were slow in coming up with any alternative suggestions, except that the CAB should dismember Capital and allot the pieces to the other allegedly deserving members of the airline fraternity—at best a long and tedious process.

The CAB was in a difficult position. On the one hand, it had no desire to hand Capital over to United, yet it did not want to endure the humiliation of having an airline under CAB stewardship forced out of business. Had other airlines presented reasonable alternatives to the CAB, the outcome might have been different. As it was, the CAB saw its choice as United's offer versus Capital's bankruptcy.

In June of 1961, the Capital Viscounts were repainted with the blue and white colors of United. With the acquisition of Capital, United once more became the biggest U.S. domestic airline. On top again, Patterson moved rapidly to consolidate his position by being the first airline to go to an all-jet equipment program. Casting his lifelong conservatism aside (and confounding his critics), Patterson broke all United traditions and ordered a foreign plane, the French Caravelle, for his short-haul routes. Thus "Pat" Patterson has at last regained for United its original position as the leader of the industry.

CHAPTER XIX

*American: Heir of the AVCO Empire*

The first airline executive to sell air transportation on a major scale, hard-driving C. R. Smith, singlehandedly raised American from the bottom to the top of the airline business in the brief period from 1934 to 1939. Unlike his benevolent and paternalistic contemporary, Patterson of United, always concerned for his company and employees, Smith ran his airline on one principle—customers come first. For twenty years his policies kept American on top, until 1960, when United took over first place in the Capital merger. Those who know C. R.'s intense competitiveness claim he will never rest until he has recaptured the crown—which CAB approval of the presently proposed merger with Eastern would accomplish.

American was born in the depths of the depression, out of chaos and confusion. Its parent was an aeronautical grab bag of unrelated and uncoordinated companies—technically an investment trust, or holding company, Aviation Corporation.

AVCO, as it was called, had been founded in 1928, to take advantage of boomtime demands for aviation stocks. Forty million dollars worth of its shares were sold to the public by a syndicate of major Wall Street houses, headed by W. A. Harriman and Lehman Brothers. Seventy directors, carefully selected from the top ranks of American industry to enhance the management (and glamorize the sales promotion for the new stock), sat on AVCO's board. With the proceeds from the public sale, AVCO began to purchase anything and everything that suggested aviation. Today, American Airlines likes to trace its heritage back through the Universal Company to another predecessor, Robertson Aircraft, for which Lindbergh flew the Inaugural mail from St. Louis to Chicago on April 15, 1926.

Out of the confusion of the AVCO airline holdings, some modicum of order gradually began to appear. In 1931, the domestic transport lines of AVCO were consolidated as American Airways. By an intricate and awkward route, a passenger could travel from Boston to Los Angeles, provided he had the time and patience to endure the detours and delays. American's operations were directed from four independent geographical divisions, with no pattern of coordination, either in operations or equipment. American operated a weird assortment of Curtiss Condors, Fords, Lockheeds, Stinsons, Stearmans, and Vultees. The safety record was nothing to boast about, and American was considered the least reliable airline when it came to on-time departures, completing flights, and providing seats for passengers who reserved them. Understandably, AVCO was not a profitable organization, sustaining losses of $3,400,000 in 1930.

More trouble brewed on the West Coast, where Errett Lobban Cord had organized Century Airlines. Cutting rates and generally harassing, Cord's airline gave American serious problems. Cord had made both a great deal of money and a great many enemies in the automobile industry. A skillful promoter, he had pyramided Auburn Motors with the help and financial backing of a group of friends. From an engineering point of view, Cord's automobile was excellent, but he seemed to lack the patience or organizational ability to develop the market properly. When the crash came, his friends discovered that the losses accrued to them.

The restless and aggressive Cord then turned to aviation. His record of financial manipulations made him an anathema to Postmaster General Brown. Cord was precisely the kind of man that Brown had determined to keep out of the aviation transportation system which he envisioned for the country. Barred by Brown from direct entry into the air transport field, Cord turned to a more devious route. He had reasoned that in the dark days of the depression, a government-subsidized Air Mail operation might be made into a highly profitable thing. If Cord could not come in by the front door, he was not above trying the second-story window. Postmaster General Brown had accepted AVCO as part of his national system, primarily because of its strong financial backing. Cord, however, believed that AVCO—with its weak management and its board of directors preoccupied with other interests—offered an ideal opportunity for his penetration.

Employing the time-tested techniques of Jim Fiske in his railroad wars with Vanderbilt, Cord set up a nuisance activity to cut rates and force American to buy him out. American reacted precisely as Cord had anticipated, and Cord received 140,000 shares of AVCO stock and a directorship in the corporation in exchange for his lines, equipment, and hangars—far more than they were worth. Within a few weeks most of his routes were abandoned by AVCO.

In addition to the substantial stockholdings acquired in return for his Century Airlines, Cord quietly began to purchase AVCO stock on the open market, where it was selling at a depressed price. He gradually acquired some 30 percent of the outstanding stock. As his holdings increased, the other AVCO directors became fearful of his intentions, recalling his past patterns of behavior. In an effort to thwart him, the AVCO management began negotiations for certain assets of North American, the other large holding company, for which AVCO would double its capitalization by issuing an additional 2,000,-000 shares of stock. (The same game Clement Keys had tried, to keep United from taking over NAT two years before.) The exchange would have had the effect of reducing Cord's interest from a threatening 30 to a more manageable 15 percent.

The proposed transaction forced Cord's hand. He obtained a temporary injunction in the courts to restrain the transfer. Simultaneously he charged in the press that American's "reigning clique" had lost $38,000,000 of the stockholders' money in three years, and that it transacted all of its important business in "secret meetings" in order to further the directors' outside interests at the expense of AVCO stockholders. The battle reached its peak in a proxy fight in October of 1932. Both sides hired squads of publicity men, Cord setting up his headquarters in the Hotel Biltmore in New York with leased telephone wires to Chicago and Los Angeles. The country's newspapers carried headlines such as FINANCIAL GIANTS LOCKED IN DEATH STRUGGLE. Cord took full-page ads in the papers, addressed to AVCO stockholders, claiming: "If we had not stopped the directors from making this North American deal, the control of your company would have passed forever from your hands." His ads then encouraged all AVCO stockholders to pass control into his hands instead.

Outside forces also played a part in the proxy fight. Operating in Cord's behalf was a brochure published by E. F. Hutton & Company, a Wall Street brokerage house, purporting to represent an AVCO balance sheet since 1929, showing losses of $20,000,000 which were attributed to its Lamont Cohu. Mr.

Cohu had only become president of AVCO earlier that very year and obviously was not responsible for its prior losses. He immediately sued for $1,000,000 in damages; nevertheless, the Hutton release served strongly to reinforce Cord's claims of mismanagement against AVCO. On the other hand, William Green, president of the American Federation of Labor, stated that: "We are thoroughly convinced that Mr. Cord is hostile to union labor," referring to a pilot strike against Cord when he was in control of Century Airlines. Ever a practical man, Cord had seen no point in paying going pilots' wages when so many wartime pilots had lost their jobs and were looking for work. Accordingly he cut all pilots' pay in half on Century Airlines and thus started the first pilots' strike—a strike also unique in that, probably for the only time, pilots struck to recover old salary levels rather than new increases.

Eventually the conflicting forces agreed to an armistice. After lengthy meetings Cord came out with control of AVCO. (There was some solace for Cohu in that Cord's frantic stock purchases in the open market had forced up the price, thereby permitting Cohu to unload his own stock at favorable terms.) Once in control, Cord moved to strengthen his organization to take advantage of the government Air Mail contracts, separating the affairs of American Airways from the other aviation activities of AVCO. American Airways was still an awkward and inferior organization, but at least it now acquired a separate personality in which its faults could be seen more clearly, and perhaps remedied.

At this point American, like the rest of its industry, was hit by the Black investigations, leading to the Air Mail contract cancellations. The whole structure of routes and payments collapsed overnight, depriving American of the $4,500,000 it expected to collect from the Post Office Department. However, for American, the cancellation was a blessing in disguise. Whereas it had previously attempted to operate with a chaotic route system, the cancellation period gave it an opportunity to consolidate. It is ironic that the worst system, in the hands of a demonstrated financial manipulator, should benefit from the Black committee. Some credit the situation with dark political motives, in that Cord was a major financial backer of Franklin Roosevelt during his campaign, making aircraft available for Democratic officials and campaigners. The real explanation is that American Airways was in such poor shape prior to the cancellation, that any change had to be an improvement. When the mail was returned, American, like the other airlines, was forced to reorganize in a face-saving move to protect the New Deal. The organizational change was minimal, involving only a shift of name from American Airways to American Airlines, but it brought in a new president, a young, tough-talking Texan, C. R. Smith.

Smith was born in Minerva, Texas, in 1899, and moved constantly through Texas and Louisiana during his early years, stopping wherever his father could find work. When he was nine years old, his father walked out of the house and was never heard from again. Smith's indefatigable mother kept the family together, taking in boarders, teaching school, and putting the children to work as soon as possible. School continued on a part-time basis, and each child's earnings went into a common fund to help the younger children. On this basis, every one of the seven Smith children finished college.

At sixteen, C. R. Smith became a part-time bookkeeper for $30 a month in the First National Bank of Whitney, Texas. Soon he entered the School of Business Administration of the State University and carried on a part-time examiner's job with the Federal Reserve Bank at the same time. In addition, he operated a one-man advertising agency, selling mailing lists of stockholders whose names he had gotten from the corporate records on file in the Texas capital. He soon broadened his operations to include the names and addresses of new parents from the vital-statistics records, selling the data to publishers of parents' magazines and marketers of baby food. Upon graduation, Smith took a job as a clerk in an accounting firm—at a substantial cut in pay. For this firm he took on the unpleasant jobs assigned to junior clerks, particularly those involving travel. From his audits he learned the operating intricacies of hotels, apartment houses, oil refineries, motion-picture theatres, and cigar factories. He soon became a specialist in public-utility accounting, and in this capacity came to know A. P. Barrett, a wealthy promoter who owned the Texas-Louisiana Power Company. At Barrett's request, Smith resigned from the accounting firm in 1926, and joined the power company as an assistant treasurer. Two years later Barrett bought Texas Air Transport, and asked Smith to operate the company. Smith protested that he was not interested in aviation, but Barrett said: "Go ahead and take it. If you don't like it, I'll get someone else."

Texas Air Transport prospered, and Barrett bought two more local lines, merging them with Texas to form Southern Air Transport. Operations spread eastward as far as Atlanta and soon passengers were carried, as well as mail. Profits were few, but Smith's strong competitive instincts kept him in the game. Taking instruction when business was dull, Smith qualified for a transport pilot's license, flying as copilot from time to time over the company's routes. In 1929, at the peak of the aviation boom, AVCO swallowed Southern Air Transport, which became the southern division of American Airways—with Smith still in charge of the operation.

From the beginning, Smith was dedicated to the concept that the future of air transportation lay in the passenger market, not in the mail subsidy. The problem was to attract passengers to the airplane. In 1933, Smith came upon an unusual mock-up model of the Curtiss Condor, while walking through the Curtiss-

Wright plant in St. Louis. This particular Condor was fitted out in a sleeper configuration, the creation of Ralph S. Damon, then president of Curtiss-Wright. Damon believed that a day spent in a hotel bed catching up on lost sleep was too steep a price to pay for sitting up all night in an airliner. To Damon the answer was in airplane berths, similar to the accommodations offered by the Pullman Company on the railroads. Damon's idea appealed to Smith, and he flew to Cord's home in California to discuss it with him. After Cord had been properly prepared, Smith telephoned Damon to rush to California. Damon picked up the miniature Condor model and filled the berths with tiny China dolls from a ten-cent store. By the time they left Cord's house in Beverly Hills, Damon had an order for ten Condor sleepers.

American put its new Condors into service in May of 1934, on the overnight hop between Los Angeles and Fort Worth. The Condors were slow and lumbering airplanes, but they were also safe and quiet; ideal sleepers. The attraction of the sleeper flight helped to establish American in the passenger market.

With Smith as president, American made rapid progress. His control was unquestioned. Cord, apparently fearful of government investigation of his past business practices (and allegedly in danger of his life from former friends and business associates), took his family to England, where he lived quietly, without interfering with Smith at American.*

The cancellation changed the character of the industry. Previously subsidy mail pay had been the dominant factor, despite Postmaster General Brown's best efforts to drive the industry toward self-sufficiency through the transportation of passengers. With the drastic cuts in mail pay following the cancellation, the

---

* Eventually Cord sold his controlling interests in AVCO and American Airlines. AVCO was subsequently reconstituted as a manufacturing company and today is active in the missile field.

airlines had no choice. Passengers were essential for survival. In 1933, American's mail revenues were nearly $5,000,000, as opposed to less than $2,000,000 from passengers. By 1937, these figures had reversed—approximately $3,000,000 in mail and more than $6,000,000 in passenger revenues. Apart from the bare fact of economic necessity, Smith attributes these changes to two factors: improved equipment and increased sales efforts.

The first change was equipment. Replacing Smith as vice-president of operations came Ralph S. Damon, formerly president of Curtiss Aircraft, producer of American's Condor sleeper planes. A good plane in its time, the Condor had given American a favorable start in the passenger market, but by 1935, it was seriously obsolete. The Douglas DC-2 was the dominant transport plane, and an improved model, the DC-3, promised to be even better. American's financial position was weak, but Smith felt that the gamble was worth it. Summoning all of his courage, he re-equipped American with DC-3's, with the help of a Reconstruction Finance Corporation loan. (Once again, jealous rivals whispered that Smith had used political influence with his fellow Texan Jesse Jones, then head of the RFC, to obtain a loan which others could not.) With the passenger appeal of the DC-3 and the economy of operation inherent in standardized equipment, American was in an ideal position to benefit from Smith's superb salesmanship.

Prior to Smith's efforts, all airlines' sales emphasis had been centered on a general attempt to popularize air travel. Smith changed this conception utterly. He believed that there was no real difference between selling an airline ticket and "a box of Post Toasties." Presently the sales department began referring to airplane seats as "perishable commodities," and when more flights were added, they talked about "increased production." American began to experiment with various credit plans, the first in the industry. Initially, scrip was sold, as early as 1934.

Other lines criticized Smith's proposals at first, but scrip proved its success, in that salesmen now had a tangible item to sell. The other lines were quick to join, thus giving birth to the airline credit card of today.

In Smith's hands the nature of airline advertising also changed from the typical ad of airplane and timetable. The most famous American advertisement appeared in the spring of 1937, under the headline—AFRAID TO FLY—challenging the great taboo of the airline industry which (like the automobile ads) never permitted discussion of safety. Weather was obviously a factor in passengers' fears, and Smith advertised American as "The Sunshine Route," implying that United's more northern flights had to face more winter weather. When a United plane crashed in the Rockies near Denver, Smith's ads promptly changed to THE LOW-LEVEL ROUTES TO THE WEST. That was going too far, and the other airlines made it clear that Smith should get back in line. But his program were highly productive and brought about a 330-percent increase in passenger revenue between 1933 and 1937—compared to an average increase of 175 percent for the other lines.

With the outbreak of World War II, air transportation was desperately needed. Hap Arnold, chief of the Army Air Corps, decided to activate the Air Transport Command, a quasi-military operation formed of both civilian airlines under contract, as well as military planes and personnel. The command of the ATC went naturally to a regular officer, but as deputy commander Arnold personally selected C. R. Smith, then generally acknowledged the most dynamic figure in the airline industry.

Smith's constant determination to get the job done, regardless of conflicting regulations, was sometimes a source of consternation and antagonism to regular military types. Nevertheless, his effectiveness was uniformly recognized in the success of the ATC. Rank did not affect old habits. Behind his desk

Smith kept his battered typewriter, fitted with a long roll of blue paper. Whenever a thought struck him, Smith would turn in his chair and bang out a terse note. The blue paper identified the source and urgency. He returned to American Airlines at the end of the war a much-decorated major general.

American had changed. Expansion had taken its toll. Smith no longer knew all the pilots and station managers personally; the easy informality of prewar days was gone. During his absence, Ralph Damon had run the show, and C. R. returned as chairman of the board. Some old friends now regarded him as aloof and distant; some even suggested that rank had gone to his head. But C. R. worked harder than ever.

In 1938, he had married a Texas girl. After a four-day honeymoon, Smith dropped her at his apartment and returned to his office, not to be seen again for thirty hours. Over the next few years the airline and his marriage fought for his time. By the end of the war the airline had won. Smith was divorced and set up New York bachelor quarters in a duplex apartment outrageously decorated with Western furniture and fittings, including a valuable collection of Remington and Russell paintings.

The ATC had given Smith a taste for new areas of endeavor, particularly the international markets. At one time during the war there apparently had been some question in his mind whether to return to American. He had discussed the possibilities of setting up a new worldwide passenger and cargo operation, using surplus C-54's and ATC personnel. However, the idea passed and Smith returned to American.

To guarantee participation in the choice North Atlantic run, American had purchased American Export Airlines. AMEX had been granted authority by the CAB before the war, but Pan American's adroit lobbying had prevented Congressional approval of the appropriation for the necessary subsidy. During the war AMEX had operated under contract to the ATC. Pan

American had gone to court to force American Export Shipping lines to sell the airline, on the grounds that a shipping company was barred by statute from ownership of an airline. Forced to sell, American Export accepted American Airlines' offer for controlling interest, and American Overseas Airlines was born as a division of American Airlines.

Smith set about re-equipping his airline—in the biggest financial transaction the airlines had ever known. As a substitute for the DC-3, he ordered seventy-five of the new Convair 240 models at a bargain rate of approximately $200,000 each. (Fourteen years later American sold the ships secondhand for more than the purchase price.) Smith had learned the advantages of equipment standardization with his DC-3's, but advances in design now prevented one model from fulfilling all the requirements of his enlarged airline system. For his long-haul routes Smith chose the Douglas DC-6, specifying that the same reliable Pratt & Whitney engines which powered the Convairs be used, to simplify maintenance problems.

Despite the fact that he had made excellent choices in equipment and had received bargain prices, financing was tricky. The immediate postwar market enthusiasm for airline securities waned rapidly. By the time Smith and the underwriters were ready with the necessary stock issue, it was touch and go whether the underwriters would go through with the deal on favorable terms. When the papers were finally signed, the market was falling so fast that Smith said to his associates: "It's lucky we got to work early today or we'd never have had a deal."

The new planes gave American a significant advantage over its rivals, particularly over United, which still operated DC-3's over its short routes. (Rubbing salt in the wound, C. R. whimsically donated American's last DC-3 to a museum.) Domestic operations prospered, but things were not going well on the international side. A $22,000,000 order for Republic Rainbows was canceled, requiring a penalty of $1,000,000. To meet Pan

Am competition, AOA's surplus C-54's were replaced; first with Connies, then with Boeing Stratocruisers. Despite a substantial government subsidy, AOA lost nearly $2,000,000 over five years. Disillusioned, Smith acknowledged the wisdom of Juan Trippe's predictions that the Atlantic was not big enough for several U.S. lines—and sold AOA to Pan Am for $17,000,000. A substantial loss, but Smith still says: "The smartest thing we ever did was to get the hell out."

Closed out of the international market, Smith returned to domestic operation with a vengeance. To him, the airlines were selling time—and speed was the essence of the operation. The greatest speed was available with the new jet engines. A jet airliner was already flying—the English DeHavilland Comet—but the Comet was far from a practical airliner. The ensuing tragic Comet accidents seemed to verify the reluctance of U.S. manufacturers to proceed with jet-transport designs. While waiting for more economical jet aircraft, Smith decided to ask Douglas for a more powerful and faster version of the DC-6—the DC-7. Initially Douglas was reluctant to build the plane; the DC-6 had been enormously successful and Douglas had planned to move directly to jets. But Smith's arguments were persuasive, and Douglas brought out the DC-7. Engine trouble prevented it from achieving the performance Smith had hoped for. On the other hand, it was a far more successful plane than Douglas had initially anticipated, and the DC-7 provided the first scheduled nonstop service coast to coast.

Believing that jets were still quite a way off, American then turned its attention to turboprops. Douglas came up with a proposal to convert DC-7's to turboprop power. Looking to the short-haul market, Convair offered its 340 model, powered with four Rolls-Royce Dart turboprop engines. But American still wasn't satisfied. Then the Allison Division of General Motors brought out its new and bigger turboprop. American again asked Boeing, Douglas, and Lockheed to come up with proposals based around the Allison engine. Douglas and Boeing were by then committed to their jet designs, but Lockheed produced the Electra (named after the first Lockheed twin-engined transport of the early 1930's). The Electra could fly sixty-five passengers at speeds over 400 miles an hour, using the short runways of convenient airports such as New York's La Guardia and Chicago's Midway, an important consideration of American's system. The Electra offered certain real advantages—but were they enough, with jets just around the corner? C. R. Smith thought so, and American ordered thirty-five.

Almost simultaneously, American ordered Boeing 707 jets for its longer routes. For Smith, the decision between the Boeing 707 and the Douglas DC-8 was particularly difficult. Douglas had earned the respect and confidence of the entire airline industry, and American prided itself on having been the first to put new Douglases in operation—the DC-3, the DC-4, the DC-6, and the DC-7. On the other hand, Boeing was ready, with a flying, tested prototype. The greater sweepback of the Boeing wings provided at least a twenty-mile-an-hour speed advantage over the DC-8. With the Boeing, American could be both first and fastest—Smith's credo. American ordered fifty 707's and entered the Jet Age, just as Smith wanted: the largest airline, offering the finest passenger service, with the fastest planes.*

But in a sense American became the victim of its own success. Smith's leadership and policies had built it into the dominant carrier in this country. But the Civil Aeronautics Board has always feared bigness, and after the war, American was at a constant disadvantage in the competition for new routes. In a

---

* Smith's constant drive for technical advances in his airplanes has not been popular with his pilots, who fear that more efficient planes may mean fewer job opportunities. American has been struck by the pilots several times on this issue, the most famous, or notorious, being the "Christmas Eve" strike—probably the all-time blunder in union public relations.

long and bitter battle American was successful in getting the CAB to put it on the backs of TWA and United in the crucial New York–San Francisco nonstop case. TWA and United immediately protested that American had used undue influence and Congressional pressure to affect the Board's decision—and they took the case to the courts. The Federal Circuit Court for the District of Columbia agreed that American's procedures were improper and remanded the case to the Board for a new trial (which eventually resulted in the same decision, favoring American. Obviously the Board could not admit that its prior decision had been the result of improper influence).

While this unpleasantness was going on, the CAB was also considering the last major route as yet unawarded in this country—the Southern Transcontinental from Miami and Atlanta to Los Angeles. American had significant advantages in its favor, but the CAB instead followed its old habits of political expediency, giving something to all the applicants—and bringing Delta, National and Continental into American territory.

The Electra decision also turned sour. Following tragic crashes on American, Braniff, Northwest, and Eastern, all Electras were restricted to two-thirds of their normal flying speeds. The unfavorable Electra publicity, operational restrictions, and jet competition, all combined to reduce revenue over the entire American system. An even bigger blow was United's acquisition of Capital. After more than twenty years of leadership as the largest United States carrier, American suddenly found itself back in second place.

Proud and intensely competitive, Smith determined to recover his lead. With no more major domestic routes to be awarded, merger was the only solution. He turned to his old friend and long-time lawyer, Malcolm MacIntyre, the new president of Eastern. A merger was agreeable, and if the CAB approves, the combined American-Eastern system will control more than one third of all U.S. airline operations.

CHAPTER XX

# Eastern: Rickenbacker, Rockefeller and the American Merger

Today, Eastern Airlines faces financial difficulties so great that it seeks a merger with American as the only solution to its troubles. Yet, of all the domestic airlines, Eastern was for years the most consistent money-maker. Part of its success was due to its route structure, primarily the run between New York and Miami over which Eastern enjoyed a virtual monopoly for the first twenty years of its existence. The second great factor was Eddie Rickenbacker, Eastern's president from 1938 until 1959 (when he stepped up to become chairman of the board).

One of this country's most colorful figures, Rickenbacker has prominently participated in two of the most important industrial and economic transformations in our history, the automobile and the airplane. Prior to World War I, he drove racing cars for such great names as Firestone, Dusenberg, Mercer, Maxwell, and Peugeot. In England preparing a racing team for the Sunbeam Motor Company when the United States declared war in 1917, Rickenbacker immediately returned to this country and offered to recruit a corps of former racing drivers for the aviation service. Because of their experience in handling machines at high speeds, he believed that racing drivers would become outstanding pilots. His project was rejected and he then sought to enlist as an individual. But at the age of twenty-six Rickenbacker was considered too old to qualify for pilot training. Family necessity had forced him to leave school halfway through the seventh grade, and although he had studied mechanical engineering and drafting with a correspondence school, his repeated requests for waivers of the age limit for pilot training were rejected on the grounds of inadequate education and experience.

Frustrated in his efforts to get into aviation, Rickenbacker accepted an offer to go to France as the personal chauffeur of General Pershing, the American Chief of Staff. Once in France, his incessant pleading finally won him permission to enter pilot training. Even so, he did not get into combat immediately. His engineering skills were then considered so valuable that Major Carl A. Spaatz, his commanding officer, refused to release him for combat.

In March of 1918, Rickenbacker was finally assigned to the "Hat-in-the-Ring" Squadron, commanded by Major Raoul Lufbery. At Lufbery's death, shortly thereafter, Rickenbacker became squadron commander. In the remaining eight months of the war he scored twenty-six confirmed victories and became America's ranking Ace. More than a great pilot, Rickenbacker was also a great leader, always willing to put the interests of the squadron ahead of his own. By the end of the war, his squadron led all others, with a total of sixty-nine victories. Those who knew him claimed that he could easily have doubled his personal score had he chosen to operate alone rather than devote himself to squadron leadership. In recognition of its wartime service, the 94th Pursuit Squadron was maintained in the peacetime years as the crack unit of the American Air Service. (Until the requirements of World War II made such personal attention impossible, the 94th Pursuit was the first U.S. squadron to receive each improved type of fighter aircraft.)

Rickenbacker returned home to a hero's welcome. The United States gave him its highest award, the Congressional Medal of Honor. Unable to find a job that appealed to him in the dull days of postwar aviation, Rickenbacker returned to the automobile business, starting the Rickenbacker Motor Company. The Rickenbacker was an advanced design, but it did not sell. The failure of his company was a blow which Rickenbacker felt deeply. Although not legally required to do so, he assumed personal liability for the company's debts.

Rickenbacker then joined the General Motors organization, initially as assistant sales manager of the LaSalle Division of Cadillac. Shortly thereafter, General Motors purchased control of the Fokker Aircraft Company, changing its name to General Aviation. Eddie Rickenbacker became sales vice-president. But the Fokker-General Motors relationship was not a happy one, and disputes and disagreements culminated with the crash of a Fokker trimotor on TWA and a resulting Congressional investigation. Disenchanted, Rickenbacker left General Aviation for Aviation Corporation as vice-president of American Airways. His American Airways career was short, terminating with Cord's victory in the proxy fight of October 1932. Once again, Rickenbacker found himself out of work.

By this time Eastern was already a successful airline, with an eventful story behind it. In 1926, the Post Office Department had invited competitive bids to transport mail between New York and Atlanta. The winning bid was $3 per pound, submitted by Harold F. Pitcairn. Pitcairn was a young pilot who flew the county-fair circuit and was then operating out of a farmyard near Philadelphia. He was also a designer and manufacturer, with several earlier designs to his credit. With the government Air Mail contract as security, Pitcairn raised the needed funds and built the first of his series of "Mailwing" biplanes. As his Mailwings were completed Pitcairn recruited a handful of World War I veterans and barnstormer pilots and began a survey of his route.

In November, 1927, before he had flown the first official Air Mail to Atlanta, the Post Office Department awarded Pitcairn a 595-mile extension, linking Atlanta with Miami. He found himself in possession of the prime component of today's Eastern Airlines, the 1,387 air miles from New York to Miami. By the standards of the times, Pitcairn's line was successful from the beginning.

Despite the success of the operation, Harold Pitcairn was torn between the manufacturing and operating ends of his business. Always more interested in design and development, he had become fascinated with a new concept in aviation, the autogyro.\* The Lindbergh-inspired airline boom was then at its peak on Wall Street, and Pitcairn was receiving attractive offers for his airline. On July 10, 1929—less than four months before the stock market crash—he sold his airline to North American Aviation for $2,500,000. North American's founder, Clement Keys, was then in the process of fleshing out his dream of a vast aviation empire. His holdings included Transcontinental Air Transport, the combined air-rail passenger service between New York and Los Angeles, and a variety of aircraft manufacturing, sales, and service operations loosely associated in the Curtiss-Wright group, as well as Sperry Gyroscope—producer of the revolutionary gyrohorizon instruments to

---

\* The depression ruined Pitcairn's plans for the autogyro, and the military turned its support to Sikorsky's development of the helicopter (which could hover, whereas the autogyro could not). Nevertheless, the simpler operation and lower cost of the autogyro present worthwhile possibilities. I recently flew a prototype model by the Umbaugh Company which was most impressive in performance. Perhaps Pitcairn's dream will be fulfilled at last.

permit flight through weather and clouds. Keys promptly changed the name of Pitcairn Aviation to Eastern Air Transport and added another colony to his empire.

The stable and strongly financed North American Aviation group was looked upon with favor by Postmaster General Brown. Eastern's pattern of service north and south along the Eastern seaboard fitted in with Brown's plans of a national transportation system, and Brown granted Eastern new route awards whenever he had the opportunity. Passenger service was soon inaugurated, using the safe and comfortable Curtiss Condor, produced by the manufacturing affiliate of North American Aviation.

In late December, 1932, Ernie Breech recalls that Rickenbacker called him and said he had an idea to discuss. Breech asked Rickenbacker to his apartment for cocktails. At the time, Breech was serving as watchdog for the General Motors aviation industries, primarily TWA and General Aviation (the renamed Fokker Company), both of which were closely involved in the complex financial structure of North American Aviation. It was Rickenbacker's idea that Breech arrange for General Motors to buy outright control of North American. The idea appealed to Breech, and with the approval of Pierre du Pont and the General Motors finance committee, the deal was consummated. With General Motors in control of North American Aviation, Rickenbacker became general manager of Eastern Air Transport.

Once again Eddie Rickenbacker made aviation history when he and Jack Frye of TWA flew the last private load of mail from Los Angeles to Newark before the Air Mail cancellations, setting a transcontinental speed record in a new Douglas DC-2. But except for that brief moment of glory, Eastern shared the general distress of the industry in the early 1930's, losing money steadily.

Under the terms of Black's Air Mail Act of 1934, manufacturing companies were prohibited from owning or controlling airlines. Faced with this edict, North American Aviation sold TWA to Lehman Brothers and the Atlas Corporation. But nobody seemed to want Eastern. Five years before, North American had paid Pitcairn $2,500,000 for Eastern. Over the intervening years North American had put in $5,000,000 more—for a total investment of $7,500,000. In 1935, North American's asking price for Eastern was $1,000,000—and there were no takers.

The immediate problem of disposal was solved by the shrewd mind of Ernie Breech, who saw that, while the Black Air Mail Act prohibited a manufacturing company from owning an airline company, the Act said nothing about one company being both at the same time. North American's counsel, Gerald Brophy of Tom Chadbourne's old law firm, agreed and proceeded to reorganize North American and Eastern into one corporate entity.

The Eastern Airlines Division, as it was then called, was in bad shape. Morale was low; revenues were decreasing; there were no prospects for improvement. New equipment was badly needed to replace the obsolete Curtisses. Rickenbacker made a whirlwind trip over every mile of the routes, going into almost every office of the airline and talking over company problems with as many employees as he could find. Ruthlessly, he cut out the "frills" and extravagances in the operation and imposed a rigid system of cost controls. He threw out the obsolete aircraft and replaced them with new Douglas DC-2's and the improved DC-3's.

Profane and aggressive, Rickenbacker drove his people hard. Under his economies, Eastern turned the corner. The 1934 loss of $700,000 was converted into a $90,000 profit in 1935. The company made progress, but it was slow and painful. Remembering the days of deep losses, General Motors' board of directors was unwilling to invest additional funds for capital improvements. In 1936, Eastern earned $168,000, increasing it to $197,000 in 1937; a small return considering the initial investment.

Representing General Motors, Breech had become increasingly dissatisfied with the airline business, its vulnerability to politics, and small and uncertain return on investment. When General Motors bought control of North American, Breech became chairman of the board. His first act had been a tour of facilities, beginning with the General Aviation Manufacturing plant, then located in Baltimore. He was flown down, crouched cold and uncomfortable in the mail compartment of a Northrup Alpha piloted by Lindbergh, who was then technical adviser for TWA. General Aviation was building a new experimental trimotor transport for TWA to compete with the Douglas DC-2. The trimotor feature had been originally favored by Lindbergh, who feared that the DC-2 could not safely hold altitude on one engine. The development of the controllable pitch propeller had remedied this defect of the DC-2, and it was clear to Breech that the General Aviation trimotor was not a profitable venture. Nevertheless, Breech liked what he saw of the aircraft manufacturing business. He moved the plant to Los Angeles and hired Dutch Kindelburger, then chief engineer for Douglas, to run the new operation.

Under Kindelburger, North American prospered as a manufacturer. By 1938, the gathering war clouds in Europe indicated ever-increasing business for military aircraft. The statutory maximum of $17,000 salary imposed on airline company executives prevented adequate compensation for Kindelburger and restricted recruitment of engineering talent in North American. Selling off Eastern Airlines would solve the problem and permit North American to concentrate on manufacturing.

With Eastern again on the auction block, a private group

of investors bid $3,250,000. The prospect was a shock to Rickenbacker—the sale meant that he would have to go. Most of General Motors' higher management was friendly to Rickenbacker, but the offer was an appealing solution to their problems. They explained that they would accept the bid unless he could better it.

Rickenbacker was not a financial man and he didn't know where to begin looking for that kind of money. He consulted a friend in the insurance business in Philadelphia. It so happened that this friend had recently seen a financial report on the aviation industry prepared by William Barkley Harding of investment bankers Smith, Barney & Company, and he suggested that Rickenbacker get hold of Harding. Harding, in turn, brought in Kuhn, Loeb and agreed to finance Rickenbacker. But some of Harding's senior partners were dubious, and Harding sought additional outside financing, taking the proposal to Nelson Rockefeller. Rockefeller explained that airlines were not in his line but that perhaps his brother Laurance might be interested. Laurance Rockefeller walked into the room with a copy of Harding's financial report under his arm, unaware of the name of his brother's visitor. "I've been reading this report," he said, "and I don't think I want to buy into a manufacturing company. Now if you gentlemen had an airline..."

The combination of Smith, Barney, Kuhn, Loeb and Laurance Rockefeller was sufficient to swing the deal—setting Eddie Rickenbacker up as president of an independent Eastern Airlines.

During World War II, Eastern released half of its fleet of DC-3's to the military services. The company's other contribution to the war effort was the formation and operation of a route extending from Miami to Brazil and across the South Atlantic to Africa. Like the other lines, Eastern was seized with the postwar optimism and enthusiasm for international expansion, requesting the Civil Aeronautics Board for an extension of its routes through South America. It is generally believed in the industry that Eastern stood to win the route now held by Braniff down the west coast of South America. However, Rickenbacker reconsidered the costs involved, and during his testimony before the Civil Aeronautics Board, withdrew his request for South American service, thereby in effect putting Braniff on the route by default. The run has never been profitable for Braniff, and the decision seems to serve as another example of Rickenbacker's canny cost consciousness.

Always strong-willed and independent, Rickenbacker deplored subsidized routes. He was one of the first airline presidents to advocate separation of Federal subsidy from mail pay. So long as subsidy was obscured in mail pay there was no standard by which to compare airline efficiency. Furthermore, the protection of subsidy encouraged airlines to seek expansion at any price. Like Trippe in this regard, Rickenbacker believed that the future of air transport lay in consolidations to reduce costs and improve efficiency. Thus, in time, fares could be reduced and the market expanded.

Testifying on this point before the CAB in 1949, Rickenbacker infuriated several other airline presidents by offering to operate their routes without subsidy. From its earliest times, air transport has been peculiarly subject to strong personalities. The airlines' tendency to overexpansion may well be traced to a desire for individual aggrandizement. (Both CAB chairmen, O'Connell in 1949 and Boyd in 1961, have cited personality factors as major barriers to sensible consolidations.) Rickenbacker put it more succinctly: "A man would be a damned fool to merge himself out of a job as long as he could get a government handout to meet his payroll."

Rickenbacker himself ran a one-man airline. Technically and

financially it was a magnificent success. His first emphasis was on safety—and after safety, economy. His objective was to fly the most planes, with the greatest capacity, at the least cost. As a result of these policies, Eastern seemed to be operating aircraft at its own convenience, rather than at that of its passengers. In order to maximize utilization, flights were often scheduled at uncivilized hours. Standby planes were few in number, and the occasional mechanical difficulties caused seemingly unnecessary and excessive delays. In the early days when Eastern enjoyed a monopoly over most of its routes, passenger inconvenience was not too important. If Rickenbacker provided the seats and the safety, Eastern profited.

Economy was the watchword at Eastern. Its pilots were famous (or perhaps notorious) in the flying fraternity for their efforts to seek advantageous positions in traffic patterns in order to minimize their flight time and gasoline consumption.*

Regardless of all of his efforts to squeeze the greatest possible net out of every dollar of operating revenue, Rickenbacker never scrimped on safety or on traffic development. He poured millions of dollars into providing service to cities where there might be potential future passenger traffic, but where the present business was insufficient to justify the service. It was his policy to fly more planes between the key cities than his competition, and often far more than available traffic warranted.

Rickenbacker's policy paid off for quite awhile. Eastern's profits amounted to $2,000,000 in 1945, rose to $8,500,000 in 1952, and reached a peak of $14,700,000 in 1956.

But there was another side to the picture. "Oh, I know we used to treat passengers badly," admits a former Eastern official,

---

* I personally have been flying in traffic patterns where Eastern pilots have misstated their positions, presumably to receive landing priorities. Of course, other lines' pilots do the same thing from time to time, but it seemed to be more of a habit with Eastern. Today, radar surveillance has almost eliminated this practice.

"but we made money every year." Increasingly, customer complaints began to bedevil the line. Despite the fact that Eastern provided far more seats than were used on most of its routes, the cities throughout the Southeast fought eagerly for additional competitive airline service. Eastern officials were deeply hurt at the reaction. Poor customer relations were taking their toll and the situation fed on itself. "Our reservations and ticket-counter people could take only so much grousing about our service," a vice-president admitted publicly. "After awhile, they began to snap back at the passengers. Then, of course, complaints grew worse. And so did Eastern morale." Passenger complaints were clearly a factor in the CAB's 1944 decision to extend National's route from Florida to New York, to provide competition for Eastern. Again in 1956, the CAB responded to complaints on Eastern's route pattern, and every mile of Eastern's domestic network was overlaid with at least one new competitor. The result was that Eastern's passenger-load factor —the percentage of the available seats occupied—dropped off alarmingly.

For the first time in years profits began to fall. Passengers on Eastern's routes were sick of poor treatment, dishonored reservations, lost baggage, late departures, first-class passengers crammed into tourist seats in order to increase revenues during the winter vacation season, and a host of other annoyances. Frustrated for years at the ineffectual results of their complaints, passengers now took out their bitterness by riding competitive airlines. Rickenbacker's basic philosophy of economy of operation was beginning to backfire. "The Captain taught us how to run a magnificent air line," said an Eastern executive, "but he never taught us how to live with competition. None of our people ever had to go out and sell before."

Besides customer hostility and new competitive services, Eastern was also handicapped by an equipment problem. An early enthusiast of jet power, Rickenbacker once considered the first DeHavilland Comet. Curiously then, when the first U.S. jets became available, Rickenbacker deliberately chose to pass the first round and to wait for more powerful engines to be available on the later models of the DC-8. George Baker, president of National Airlines and a most aggressive salesman, jumped at the opportunity. By an intricate and cunning transaction with Pan American (described elsewhere) Baker acquired 2 Pan American 707 Jets and pressed them into service during the winter Florida vacation season. National's jet competition cut deeply into Eastern's revenues. Already one season behind in jet deliveries, Rickenbacker then cut the number of DC-8's he had ordered from 20 to 16. From the point of view of Eastern's internal needs, the cutback was probably wise. However, from a competitive viewpoint, it was a serious error; it prevented Eastern from providing a full pattern of jet service to compete with other carriers. Offered a choice between jet and piston equipment—particularly Eastern piston equipment, notoriously uncomfortable and crowded—passengers inevitably chose other lines if given the opportunity. With the jet cutback, Eastern was left to stretch its limited aircraft as best it could. For the past two winter seasons, when the New York, Detroit, and Chicago to Florida business was at its peak, Eastern's competitors had more jets over each major route by a ratio of four to one.

Another major equipment problem involved the Lockheed Electra. In addition to its long-haul service between Florida and major northern cities, Eastern provides service to a number of smaller, more closely spaced cities. To fly the shorter route segments, Rickenbacker felt that the large jets would prove uneconomic. Accordingly, he ordered 40 Lockheed Electras—more than any other airline. There followed the tragic series of Electra accidents. Electras of Braniff and Northwest came apart in flight; an Eastern Electra lost power on take-off from Boston and crashed into the harbor, apparently having ingested a flight of starlings into its engine air intakes. The unfavorable publicity severely handicapped all lines operating Electras, particularly Eastern, since it had more of these planes than any other. For the Electras it did continue to operate, there was the further problem of the speed restrictions imposed during the Civil Aeronautics Board investigation. Flying at only two-thirds of its programed flight speed, the Electra's operating costs mounted rapidly.

In the face of these compounding difficulties, Rickenbacker, to his great credit, himself recommended that he turn over operating responsibility to a new president.

To replace Rickenbacker, Laurance Rockefeller selected Malcolm MacIntyre, a former Rhodes scholar and a successful corporate lawyer from the major New York firm of Debevoise, Plimpton, Lyons & Gates. For four years during World War II, MacIntyre had served with distinction in the Air Transport Command, where he became a close friend of C. R. Smith. Following the war, MacIntyre took American's corporate legal business with him to New York. During the latter days of the Eisenhower Administration, MacIntyre served for a time as Assistant Secretary of the Air Force.

To succeed as vital, famous and strong-willed a man as Rickenbacker would be an enormous problem under the best of circumstances; faced with Eastern's many problems, it was doubly difficult. The short-haul nature of most of Eastern's routes was intrinsically low in profit potential. Only Eddie Rickenbacker's remarkable operation efficiency had kept Eastern's head above water for as long as it did. But now Eastern's routes were overlaid with new competition which generally enjoyed substantial advantages in jet equipment. Furthermore,

Eastern was additionally handicapped by its reputation for poor passenger service.

MacIntyre immediately embarked on a three-part program to establish a new public image; to introduce new and improved passenger service; and to re-equip Eastern with jets as quickly as possible.

One of MacIntyre's first major policy moves was to reduce operational expenses by cutting back uneconomic flight schedules. He promptly grounded and subsequently sold many obsolete planes, lopping off more than 15 percent of Eastern's former 838,000,000 seat miles per month. Having thus reduced expenses, MacIntyre then turned toward organizational problems, determined to restore Eastern's respect among the traveling public.

Passenger service at Eastern had formerly been scattered among several departments. MacIntyre set up a completely new department, directly responsible to him, that took over every function in any way related to the passenger, from first phone call to final baggage delivery.

MacIntyre also quickly reorganized schedule practices. Of Eastern's 39 remaining Electras, 18 were exclusively devoted to commuter patterns—flying between pairs of cities 300 to 500 miles apart, leaving earlier in the morning and later in the afternoon, to permit a businessman to transact a full day's business and still be home at night. Over many of these routes Eastern competes with local service carriers, and the Electra's greater speed provides a certain competitive advantage. On the other hand, over the longer routes, where Eastern would be in competition with pure jets of other lines, the past Electra safety record was a handicap. To cover these routes, MacIntyre ordered 15 Boeing 720's, most of which are already in service. He has also ordered 20 Boeing 727's, the 3-jet short-haul aircraft which will be used to replace the Electras over the shorter route segments beginning in 1963. Thus in the not too far distant future he hopes to have Eastern operating as an all-jet operation.

From the public's point of view, MacIntyre's greatest achievement is the new "shuttle" concept. Searching around for a means of utilizing Eastern's fully depreciated Constellation aircraft, for which there was no commercial resale opportunity, MacIntyre determined to put into effect a minimum-cost, no-frills service designed to compete with bus transportation. The spectacularly successful shuttle flights between Boston, New York, and Washington leave every hour and require no reservations. The obvious convenience of this service has succeeded in taking away a major portion of the business of American and Northeast. Airline critics frequently point out that the Ludington Line had offered shuttle service thirty years before, between Philadelphia and Washington, and various nonscheduled operators had implored the CAB to permit them to provide it years ago. In any case, it was MacIntyre of Eastern who finally put it into effect and deserves the credit for its striking success.

Today Eastern is making every effort to provide its passengers the best service available. By dint of hard work and more realistic scheduling, Eastern has changed from having one of the worst on-time records in the industry to one of the best. The new slogan is, "Eastern has standby airplanes instead of standby passengers."

Despite the success of his innovations, MacIntyre believed that Eastern would remain in a marginal position at best unless some means could be found to reduce costs and improve aircraft utilization. The means he chose was merger. Several candidates were considered, including Delta, Northwest, TWA, and American. But Delta seemed too small, and TWA and Northwest both presented problems as to the future of their international routes. Accordingly, MacIntyre embarked on intensive negotiations with his old friend C. R. Smith at American.

MacIntyre estimates that the proposed merger will save more than $100,000,000 in capital costs, by reducing the need for additional aircraft and through better utilization of existing fleet. Furthermore, annual operating savings of more than $50,000,000 are predicted through integration and consolidation of maintenance, office, ticketing, and terminal facilities. Not the least of Eastern's advantages for American is the prospect of MacIntyre as president of the merged line. (Like many dynamic individualists, Smith has never been able to bring along a clear heir apparent, and his inevitable retirement would leave a serious gap at American.)

Despite all these advantages, the merger line would control more than a third of the U.S. market. As might be expected, any proposal to put more than one third of an industry into the hands of a single company has raised protests and dark charges of monopoly. A recent Congressional staff report prepared for the House Judiciary Subcommittee denounced the proposal as creating a "supercarrier" and questioned the role that "a small group of major insurance companies and banks" play in shaping the destiny of the airlines. The report implied that part of the motivation for the merger could be attributed to the fact that American's lead bank, the Chase, is headed by David Rockefeller, brother of Eastern's dominant stockholder, Laurance. Despite a certain gossip-column charm to such a charge, the report is unclear as to whether David Rockefeller might be seeking to protect existing bank loans to American by increasing the company's earning power or to enhance the value of his brother's stock interest in Eastern. Apart from name-dropping, the report does not pursue the real question of whether the merger is a suitable solution to the problems facing the airline.

*CHAPTER XXI*

---

# TWA and the Enigma of Howard Hughes

Howard Hughes' battle with the banks is the most intriguing tale of corporate finance since the stirring struggles of the railroad robber barons half a century ago. The current conflict has an additional contemporary interest in that it opposes one of the last "loners" in U.S. industry, a true maverick, against the "organization men" and entrenched power of several of our strongest financial institutions.

The stake is control of TWA, on paper potentially the most profitable airline in the world. The only airline flying both the richest transcontinental and international runs, TWA is also the only airline with outright stock ownership in the hands of a single man, the enigmatic and inscrutable Howard Hughes. (As a comparison, for all his personal power, Juan Trippe owns less than .01 percent of Pan American.) There is no question of Hughes' many contributions to TWA. Ever Hamlet-like, TWA's greatest opportunities have been lost through hesitancy and indecision. Threatened with bankruptcy, Hughes surrendered his voting control to bank-appointed trustees. He now claims that the financial institutions entered into a conspiracy to steal his company and the two groups are locked in a bitter law suit.

TWA had its origins in 1928 as Transcontinental Air Transport—a combined air and rail passenger service between New York and Los Angeles. TAT was soon merged with Western Air Express to form Transcontinental and Western Air, Inc., or TWA. With Lindbergh as technical advisor, TWA became famous as "The Lindbergh Line." Originally part of the North American Aviation holding company complex, TWA shifted under the control of General Motors, who nominated one of their able young vice-presidents, Ernie Breech, as chairman (to return twenty-six years later as a trustee of Howard Hughes' stock). After the shake-up of the airline industry following the Black hearings, operational control devolved upon a young pilot, Jack Frye.

Jack Frye's career in aviation began during World War I. With the armistice, Frye moved to California, set up a small flying school, and flew with the "Thirteen Black Cats," the Hollywood stunt pilots who performed in the early movies. With a Fokker demonstrator purchased at cost, Frye soon began to operate a scheduled passenger service between Los Angeles and the Arizona desert. His one-ship operation depended primarily on the travel of movie stars who had desert hideaways, highly fashionable in those days. The big bulge of traffic occurred on the weekends and the demand was so great that Frye was sometimes prevailed upon to carry passengers in the pilot's cockpit. Overloaded, Frye frequently had to stop for extra gas before crossing the Sierras. (Old-timers recall that the refueling stops were also welcomed by anxious passengers who had been drinking prior to takeoff and did not feel their own tankage adequate to complete the flight.)

*Jet Age Giants* [ 245

In 1930, Frye's company was absorbed by Western Air Express. With the union of Western Air Express and Transcontinental Air Transport in 1931, Frye moved on to TWA. His abilities were immediately apparent and, by 1934, Jack Frye was vice-president in charge of operations—the title he carried at the time of his record-breaking transcontinental flight prior to the Air Mail cancellations. Barred by the Black legislation, General Motors sold TWA to Lehman Brothers and Atlas Company and Frye moved up to the top job.

For Frye, flying was his first love. When the Boeing Model 247 demonstrated the enormous possibilities of the modern airliner, Frye urged the TWA management to try to purchase the new Boeing. United, however, had placed such a large order that Boeing's facilities were tied up for 18 months. Frye did not want to wait that long for delivery and he turned instead to Donald Douglas. He explained that he wanted the Boeing but couldn't get delivery. Douglas, with the example of the already proven Boeing to work from, promised something even better. The result was the DC-2—with which Frye set a new transcontinental speed record—and which was to become the parent of the world-famous DC-3.

Frye maintained his air transport license by flying some routes on the line—the only top airline executive who did so on a regular basis. He pioneered high altitude, "over weather" flying, most of the work being done in the Northrup "Gamma" which he used to break his old DC-2 transcontinental record with the first load of mail after the service was returned to private airlines in 1934. High altitude flying offered many advantages in smoothness, speed and economy but it also imposed the requirement of either oxygen or pressurization for passengers.

As a step toward a better transport plane, Frye had pledged TWA, along with United and American, to help Douglas underwrite the cost of the development of a new four-engine airliner,

246 ] THE SKY'S THE LIMIT

which was to become the DC-4. But the DC-4 program proved to be substantially more expensive than anticipated. Furthermore, the production models would lack pressurization for high-altitude flying, essential to the full utilization of the range and potential of a four-engined transport plane. Frye then turned to Boeing and their model 307 Stratoliner, which had been developed as a transport version of the B-17, "Flying Fortress." The Boeing Stratoliner was smaller and more limited in capacity than Frye's objective, but nevertheless it was a four-engined, pressurized transport plane—flying before any other. Frye ordered five of the Boeings and put them in service—the first domestic airline to operate four-engine transports capable of transcontinental or over-ocean flying.

By this time in the affairs of TWA, Howard Hughes had entered the picture—and was almost immediately to become the dominant factor in the airline. Over the years, almost everyone has tried to explain Hughes' behavior in complex psychiatric terms. My opinion is quite simple. I think Howard Hughes has grown old without changing his little boy's fascination for airplanes, movies and girls. To the tired, middle-aged ethos of our business world, Hughes' intrigues and eccentricities are an enigma—but any small boy would instantly understand and appreciate the secret night negotiations and delight in his complicated dealings. Unpressed, unshaven, tieless and in dirty sneakers, Howard Hughes is the Huck Finn of American industry.

His personal peculiarities tend to obscure his keen business sense. Behind his eccentric behavior, Howard Hughes acquired the largest modern pool of industrial wealth under the absolute control of any single individual. His Hughes Tool Company is the principal supplier to the entire oil industry of its most essential tool, the drilling bit. At one time, his control of RKO made him a major factor in the motion picture industry.

His Hughes Aircraft Company in Los Angeles is one of the dominant companies in the electronics field and TWA had every opportunity to be the greatest airline in the world.

The first step in this fabulous fortune was the Hughes Tool Company (sometimes also known as Toolco) which Howard Hughes inherited from his father when he was nineteen. His father was an Iowa lawyer who drifted into Texas—and the oil game. Through his wife, Hughes met a successful independent driller. Over cocktails one night, they decided they could produce a better drilling bit for oil wells. Before long, Hughes came up with a rotary bit, so great an improvement over the existing hard-rock drills that no one else was permitted to see or touch it. Hughes himself always carried it to the well head wrapped in burlap. Other workers were sent away until he had the bit out of sight down the hole.

When his partner died, the elder Hughes had a series of difficulties with his widow but eventually he reacquired all of the company stock. From this experience, he warned young Howard, "Son, don't ever have partners. They're nothing but trouble." The warning took and Howard Hughes has been a loner all his life.

Suspicious, secretive, introverted and independent, the thinly mustached, darkly handsome Hughes lives in a world of his own. To this day, nobody knows what Howard Hughes calls home (private detectives have sought him vainly for the past eight months). He generally lives out of various hotel suites, their sterile interiors unrelieved by any trace of personality. He seldom visits his office in Los Angeles \*; transacts his business almost entirely by phone (although he has been known to

---

\* A fantastically equipped command post, with an almost childish collection of electronic gadgetry and warning devices. In a pending litigation, Hughes' attorney recently astonished the staid Wall Street counsel of the opposing banks and insurance companies by accusing them of attempting to take surreptitious X-ray photographs of documents in the office. It developed that the battery had run down on one of Hughes' anti-X-ray warning devices, which had therefore sounded a false alarm.

conduct major negotiations in such unlikely places as hotel men's rooms); and is served personally by a small staff, all sworn to secrecy—and all Mórmons whose abstemious principles Hughes values highly.

His father's sudden death left young Howard a well-run, and very profitable company. Feeling that there was no need for him in Houston, he moved to Hollywood to pursue his dominant interests in life—girls, movies and flying. He bought RKO studios, produced "Hell's Angels," probably the greatest movie of World War I aviation, fell in love with Jean Harlow, his leading lady, gave fantastic parties, and set out to break all of the world's aviation speed records. Gifted with a high degree of technical and engineering skill, Hughes was an exceptional pilot. Flying a small racer of his own design, the H-1, he broke Jack Frye's transcontinental record and followed that with a new round-the-world speed record in a Lockheed 14.

The speed records brought Hughes and Frye into close contact. Together, Hughes, Frye and Lockheed embarked on a development program for the Constellation transport for TWA. (Hughes is also credited with an important role in the design of Lockheed's famous wartime P-38 pursuit plane.) The "Connie" was far advanced over any transport then on the drawing boards and with it Hughes and Frye had dreams of making TWA the greatest airline in the world. At Frye's urging, Hughes bought control of the company in 1939. Over the years, Hughes has increased his stock holdings to the present 78 percent—at an average cost of 12 dollars per share. In addition to his stock interest, Hughes also holds more than 100 million dollars worth of TWA debentures.

In the hands of Hughes and Frye, TWA became the most technically advanced of all the airlines. With its Boeing 307's, TWA pioneered "over-weather" passenger operations, a significant step forward in safety and comfort. At the beginning of the war, TWA was the only domestic airline with four-engine equipment and experience and TWA's five Boeing 307's became the original nucleus of the Air Transport Command.

For its technical pioneering and progressiveness, TWA was richly rewarded by the CAB in postwar route decisions. The most favored of all airlines, it was awarded more than 21,000 miles of new international routes, including the choice "Blue Ribbon Run" across the North Atlantic, with additional service through Egypt and India to the Orient. (Plans for a round-the-world service via a hookup with Northwest in Shanghai were precluded by the Chinese Communist take-over in 1948.) In keeping with its international expansion, the former corporate name of Transcontinental and Western Airlines was changed to Trans World Airlines.

Inexplicably, Hughes' interest in the airline began to change. Operational details bored him and he seemed to take increasing refuge in the esoteric world of airplane design and detail, often of such minor character as galley layouts or color schemes. Major corporate decisions waited upon his whims. At one point, he commandeered a new Constellation out of the operational fleet and disappeared for several weeks. It later developed that he had taken it to Nassau where he practiced landings daily, trying to improve piloting techniques. Regardless of his motives, his mysterious absences (not to mention the airplane's) caused difficulty in the company.

With Hughes out of touch, Jack Frye attempted to develop programs and policies to meet the anticipated requirements of TWA's new routes. But Frye's financial plans soon ran headlong into the objections of Noah Dietrich, the fiscal watchdog for Hughes Tool and general overseer of the Hughes' empire. Dietrich feared that Frye was attempting too much pioneering with Hughes' money. Furthermore, Dietrich predicted, quite correctly, that all the airlines were too ambitious in their postwar expansion plans and would soon be in serious financial trouble. Dietrich eventually convinced Hughes that certain operating economies were absolutely necessary to the welfare of TWA and that the existing management was not disposed to put them into effect. Before Hughes, Dietrich and Frye could reach any kind of an accord on new policies, the securities market took a sharp downward drop and the opportunity for a successful stock offering to finance new aircraft had been lost. By 1947, TWA's financial condition had become critical. All efforts toward bank refinancing had failed and TWA faced bankruptcy. At this point Dietrich, speaking for Hughes, required Frye's resignation as a condition to further financial assistance from the Tool Company.

Meanwhile, Hughes was having problems with other parts of his empire. His long awaited postwar movie, "The Outlaw," starring the buxom Jane Russell, was being delayed by censors. Television was cutting heavily into the movie industry. In addition, things were not going well at Hughes Aircraft. The Aircraft Company had been set up as a division of Hughes Tool in 1934, to permit Hughes to indulge his aviation interests. Not surprisingly, Hughes Aircraft failed to achieve financial success. It appeared that Hughes' primary interest was to develop the world's fastest and largest airplanes. His F-11 Pursuit, an effort towards this end, was never put into production. The largest, a huge wooden flying boat, begun by Hughes in partnership with Henry J. Kaiser, allegedly absorbed $55,000,000 in government financed development costs and was flown (by Hughes himself) for only a few seconds.

The flying boat fiasco brought on a Congressional investigation, fascinating in color and complexity. Hughes' Washington representative, a suitably obsequious, plump little man reminiscent of a harem eunuch, told of arranging lavish entertainment with beautiful movie starlets for government officials. As the case against him mounted, Hughes himself appeared before the Senators, tieless, unshaven, wearing a rumpled jacket borrowed from his valet. Despite the incongruity of his attire and in the face of the unfavorable prior testimony, Hughes counterattacked, charging that Senator Owen Brewster had rigged the case against Hughes Aircraft as part of a plan of blackmail and bribery. Hughes offered to present evidence of Brewster's extortionary proposals (supposedly demanding control of TWA as the price of calling off the Hughes Aircraft investigation). With the tables turned by Hughes' charges, Brewster and his fellow Senators dropped the whole matter, significantly without asking for confirmation of Hughes' statements. Brewster lost his Senate seat in the next election.

For the rehabilitation of the Aircraft Company, Hughes brought in a team of former Air Force officers, the key man being Charles B. Thornton. "Tex" Thornton had been the leader of the famous Air Force "Whiz Kids," who had set up the wartime Air Force statistical control system. After the war, Thornton had suggested to his group of brilliant young men that they sell themselves as a unit, rather than seeking jobs as individuals. Many companies fought for their services, but Ford won out and Thornton took the Whiz Kids with him to Detroit in 1947. But things weren't moving fast enough for him at Ford and he left two years later, together with several of his former associates, to take up the new challenge at Hughes Aircraft. (Several of the "Whiz Kids" remained at Ford, among them Robert McNamara, who was destined to become Ford president in 1960 and President Kennedy's Secretary of Defense in 1961.)

Thornton immediately recognized the promise of a small electronics research laboratory operated by two scientists—Dr. Gene Wooldridge and Dr. Simon Ramo. Anticipating the Air Force need for an all-weather interceptor, he turned the scientists' energies toward the development of the two vital elements of an interceptor system: an airborne fire control system and an air-to-air missile. When the outbreak of the Korean War sent a new flood of orders surging through the aircraft industry, Hughes Aircraft was in a strategic position. It became the sole source of supply for fire control systems for the entire interceptor program—equipping the North American F-86, Northrup F-89, Lockheed F-94 and the Navy's McDonnell F2H. Similar success followed with the development of their "Falcon" air-to-air guided missile. Hughes Aircraft had clearly demonstrated its superiority over all other companies in these new and highly sophisticated electronic weapon systems. The company's growth was fantastic; its staff multiplied nearly 200 times. The scientific talents ranged around Wooldridge and Ramo became the most versatile single pool of electronics specialists in the country.

With the rapid expansion of Hughes Aircraft, the company's requirements for capital increased. Typically, Hughes deferred decisions. Matters reached a climax with the need for a new research laboratory. Weeks passed without a decision. Finally word came back through intermediaries that Hughes desired to have a new laboratory built near his desert home in Las Vegas rather than near the main Hughes Aircraft plant in Culver City. Thornton, Ramo and Wooldridge refused to agree with the seemingly capricious desire to move to Nevada, objecting to the physical separation of the laboratory staff from the manufacturing plant at this critical stage in their development. Finally forced to give in on the location of the new plant, Hughes got his revenge in other ways. He required that all design drawings of the new facilities be submitted to him personally for review, thus delaying construction for weeks. He took personal interest in the decision for colors of interior paints and other similarly frivolous determinations. At a crucial stage in the development of an airborne guidance system, he deprived the company of the services of the flight test director, whom

Hughes requisitioned as technical adviser for a film called "Jet Pilot" which he was then making at his RKO studios.

Fresh from his victory over Jack Frye at TWA, Noah Dietrich arrived on the scene at Hughes Aircraft and began to intrude into management. Daily, the personality conflicts became more intense. There were rumors that Hughes would sell out. The Air Force group within the company determined to try to find a buyer to their liking. Thornton rounded up substantial interest, but because of Hughes' recalcitrance, each deal fell through. Finally, the management group sent Hughes a formal notice that they could no longer be responsible for meeting the company's commitments for the Air Force, so long as Hughes and Dietrich continued to meddle in management.

The Air Force naturally became increasingly concerned because of the critical and sole-source nature of the products of Hughes Aircraft. Harold Talbott flew to Los Angeles and bluntly told Hughes, "You have made a hell of a mess of a great property. By God, so long as I am Secretary of the Air Force, you're not going to get another dollar of new business." Hughes was not to be outdone, "If you mean to tell me that the government is prepared to destroy a business merely on the unfounded charges of a few disgruntled employees, then you are introducing communism."

Roger Lewis, then the able Air Force Assistant Secretary for Materiel (subsequently vice-president of Pan American and most recently chosen president to pick up the pieces at General Dynamics), tried to give the situation time to work out. Before he left Los Angeles, Lewis made it clear to the surrounding aircraft industry that the Air Force would "look with disfavor" on any attempt to pirate Hughes' talent. But the conditions at Hughes Aircraft were beyond remedy. Wooldridge and Ramo left to form their own company. Tex Thornton, financed by Lehman Brothers, started building his remarkable Litton Industries. The Air Force, determined to free itself from its dependency upon the capricious monopoly of Howard Hughes, rapidly brought along other companies in the sophisticated electronics areas.

As if suddenly bored with the whole situation, Hughes set up a charitable medical foundation and turned over to it all of the stock of Hughes Aircraft, thereby depriving himself forever of the future profitability of this still great electronics enterprise.

Following the ouster of Frye in 1948, TWA passed into the hands of Ralph Damon. Previously, Damon had served as president of American during C. R. Smith's wartime absence in the Air Transport Command. After the war, frictions developed between the two, culminating in Smith's decision to sell American's international division to Pan Am. Damon wanted to stay in the international game and jumped eagerly into TWA. Despite Damon's best efforts, the company did not progress as it should have. For some obscure reason, Hughes decided to restrict advertising and promotion. Furthermore, TWA's Constellations were steadily being outclassed as DC-7's came into service with all of TWA's major rivals. Frustrated and embittered, Damon died of a heart attack in 1955.

He was replaced by Carter Burgess, a former protégé of Jack Frye, then serving as Assistant Secretary of Defense. Burgess lasted only 11 months, during which time he never met Hughes in person. The final parting occurred, not surprisingly, over the re-equipment program. In an effort to maintain a competitive position until jets were available, TWA had been forced into a costly interim decision to buy an improved model of the Lockheed Constellation, which TWA press agents called the "Jetstream." Other carriers protested, claiming that the title gave the impression that the aircraft were, somehow or other, jet-powered. TWA, on the other hand, maintained that the name implied only that the aircraft was sufficiently long-ranged to fly pressure pattern routes and take advantage of the jetstream winds.

The crucial competitive element for TWA became the early delivery of jets but Hughes seemed unable to decide on either the Boeing 707 or the Douglas DC-8. For a time, Hughes himself considered building a jet transport of his own for TWA. Then, he and Convair began a curious, coy courtship. The negotiations were lengthy, almost always conducted at night and sometimes marked by bizarre occurrences, such as Hughes impulsively interrupting talks at 3 A.M. to take the tired engineers to see a private showing of his latest movie, complete with the presence of the leading actresses. Long after his competitors had made their decisions, Hughes suddenly placed his orders, totalling 33 Boeing 707's, 30 Convair 880's and 13 Convair 990's —considerably more aircraft than TWA could then afford.

Already seriously behind in jet delivery schedules, Hughes apparently thought he saw an opportunity to "corner" the jet engine market. Accordingly, he entered into large contracts with Pratt & Whitney and General Electric for jet engines, substantially beyond any foreseeable requirements of TWA. It seemed to be Hughes' plan that the other airlines would have to come to him for engines, which he might then trade off for improved delivery positions for the jet airframes themselves. In fact, Hughes' strategem failed and he was stuck with additional financing requirements to cover his contractual obligations for the engines.

Financial pressures began to mount, at a particularly awkward moment. The fabulous profitability of Hughes Tool was impaired by the recession in the oil industry in the late 1950's. By turning over the stock of Hughes Aircraft to the charitable foundation, Hughes had cut himself off from assistance from that quarter. The banks refused to make further commitments. To defer delivery and delay the due date of payments, Hughes allegedly began a program of harassment at Convair. TWA inspectors made daily visits, specifications were changed, and at one point Hughes' men actually pulled incomplete planes off the production line under armed guard and refused to let Convair people touch them.

Bob Gross of Lockheed then came forward with a proposal to buy Hughes Aircraft. Lockheed needed a sophisticated electronics company to move forward from aircraft into missiles and Hughes Aircraft would be an ideal acquisition. Although Hughes no longer owned the stock of Hughes Aircraft, the Tool Company held some $70,000,000 worth of Aircraft's notes, real estate and mortgages. With the proceeds from the sale to Lockheed, the debts to the Tool Company could be paid off, providing Hughes with cash to finance jet purchases for TWA.

While negotiations for the purchase of Hughes Aircraft were going forward, Gross recommended his friend Charles Thomas for the job of president of TWA. Thomas had been head of Foreman and Clark, a Los Angeles clothing manufacturer, and was then serving as Secretary of the Navy. Despite his lack of airline experience, Thomas' presence seemed to produce results. By a series of intricate leasing arrangements, some Boeing 707's were put in service and TWA began to make money.

If the sale of Hughes Aircraft had gone through, the difficulties would have been over. But, at the last minute, Hughes changed his terms. He demanded the price of the Aircraft Company be determined by the price-earnings ratio accorded by the market to Litton Industries, Tex Thornton's rapidly growing electronic complex. Apparently Hughes could not bear the thought that his former employee could put together a more valuable company. The other participants in the transaction disagreed—and the deal fell through.

Hughes had already delayed more than four years in financing his jet fleet. Apart from his characteristic trait to postpone all decisions, there were some valid considerations. Apparently he hoped that favorable market conditions and perhaps improved profitability in TWA would open the door to an equity financing. Furthermore, there was the possibility that lower interest rates might make debt financing easier. Perhaps most significant of all were the tax considerations. Hughes Tool was earning as much as 50 million dollars a year. If Hughes paid the earnings out to himself as dividends, the government would immediately seize 90 percent in taxes. Yet Hughes could not leave the earnings idle in the company without having them taxed as an unreasonable accumulation of surplus. Hughes put them to work buying aircraft. It was his plan to lease the planes to TWA, thus not only avoiding the accumulation problem but also gaining tax advantages in depreciation write-offs and perhaps capital gains on the eventual sale of the planes as well. However, Thomas and others in TWA began to oppose the lease plan as being a benefit to Hughes at the expense of TWA.

As the delivery dates neared, the pressure on Hughes became acute. To arrange financing, he retained three major Wall Street houses, Dillon Reed, Lehman Brothers and Lazard Frères. Dillon Reed assumed the lead position and evolved a plan which, although changed in minor particulars, generally provided for a combination of long-term loans from insurance companies and interim, short-term loans from commercial banks. According to Hughes, the major insurance companies, Metropolitan, Prudential and Equitable, had previously agreed to a pattern of conduct known as the traditional senior lender's concept, whereby no company would deal with a major airline without the consent of that airline's traditional senior lender. By this time Equitable had established itself as TWA's senior lender and the Irving Trust Company was the chief commercial bank. Accordingly Dillon Reed worked with these institutions in developing their plans. The amount of the loan was so large that Equitable shared the long term debt with the Metropolitan and Irving arranged a syndicate of banks.

At this point the ensuing events become subject to intense controversy and dispute, particularly regarding the motivations of the individuals involved. Always a recluse, Hughes had become increasingly secretive (some said because of his sensitivity over his gradual loss of hearing) and whenever possible conducted his business through agents and intermediaries. Moreover, it seemed to be a fixed business practice with Hughes to change agents at a moment's notice. Thus the other parties to the negotiation never knew from one minute to the next whether the man they were dealing with would continue to have authority. Despite the awkwardness of this situation, the financial institutions were at first willing to play along with Hughes so long as Thomas, whom they trusted, was president of TWA. At least they knew where to reach Thomas and what authority he had. But Thomas had agreed to stay in TWA only for two years, unless he received a long term contract with additional compensation. When Thomas raised this subject with Hughes (by phone, of course) Hughes hesitated. Thomas was too valuable to lose at this point but a long term contract from TWA would free Thomas from direct subordination to Hughes. Instead, Hughes offered an equivalent contract from the Tool Company, where he could keep Thomas squarely under his thumb. Thomas rejected the proposal and resigned from TWA.

TWA had run through five presidents in the preceding 15 year period and there had been a gap of more than a year prior to Thomas' appointment. Such instability of management unquestionably interfered with TWA's development and was a legitimate source of concern to anyone interested in the airline. However, Hughes claims that James Oates, of the Equitable, Harry Haggarty, of the Metropolitan, and Ben-Fleming Sessel of Irving Trust, got together and decided to use Thomas' resignation as an excuse to seize control of TWA by insisting that

Hughes place his stock in a trust under their domination, as a condition to any future financing.

The financial men justified their action on the grounds that they felt a sense of obligation to assist in the financing of TWA as a vital part of the national transportation system. Yet, they could not with a clear conscience put outright depositors' funds into the capricious hands of Howard Hughes. If Hughes would not deal with them directly and openly, they demanded that control be put in the hands of men who would. As their trustees, the institutions nominated two outstanding U.S. industrialists, Ernest Breech, recently retired as chairman of the Ford Motor Company, and Irving Olds, formerly chairman of U.S. Steel. By now Hughes' back was to the wall. He tried other sources of financing but all doors seemed closed. He fired his long time attorney, Ray Cook, and hired Hollywood lawyer, Greg Bautzer, husband of actress Dana Wynter. Despite Hughes' twisting and turning, the banks were relentless. Sessel of the Irving dealt the final blow. In a prior transaction secret to this day, Hughes had personally borrowed many million dollars from the Irving, pledging as collateral all of his stock in the Tool Company. Sessel threatened foreclosure simultaneously on all loans, both to TWA and to Hughes.

Speaking for Hughes, Bautzer finally accepted the trust arrangement. Papers were drawn and all parties signed the agreement; that is, all except Hughes, who sent word through Bautzer that the banks had increased the interest rate without notice. The day dragged on and Bautzer was unable to locate his client for further discussion. Bautzer pleaded for an extension. The following day the bankers went to Bautzer's hotel with their final ultimatum and were told by Bautzer's beautiful wife that he was too sick to meet with them, having exhausted himself by negotiation with the bankers during the day and Hughes during the night. Nevertheless, Bautzer advised them that Hughes' trustee, Raymond Holliday, would sign the agreements the following morning in Hughes' behalf. When Holliday arrived at the Chemical Bank at the appointed hour, he claimed that there were too many documents and issues for one man to cope with, particularly since one of his lawyers had been fired and the other was sick. The bankers suggested that perhaps Bautzer might get better in time to help Holliday look over the documents. Upon calling, they discovered that Bautzer had gone to the hospital. Time was now of the essence. The agreements terminated at the end of the day and it was necessary for the plane mortgages to be registered with the Federal Aviation Authority office in Oklahoma City—which closed at 5:30 P.M., New York time. Holliday asked for more time. The bankers refused. Holliday retired to a room to make some calls in private. The bankers phoned the FAA and requested the registration deadline be extended to 7:30 P.M. As the hands of the clock in the board room at the Chemical Bank passed 7:00, the prospects for successful completion looked dim. Bautzer could not be reached; Hughes could not be reached. But suddenly, at 7:15, Bautzer got well. By 7:25 the mortgages were registered and stamped.

With the signing of the trust documents all concerned seemed to breath a sigh of relief. But the real bitterness was just beginning. The bankers were now in a position to dictate the terms of the financing and they demanded 6½ percent interest on the long term debt, which Hughes claimed was higher than any interest rate charged by them to any other corporation in 1961. Furthermore the banks introduced a clause requiring a 22 percent penalty for prepayment to prevent Hughes from regaining control by paying off the loans.

Hughes fought these conditions, on the grounds that they had not been explained to him in advance. Relations between the parties deteriorated rapidly. The financial men took the view that they were dealing with an erratic and irrational man who "had made a hell of a mess of a great airline" (echoing Air Force Secretary Harold Talbott's comments regarding Hughes Aircraft).

At TWA, Ernie Breech took the lead role, becoming chairman of the board in addition to his trusteeship. Independently wealthy and retired from a brilliant business career as, consecutively, vice president of General Motors, president of Bendix and chairman of Ford, Breech took on the responsibility at TWA at least partially out of sentiment because of his part in the early days of the company's existence. Breech's entire business career had been that of a professional manager of great public corporations and he had no patience for the idiosyncracies of Howard Hughes.

As president of TWA, Breech installed Charles Tillinghast, a former Wall Street lawyer who had earned Breech's respect at Bendix. Breech and Tillinghast assessed TWA's equipment program and determined that more planes were needed. Hughes still held title to ten Convair 880's and thirteen 990's which he had ordered for TWA. But TWA was under no legal obligation to accept them. Instead Tillinghast ordered new Boeing 720's. The new order was financed by an additional 146 million dollar loan arranged through the same financial institutions who had participated in the first financing—with the additional provision that this second financing must be prepaid if the trustee's control should ever revert to Hughes. Thus Hughes was faced with an almost insurmountable barrier to the recovery of his airline: first, the original 165 million dollar loan with its burdensome 22 percent prepayment penalty; next, the 147 million dollar loan for the new Boeings, due and payable on any attempt to pay off the first loan; and finally, the problem of payment for the already ordered but now unwanted Convairs.

Obviously, Hughes did not take such treatment lying down. But before he could mount a counter-attack Tillinghast struck another blow—an antitrust suit charging that Hughes Tool had monopolized aircraft purchases to the damage of TWA. Actually, the wording of TWA's complaint leaves a strong impression that it is more in the nature of stockholder's derivative action for mismanagement than a true antitrust suit. (All of the transactions between Hughes Tool and TWA were approved by the CAB, thereby becoming automatically exempt from the operation of the antitrust laws.) Regardless of its validity on antitrust grounds, the suit served the purpose of critically presenting the record of Hughes' management of TWA.

Hughes responded with counterclaims against the financial institutions of more than 300 million dollars. He charged that the institutions had conspired to steal control of his company; that they had unlawfully excluded other financial institutions from participating in the financing; that they were seeking to perpetuate their control by self-dealing; all as part of a general plot to acquire control of the market for major airline financings for themselves. Perhaps the most telling of Hughes' arguments was the fact that the financial institutions had acquired control without the approval of the Civil Aeronautics Board, apparently a clear violation of law. (Louis Hector, a former member of the CAB, charged in his 1959 resignation statement * that, among other failings, the Board had cravenly sidestepped their responsibility to investigate the question of whether financial institutions, through the terms of their loans, were acquiring domination of the airline industry.

Meanwhile, Hughes had gotten himself involved in a complex deal with Northeast Airlines. Northeast started as a small regional carrier, cursed with the dual hardships of bad weather and short routes. In an effort to strengthen it, the CAB in 1955 granted Northeast a New York–Florida route. The company hurriedly embarked on a costly expansion program and was

* A scathing denunciation of the CAB, reported in full in 69 Yale Law Journal 931.

badly set back by the adverse publicity of a crash of one of its aircraft on Rikers Island, where survivors were interviewed by television on the spot, an ordeal no other airline has had to face in its public relations efforts.

Northeast had been controlled by the Atlas Corporation. Some years before Hughes had sold his RKO movie studios to Atlas in exchange for stock. The CAB questioned the transaction on the grounds that Hughes was thereby in a position to control two airlines without CAB approval. The case dragged on and on and before the CAB could reach a decision, the financial situation at Northeast became critical. The British Vickers Company, builders of Northeast's Viscounts, threatened foreclosure. A proposal by Eastern and National to take over Northeast's Florida route and for Mohawk to handle the regional situation within New England was turned down by Atlas. Hughes then offered to bail out Northeast in exchange for full control.

His offer hung the CAB on the horns of a dilemma. On the one hand they hated to see Northeast fall into Hughes' hands. On the other, the Board was most reluctant to have an airline go bankrupt, fearing criticism of CAB stewardship. At the present moment, it appears that the CAB has decided in favor of Hughes, who has announced his intention to merge Northeast into TWA, if and when he regains control. Meanwhile there is considerable speculation that the trustees will sell TWA to Pan American. The last thing anybody seems to want is to let Hughes get back in the airline business.

CHAPTER XXII

## The Stormy Career of National Airlines

National's stormy career is the direct result of the mercurial character of its founder, George Baker. A big, bulky man with beard-shadowed jowls, Baker is addicted to black cigars and blunt language. His antecedents are shrouded in mystery. There is a rumor that he entered aviation flying bootleg whisky into Chicago for Al Capone during prohibition. It may not be true but the rumor suits him. The records show that Baker was born in Chicago, attended the Montana School of Mines, and left college to join the U.S. Forestry Service in Montana. He worked briefly on a ranch and came back to Chicago with a cattle run during the fall. In 1918 he entered the Army Tank Corps on his eighteenth birthday. After the war, Baker had several jobs, among them selling Whitman candy, and then typewriters, across the Middle West. He soon found himself a used-car salesman, then entered the factoring business, financing car dealers. With a reputation as a tough and ruthless negotiator, he shortly had repossessed enough cars to go into the used-car business on his own. Somewhere along the line Baker learned to fly—and became an airplane salesman in Chicago. When the depression caused a drop in his business, Baker took his last two remaining planes and set up National Airlines Taxi Service, doing odd jobs anywhere.

In 1934, when the Air Mail was returned to private operators, Baker bid on the 124-mile route over Florida swampland between St. Petersburg and Daytona Beach, claiming that he picked this route simply because it was the shortest one available. When his bid was accepted, Baker moved to Florida and set up operations, with himself as pilot, ticket agent, mechanic, and baggage smasher combined. (To this day he is carried on National Airlines seniority lists as Pilot #1.)

From the beginning, Baker was a thorn in the side of Eddie Rickenbacker's Eastern Airlines. Gradually, and against the bitter opposition of Rickenbacker, Baker expanded his operations within Florida and as far west as New Orleans. The big break came in 1944, when the CAB awarded him a route between Miami and New York. He had applied for the route four years previously, but frankly admits that he had not thought too highly of his chances. Apparently the CAB rested its decision on two factors: first, it wished to provide competition for Eastern on the New York–Miami run; secondly, the CAB did not wish to make any of the other large lines yet bigger by cutting them into such a rich market. Of the decision, Baker says: "I guess they gave it to us because we needed it so badly. We didn't have anything to offer. Any one of the big carriers could probably have operated it better."

The New York–Miami route was the making of National. At the end of the war, Eastern was still flying DC-3's when Baker introduced DC-4's and inaugurated the first nonstop service to Miami. For the first time, Eastern realized the degree of the threat. Baker claims that years before, Rickenbacker had told him: "Get in my way again and I'll take you over." Baker was determined that this would not happen. On paper, Eastern had every advantage over National. With its financial reserves and equipment potential, it could bracket National's operation. There is an old maxim in the airline business that traffic ordinarily flows to the carrier offering the most frequent service. Against Eastern, Baker was hopelessly overmatched in trying to offer flight for flight. Instead, he used showmanship and every salesman's trick to lure customers away from Rickenbacker.

A good start was pretty girls. While Eastern offered only male stewards on its planes, Baker adopted the policy of hiring the prettiest girls he could find as his airline hostesses. In seeking beauty, Baker was among the first to break with the old airline tradition that hostesses had to be nurses. Before long, National's reputation for beautiful hostesses had grown to the point that a story was started in the industry that Baker had once hired the entire chorus line of a show stranded in Pittsburgh. National executives liked to claim that they had beaten Eastern with Service, Safety and Sex.\*

After Baker had jumped to an early lead with the DC-4 nonstop flights, Eastern retaliated with Constellations. But the Constellations were outfitted for five-abreast seating, for maximum revenues. Passengers resented what they did not regard as first-class treatment.

With his keen salesman's sense, Baker examined his New York–Miami markets and intuitively perceived certain special characteristics. He concluded that most passengers on that run were acutely cost conscious, therefore probably particularly susceptible to lower coach fares. At the same time, Baker thought

---

\* National's safety record was among the best in the industry until 1960, when two unusual accidents, perhaps both sabotage, occurred: the fantastic suicide bombing of a National flight in South Carolina; and the still unexplained disappearance of a National plane over the Gulf of Mexico.

he detected a reverse psychology, in that certain passengers, however attracted by the lower fares, would not wish to be seen on coach flights. To take advantage of this emotion, Baker also offered the pretentious and flamboyant "Star" flights, where red carpets were actually rolled out on the runways.

Highly successful in his sales policies, he had serious difficulty with the labor-relations problem. In 1945, one of Baker's pilots landed too fast, overshot the field, and crashed through a sea wall at the end of it. Furious, Baker fired the pilot. The pilot appealed to National's grievance board, and the board—composed of two management men and two airline pilot union members—deadlocked. There was no machinery for bringing in an impartial fifth man, and Baker refused to take the issue to arbitration. The case remained deadlocked for two years, and relations between Baker and his pilots steadily grew worse. Finally Baker agreed to let the National Mediation Board pick an arbitrator. At this point the pilots' union got stubborn and rejected the choice of the Mediation Board. At the height of the winter tourist season and National's peak profit period, the pilots struck.

Baker fought on. He hired former Air Force pilots who were not union men and attempted to maintain the full schedule of flights for the winter tourist season. Frequent fist fights occurred between the strikers and the pilots. At the peak of the difficulty, National's four new DC-6's were grounded as a result of the crashes by DC-6's on other lines. All kinds of pressures were brought to bear on Baker to give in to the union. The CAB ordered an investigation. A proposal was introduced that Pan American would get the New York–Miami route and Eastern and Delta would split National's other services. The CAB seemed determined to force Baker to settle with his pilots or lose his airline. Baker believed that the CAB's decision was motivated not only by the political pressure of the pilots' union, but behind it all he suspected the Machiavellian hand of Juan Trippe. For years Trippe had coveted a New York–Miami route which would give Pan American access to the great traffic center of New York and also would integrate his maintenance operations, now split between Miami for the Latin-American division and New York for the Atlantic divisions. Baker knew that Pan American would keep pressing the CAB to dismember National unless Baker could convince Trippe that a better deal could be worked out—preferably a deal that would preserve National under Baker's control.

Almost from the beginning, Trippe and Grace had been feuding over Panagra, which they owned jointly. Into the breach stepped Baker. He suggested that National fly Panagra planes between New York and Miami on an interchange basis. Initially, Trippe was cold to the proposal, but Baker offered an additional inducement—a stock interest in National, if Pan American would agree to the interchange. Meanwhile, desperate for cash, Baker sold 174,000 shares of National stock to Grace. When Trippe heard about the deal, he demanded a bigger chunk of stock than Grace had. An agreement was signed whereby Trippe would receive an option to buy 30 percent of National's stock and Grace would have an option to increase its holdings up to 18 percent. This would leave Baker with only 12 percent of the stock, but he counted on the support of friendly stockholders, particularly Grace, whom he could play off against Pan American to preserve control. These terms were incorporated in a memorandum of understanding signed by Baker, Peter Grace, and Trippe at 4 o'clock in the morning of the very day an executive of Pan American was to go on the stand before the CAB and present Pan American's case for dismembering National. The executive received instructions to change his tune while waiting to be sworn in to testify. The CAB immediately suspended hearings and took under consideration the contract between Grace, Pan American, and National. And, while the Board considered, Baker had the money and time he needed to repair his damaged airline.

With this breathing spell Baker was able to settle the strike and get his airline back in profitable operating condition. Meanwhile, his relations with Trippe deteriorated. Trippe contended that he had the right to buy additional stock on the open market and thus acquire outright control of the airline. Baker maintained that under the memorandum agreement, Trippe's stock ownership was limited to the 30 percent set forth in the document. Before long (with National once again profitable) Baker tore up the deal with Pan American, claiming that Trippe had breached the contract. The Panagra-National interchange went into operation over Trippe's violent protest.

The Grace stock purchase in 1949 had been the turning point. By 1951 National was clearly out of the woods and Grace offered to sell the stock back for a $1,500,000 profit. Baker accepted eagerly. The deal was promptly challenged by a National director (whom Baker claimed was in cahoots with Trippe). A proxy fight was started and the ensuing board meeting was attended by armed guards, but Baker's control was preserved.

Seeking expansion, Baker tried to buy Colonial Airlines, but was beaten out by Eddie Rickenbacker. Baker then unsuccessfully tried to acquire Northeast Airlines, which was subsequently certified by the CAB to become the third carrier on the New York–Miami route. Baker also wanted a Great Lakes–Miami route, and had been recommended by the CAB hearing examiner for the lucrative Chicago–Miami run. But before the final decision of the Board, Baker was again in trouble.

Some years before, in an effort to broaden the opportunities of National Airlines, Baker had acquired TV Channel 10 in Miami. The circumstances of the acquisition were suspicious. Baker's lawyer was discovered to have made substantial loans to the FCC commissioner who had cast the crucial vote in the award. The commissioner and Baker's Miami attorney were arraigned on charges of conspiracy to defraud the U.S. Government. Naturally such behavior was not helpful to Baker's case before the CAB. In short order, National—which would otherwise surely have been favored—lost the Chicago–Miami run to Northwest and the St. Louis–Miami route to TWA.

These blows were followed by the bad winter season of 1957–1958, which drastically cut into National's revenues. Looking forward to the fall, Baker saw more trouble. Eastern would be equipped with the new Lockheed Electras. Baker had ordered some, but they would not be delivered until after Eastern's and he feared that the new aircraft would provide Rickenbacker with a substantial competitive advantage in the crucial tourist season. Baker could not afford another bad winter.

There was a possible solution. Baker and Rickenbacker had both ordered DC-8 jets, but they would not be available for another two years; but Boeing was making deliveries on 707's. Baker felt that he would get a jump on Eastern if he could rent a couple of 707's for the winter of 1958. He approached C. R. Smith of American Airlines, but Smith said American needed all the jets it had for its own routes. The only other alternative was Pan American. In view of their past differences, it is almost unbelievable that Trippe would get together with Baker again, but each wanted what the other had. There was a certain logic in the deal Baker proposed. Pan American enjoyed its heaviest traffic during summer months and could well spare the equipment that Baker needed during the winter. Jet financing was expensive, and Pan American could use the cash. Financially, the deal made sense for both Pan American and National. And Baker was willing to throw in the extra inducement—an exchange of 400,000 shares of National and Pan American stock on a one-for-one basis (highly favorable to National). However, Pan American would get an option on an additional 250,000 shares, enough to give Pan Am control. The prospect of acquiring access to the rich Miami–New York market was too much for Trippe to resist.

The deal was quickly completed and enabled National to fly the first jet transport in domestic service in December of 1958. Operating the two Pan American jets during the winter, Baker took a great volume of business away from Eastern. It was a coup of the highest magnitude. For the use of the jet, Baker paid Trippe operating expenses and a minor profit. The real inducement for Pan American had been the stock options, but that part of the deal had to receive CAB approval. CAB consideration dragged on through the winter, every day of which Baker made money with Trippe's airplanes. By the end of the Florida season, when Baker had no further use for Pan American's jets (his own would be delivered before the following fall), the CAB disapproved the entire transaction. Baker acted crestfallen and Trippe was furious.

The success of the Pan Am jet deal was followed by the CAB award of a rich transcontinental run from Miami to Los Angeles, which should assure National permanent prosperity. But sedate security is not Ted Baker's style. Ever restless, he embarked upon a merger proposal with Bob Six of Continental. Under the terms filed with the CAB, Baker was to become chairman of the merged company, with Six as president. Insiders rubbed their hands in glee at the thought of the titanic battles to come. (One of Baker's old executives says: "Ted's a great guy until you go to work for him. Then he hates you because he thinks you're taking his money.")

But the conflicts were never to develop. Immediately following the announcement of the American-Eastern merger, the Continental-National merger was called off, for reasons never explained publicly. Instead, Baker sold his stock in National to thirty-five-year-old Lewis Maytag, Jr., heir to the washing-machine fortune, who had previously indulged his aviation enthusiasm as president of Frontier, a Western local service airline. Not surprisingly, the terms were remarkably favorable to Baker (nearly twice as much as a stockholder not enjoying Baker's position could have received on the open market) and his old top management team was pushed aside to permit Maytag and his associates to take over at once.

Whatever the future may hold for National, it won't be the same without Ted Baker.

*CHAPTER XXIII*

# Northwest and the Great Circle Run to the Orient

From the earliest days of navigation, men have dreamed of the Northwest Passage—the short cut to the Orient. Today Northwest Orient Airlines is the only United States airline to fly the Great Circle run to the Far East, saving nearly 20 percent of the mileage between New York and Hong Kong.

How Northwest came to enjoy this advantage is not only a dynamic story of company growth, but also reflects the remarkable progress in aircraft performance—as well as dramatizing the problems facing our international airlines today. Northwest was awarded the choice Great Circle route seventeen years ago, when only the most visionary airline prophets could foresee its true significance. At that time no aircraft were available with sufficient range to take full advantage of the distance savings over the Great Circle route. When fueling stops were necessary, there was far greater traffic potential on a route via New York, Chicago, San Francisco, Honolulu, and Tokyo—rather than over the frigidly forbidding and sparsely populated Aleutians. However, the advent of long-range jets changed the picture considerably; on a nonstop flight the Great Circle route is almost an economic necessity.

Recognizing its importance, foreign airlines have demanded and received access to the Great Circle route. Logically, America's dominant international airline, Pan Am, should be permitted to compete on an equal basis on a United States route with its foreign competitors. On the other hand, Northwest argues, with justification, that putting Pan Am on the route would seriously impair Northwest's position. Thus, changes in circumstances occasioned by improvements in aircraft performance—unforeseen or inadequately considered at the time of the original route award to Northwest—pose a particularly troublesome problem today.

Northwest had its beginning in 1926, on the 400-mile run between Chicago and the Twin Cities of Minneapolis and St. Paul. The entire passenger travel in 1927 was less than a single load on one of Northwest's jets today. Yet from 1927 to 1933, Northwest gradually extended itself westward, through the Dakotas and Montana, then across the Rockies to the Pacific at Seattle. Early aircraft included Stinsons, Wacos, then Ford Trimotors—even a Sikorsky amphibian flying between Minneapolis and the Duluth yacht harbor. By the time Northwest reached Seattle, its pilots were braving the snowy passes of the Rockies in the first Lockheed Electras. Even then Croyl Hunter, Northwest's president, had dreams of a transcontinental route across this country and on to the Orient. The first element was a link between Minneapolis and New York, but the war came along before such a route could be secured.

Japanese landings at Kiska and Attu, at the tip of the Aleutians, threatened our position in Alaska. To obtain assistance, Northwest planes and pilots were requisitioned. Under the guidance of George Gardner, Northwest manned the Air Transport Command routes across Canada to Alaska and the Pacific.

The influence of these dangerous and exciting times can be seen today in the solid red tail on all Northwest aircraft. In Northwest's Arctic operations, the prospect of a crash or forced landing in the snowy vastness was a distinct possibility. To increase visibility and air rescue, the tail (usually the part of an aircraft more likely to remain intact in the event of a crash) was painted bright red. Today Northwest's red tails are not considered a safety factor but are a memento of those colorful days of its wartime career in the Arctic.

As its military operations increased, so did Northwest's domestic route patterns. Toward the end of the war, the CAB granted Northwest's earlier requests for an extension from Minneapolis to New York by way of Milwaukee and Detroit— making Northwest the fourth transcontinental airline. The following year, in the Pacific route case, the CAB recognized Northwest's wartime accomplishments by the award of the Great Circle route to the Orient. This decision was hotly contested by Pan Am, which felt entitled to more consideration because of its early pioneering on this route with Lindbergh's flight in the early thirties. However, at the time, transpacific travel was preponderantly across the Central route, via Hawaii, and the CAB intended to provide competition for Pan Am by granting Northwest the only other significant route in that area of the world. Although colder and less romantic, Northwest enjoyed the shortest route via Seattle, Anchorage, Korea, and Tokyo, terminating at Shanghai, where Northwest was to meet TWA to complete a round-the-world service. Northwest was also in line for a trans-Siberian route to Moscow.

To compete on its expanded system, Northwest set about modernizing its aircraft fleet. In a bold move, Croyl Hunter determined to inaugurate two new aircraft simultaneously: the

Martin 202 for short domestic runs; and the Boeing Stratocruiser for the transcontinental and Pacific routes (the Boeing purchase had the added advantage of generating local political support for Northwest in Seattle).

Unfortunately, the high hopes of the early postwar days were subject to severe setbacks. Rapid deterioration of United States-Soviet relations ruined the prospects of the Moscow route. The take-over by the Red Chinese precluded the Shanghai hook-up with TWA. Domestic operations were impaired by a series of accidents with the new Martins (7 crashes out of an original fleet of 25). Furthermore, the Boeings, although popular with passengers because of their spaciousness, were proving costly to operate. Reluctantly Northwest sold off its Martins and re-equipped with DC-4's. Yielding to stockholder pressures, Croyl Hunter gave up his operational responsibilities and moved up to chairman of the board.

As if jinxed in equipment decisions, Northwest—under the presidency of Don Nyrop, former chairman of CAB—ordered Lockheed Electra Turboprops, and was hurt by the resulting crashes and operational restrictions on these aircraft. Despite its equipment problems, Northwest's route patterns were enhanced by the award of lucrative Florida routes, particularly valuable in providing seasonal balance to utilize equipment during the long, cold winters in the Northwest, when Florida travel seems particularly appealing.

Today Northwest's equipment problems appear to be over, and the company operates a mixed fleet of DC-8's, Boeing 720's, Electras, and some DC-6's and -7's. But the crucial question of the Great Circle route remains. The nation's prime international carrier, Pan American, cannot compete effectively with its foreign competition without the Great Circle route—and Northwest cannot compete effectively with Pan American on the same route. The threat hangs heavily over Northwest's future.

## CHAPTER XXIV

## Delta: A Crop Duster's Progress or Virtue Rewarded

The progress of Delta from a one-plane crop-dusting outfit into the nation's fifth largest airline almost qualifies as a fairy-tale classic of virtue rewarded—for Delta has earned its way on those fundamental virtues of thrift and hard work, and the consistent application of the Golden Rule in its customer relations. President and founder is C. E. Woolman, who, together with Juan Trippe of Pan Am, is the only remaining airline chief executive occupying such a role (Woolman is also the second largest Delta stockholder after Richard Reynolds of the tobacco clan).

An old pilot in the truest sense, Woolman's lean, lined and weather-beaten face proclaims his long hours in an open cockpit. When crop dusting was slow in the Georgia cotton fields, Woolman sometimes carried passengers—and the mail when the government gave out the first contracts in the late twenties. With his mail pay, Woolman added planes and pilots and turned in a very creditable performance in and around Atlanta. A highly efficient line but a small one, Delta was an innocent victim of Postmaster General Brown's plans for a transcontinental system in 1930. Brown apparently regarded Woolman favorably and had intended to work him into a portion of the proposed transcontinental route through a combination of extensions and subcontracts. However, political difficulties made such integration impractical, and Brown dropped Woolman from his plan. Naturally Woolman protested bitterly, but the Postmaster General was adamant, claiming that Woolman could either sell out to American or forfeit his mail contract, since the only contract would be awarded on a transcontinental and not a local or regional basis.

Squeezed out of the Air Mail business, Woolman returned to crop dusting to keep the nucleus of his organization intact. Before too long, the mail contracts let by Postmaster General Brown were canceled by the New Deal. When new contracts came up for bidding, Woolman was ready and waiting—and won back his old routes.

Since then Delta's growth has been steady, expanding throughout the southeastern United States and strengthening its position with the acquisition of Chicago and Southern Airlines. With the 1961 award of a transcontinental route from Atlanta and the Space Age complex at Canaveral to the Pacific Coast, Delta became the fifth largest domestic airline.

The secret of Delta's success has been the careful, conservative management of C. E. Woolman—and the relative lack of competition by major carriers during Delta's most formative years. Instead of expensive terminals and ticket offices, Woolman concentrated on service. On his important routes, Woolman faced Capital and Eastern—and was able to demonstrate significant superiority over each, both in operations and public relations. Capital's increasing financial difficulties (which eventually

*Jet Age Giants* [ 279

forced it to merge with United) adversely affected its efforts, and until recently, Eastern's reputation for poor passenger service was a severe handicap in the face of Delta's Golden Rule approach. Furthermore, when Eastern unaccountably canceled its orders for early J-57-powered DC-8 jets in order to wait for the more powerful J-75 engines (the advantages of which are not too significant on short domestic runs), Delta quickly slipped into the early delivery position— and was able to offer jet service far ahead of Eastern.

Today, Eastern has plenty of jets and under its new president, Malcolm MacIntyre, has embarked on a new program to improve passenger relations. Furthermore, by its acquisition of Capital, United presents a far more formidable threat. On the other hand, Delta today is in a much stronger position itself. The major portion of our evergrowing space activities lies along the Gulf coast from Florida to Texas. The only major airline to link these crucial areas, Delta's future seems assured. The only remaining question seems to be who can possibly replace the irreplaceable C. E.

*CHAPTER XXV*

*Continental and the Furor over Fares*

Fears and fares have been the two basic barriers to the acceptance of air travel. Every man in the industry is deeply and genuinely concerned with safety, and every reasonable precaution is carried out. Regrettably, despite all efforts, accidents do occur. At the same time, airlines are several hundred percent safer than automobiles, and it seems apparent that fears are steadily becoming a less significant deterrent to air travel.

Fares, on the other hand, are an obvious deterrent and are readily susceptible to management control. It is somewhat surprising, therefore, that more attention has not been paid to fare policy. There are at least two good reasons for this apparent neglect. First of all, during their formative period, the airlines were primarily competing with the railroads and were forced to set their fares on that basis alone. It wasn't until after World War II that airlines really began to make serious inroads into rail travel (airline passenger income did not exceed mail pay until 1943). Secondly, there is a widespread body of opinion in the industry that any individual reduction in fares will immediately be followed by other lines, thereby negating any advantage to the originator and resulting solely in a decline in revenues for all.

It is generally acknowledged today among airline executives and transportation economists that nearly all of the potential traffic has been absorbed from the railroads. Thus future airline passenger growth will be very slow—unless some inroads can be made into the vast intercity automobile market. In the face of this situation, fare policy has suddenly become a burning issue —and the chief torchbearer is Bob Six of Continental.

Another rootin', tootin' Texan in the early C. R. Smith tradition, Six has parlayed a thin Texas–Oklahoma route into a major factor in the airline industry. Big, bluff and flamboyant, once married to singing star Ethel Merman, Six is a master of salesmanship and efficiency. His success is all the more remarkable in that over his major routes (roughly a triangle between Texas, Los Angeles, and Chicago) Six has faced the strongest possible competition—American, United, and TWA. Yet Continental was the first to introduce jet service on these lucrative routes, and Continental gets the highest utilization on its big Boeing 707's of any company in the business—undeniable evidence of Six's management ability.

The economies and efficiencies he has achieved at Continental cause Six to take an unusual view of the present traffic plateau —and place him in direct conflict with the older leaders of the industry. Chief spokesman of the traditional view is Patterson of United, who argues that higher fares are the only means by which the airlines can attain sufficient revenues until passenger growth resumes. Six regards this argument as unimaginative, lacking in public spirit, and just plain wrong. The only suitable solution, as he sees it, is more passengers. Raising fares will merely reduce the market, and not raise revenues significantly. Granting that only a fraction of the automobile travel market is susceptible to movement by air, nevertheless, penetration of only 4 percent of the automobile market would double present airline volume. To Six, the way to achieve this growth is lower fares. In this basic approach he is joined, with some minor differences, by the new members of the airline presidents' circle, MacIntyre of Eastern, and Tillinghast of TWA. (The argument almost boils down to the young versus the old—and the airline old-timers seem as sensitive to the thought of lower fares as die-hard Southerners to integration—perhaps as a hangover from the bitterness of the nonsked arguments.)

Despite the magnitude of his opposition, Six recently filed a sharply reduced tariff for the required prior CAB approval—a rather hot potato for the tender hands of the CAB. Clearly, lower fares are a public benefit, but what if such lower fares were to prove harmful to other airlines? Once again the Board found itself torn between its responsibilities to the public and to the other lines. So far the Board has avoided facing up to a decision by suspending Continental's proposed tariff pending an investigation. There is considerable doubt whether the Board genuinely intends to make such an investigation or whether it is simply hoping the problem will go away if it ignores it long enough. (In the nearly twenty-five years of its existence, the Board has never publicly considered the question of proper fare structure.) However, there is some reason to hope that it means what it says this time. Chairman Boyd has publicly stated that he considers fare policy the toughest question the Board will have to face—but that was before the major mergers were proposed. Under the circumstances, it's probable that almost everybody would like to sweep the fares question back under the rug for awhile—but will Bob Six let that happen?

*PART EIGHT*

# A Dark Horizon

*CHAPTER XXVI*

# Technical Triumph and Financial Failure

The airlines' magnificent new jets represent a technical achievement undreamed of only a relatively few years ago. Capable of cruising comfortably with 180 passengers at nearly the speed of sound, the jets seem to be the ideal vehicle to achieve the airlines' dream of low cost, mass air transportation. Instead, the introduction of jet service has brought about a deepening financial crisis in the industry, with losses exceeding 36 million dollars in 1961.

The cause is simple—but the cure is not. The big jet cabins carry nearly twice as many passengers twice as fast as their piston-powered predecessors. Therein lies the difficulty. While the technical capabilities of the airlines have expanded enormously, the passenger market has failed to keep pace. Our present passenger market could be fully serviced by less than half of the jets already flying.

But, conditioned by old competitive attitudes, each individual airline flies its same full pattern of scheduled flights to maintain its position in the market. Offering many more available seats for the same number of passengers, all lines fly half empty. No industry can survive if half its production goes to waste. Airlines do not have even the normal industrial flexibility of placing unsold production into inventory. An unfilled seat is lost forever.

To those not familiar with the particular background of the airline industry, it must seem incredible that otherwise intelligent businessmen should have knowingly put themselves in this lamentable position. The airline executives attempt to excuse themselves by pointing the finger of fault at the CAB for having authorized too much competition. However, the airlines had five full years following the critical CAB decisions in which to make the necessary economic adjustments. They did not do so.

At least a partial explanation for this failure seems to be the old habits formed in the early days of development when improved airplane performance and efficiency, together with a steady growth in national population and income, accustomed management to expect constant expansion. As a practical matter, the airlines' early problems were technical and political, not economic.

Since their beginnings, the airlines have heedlessly sought expansion at any price, fighting for new routes like sharks in a feeding frenzy, devouring each other. Protected from price competition by CAB rate regulation, the airlines poured fantastic sums into relatively incidental improvements in service, throwing ever more, bigger and costlier planes onto their routes (planes made even more expensive by minor interior differences intended to distinguish one airline from another), duplicating palatial terminals and ticket offices in a desperate race for passenger favor. It's a good question whether passengers might not have preferred less "service" in return for lower fares.

## A Dark Horizon [ 285

Of course, the CAB cannot escape a major share of the responsibility. Uncertain and insecure, the politically vulnerable CAB always seemed willing to give in to pressures for new competition on markets already crowded by the growth of nonstop services. For instance, in the early days, Chicago–New York was served by three lines, all flying different routes with stops along the way: United, via Cleveland; TWA, by way of Pittsburgh; and American, through Buffalo and Detroit. When the DC-3 made nonstop flights possible, the New York–Chicago market was already saturated, even before the CAB authorized additional airlines. Nonstop jets have now done the same thing in the New York–Los Angeles and New York–San Francisco markets.

Only a nearly constant 15 percent yearly traffic growth saved the airlines from feeling the consequences long ago. But the sands ran out just as the jets came in. Over the years the airlines had gradually absorbed nearly all the long-haul train and bus traffic. Only drastic new fare reductions (which most airline managements are reluctant to consider) could penetrate the automobile market. So airline revenue growth dried up just when it was most needed.

Internationally, the problems are at least as serious—but the causes are somewhat different. Except for occasional romantic adventures on Pan American's prewar flying boats, large-scale international air travel developed since World War II. In the beat-up, war-weary world of 1945, the United States was the only country technically or economically able to provide international air transportation. Those were also the peak days of U.S. altruism and international idealism and our international aviation policy was made in that context.

The sole Cassandra, Juan Trippe, argued for the "chosen instrument"—one U.S. international airline. In vain, Trippe pointed out that the prestige and foreign policy of every emerging national would demand an international airline as a symbol of independence and national dignity. (One wag has observed that aeronautical activities in some of these emerging countries have progressed from swinging through tree branches to jet transports in one generation.) To offer reciprocal rights between the U.S. and all foreign nations desiring them would soon saturate the available passenger market. Furthermore, the great majority of international traffic would come from the United States and, Trippe argued, our national policy should be to retain our share of the market. Trippe's proposal was to concentrate all our traffic on one line (preferably his own), and fly planes big enough to spread the cost over sufficient passengers to bring fares down—and thus expand the market.

But our policy-makers ignored Trippe's arguments. In 1945, the United States was so clearly dominant that the threat of foreign competition was remote. Our more immediate duty seemed to be to help build up the war-torn nations of the world. Besides, competition was the American way. Accordingly, the CAB certificated three U.S. carriers on the North Atlantic—American and TWA, as well as Pan Am. Within three years tough competition and low load factors forced American out. Fearing a price war, British bulldog obstinacy kept fares at artificially high levels through rate regulation by IATA, the international cartel. Without price competition, rivalry took the form of prettier hostesses, more orchids, better wines, thicker steaks, and other such trivial nonessentials. When coach service was finally introduced, a major international incident arose over what constituted a "sandwich," since U.S. lines feared foreigners were getting away with serving supposedly prohibited free meals on coach flights.

Even so, the full effect of foreign competition did not build up at once. United States equipment advantages and foreign dollar shortages combined to preserve the U.S. lead for a time. Gradually the gap narrowed, closing in 1960 as foreign airlines equipped themselves with the new Boeing and Douglas jets. Today on the North Atlantic substantially more than two-thirds of the total traffic is produced from the United States. Competing for this traffic are two U.S. and seventeen foreign lines, all offering substantially identical equipment, fares and service. Included in the present group are not only such great airlines as BOAC, Air France, KLM, SAS, but also Ireland, Israel, Iran, and Pakistan. Soon to come are Ghana and the United Arab Republic, and others will shortly follow. These smaller lines carry far more than their proportionate share of the traffic flowing between their countries and the United States. Even more galling, their new jets are usually financed out of U.S. Foreign Aid funds, and often the airline itself was started with U.S. Technical Assistance programs.

Perhaps even greater problems lie ahead. Our labor costs spiral ever upward. A U.S. airline captain is paid more than the entire crew of most foreign lines—with similar wage-cost comparisons throughout the systems. Another major threat is Russia's Aeroflot. Flying converted military jets on her European runs long before the U.S. offered passenger jet service, Russia has yet to make her presence felt in the transatlantic market. The whole industry shudders at the thought of Communist jets undercutting the world fare structures. As a matter of economic philosophy, it is fascinating to note that the Communist Aeroflot promotes its pilots on ability, rather than seniority, as in this country. At the same time, a recent Soviet newspaper article severely criticized Aeroflot for those ubiquitous airline ills: late departures, lost baggage, changed schedules and poor service. Apparently things are really not too different over there, after all.

The present problem of the airlines can be simply stated: too many airlines flying too many planes for too few passengers. Faced with this situation, common logic would seeem to suggest adjusting flights or combining schedules. However, the competitive habits and antagonisms of the past are hard to break and such solutions are not appealing to most airline executives, who feel that any schedule curtailments would impair their competitive position. Instead, several airlines publicly urge higher fares—at best a temporary solution and hardly in the public interest. The CAB, on the other hand, has countered with the suggestion of mergers as a more appropriate means of reducing competition, serenely ignoring the paradox that such overcompetition was an outgrowth of the CAB's own prior actions.

But what kind of mergers? Presumably the CAB intended the strong with the weak. But such unions are not likely to appeal to stockholders of the strong (who don't want to pick up a deficit) or to managements of the weak (who don't want to merge themselves out of a job).

The first step would seem to require a reduction of excessively duplicating services. As C. E. Woolman of Delta puts it, "You can't keep three cows indefinitely in a pasture where there's only grass for two." Some in the industry jump from this obvious truth to the conclusion that mergers are the only solution to the problem. However, the most serious areas of overcapacity are on the major transcontinental markets served by the Big Four. Any merger between these carriers would produce a giant out of all proportion to the rest of the industry. Woolman, and several others, fear the dominance of such merged companies, regarding them as leading inevitably to nationalization. Instead, they believe that substantial improvements can be made by private inter-line route adjustments, if given time to work out.

Both the strengths and weaknesses of the merger theory are presented in the present proposal to join American and Eastern. No one denies that the union would profit the combined companies. But opposition centers on the sensitive issue of size.

Between them, American and Eastern now carry nearly one-third of all domestic air traffic. Combined, they would doubtless increase this percentage, perhaps to 50 percent or more, from so-called "back-up" traffic—such as Eastern passengers who now connect to United or TWA but would doubtless travel via American if the merger went through. Another drawback is the fact that the merger will not affect the critical overcapacity on the transcontinental markets.

In view of the opposition, it seems unlikely that the CAB will approve the merger, particularly in an election year. Actually, the final decision lies in the White House, since a few foreign routes to Canada and Mexico are involved and their transfer requires Presidential approval. The President's brother, the Attorney General, is already on record as disapproving of the merger, perhaps an indication of what may be expected at the White House. But meanwhile the airlines are virtually paralyzed in their planning, since no executive will commit himself to any alternative arrangements until a decision has been reached on American-Eastern.

Across this controversy lies the shadow of Juan Trippe. Just before CAB hearings were to open on American-Eastern, Trippe disclosed that Pan Am was considering merger with TWA. As usual with Trippe, the timing was as significant as the action itself, adroitly forcing the CAB's hand, for approval of American-Eastern would therefore imply approval of Pan Am–TWA, creating Trippe's cherished "chosen instrument."

Furthermore, the disclosure forced into the open a secret CAB staff study which would have drastically realigned transatlantic service to Pan Am's detriment. Concerned over the mounting losses of TWA, the CAB staff recommended restricting Pan Am to London and Frankfurt, giving TWA exclusive U.S. rights to Paris and Rome. Under this plan, TWA's Middle-Eastern routes would also be terminated at Cairo, thus ending any attempt to maintain competitive round-the-world service by two U.S. airlines.

The net effect of this plan would be to make Pan Am the "chosen instrument" for round-the-world service, with all its implications of national prestige, and at the same time penalize Pan Am severely on its most important Atlantic routes, where its foreign competitors would enjoy the enormous advantage of access to all the principal gateway cities. The same paradox would exist in the Pacific where Northwest and foreign airlines fly the shorter, superior Great Circle route presently denied to Pan American. There is something supremely ironic that Trippe should achieve his "chosen instrument" dream at the expense of crippling handicaps on the Atlantic and Pacific ocean routes which he pioneered.

A major figure in the industry recently gave me a more colorful and succinct analysis (simultaneously providing a revealing insight into the typical attitude of one airline president toward another and toward the CAB). "I don't like Trippe personally and I never have," he said, "but it's a hell of a thing for those petty little bureaucratic bastards at the CAB to turn him loose at last and then break both his legs at the same time."

One possible alternative avenue for the CAB would be to set out some general guidelines to assist the individual airlines in working out more acceptable private arrangements. For instance, the Board might well declare that it contemplated an eventual readjustment of the present route system so that only two carriers would serve each major market. Repeated studies have demonstrated that two strong carriers provide suitable competition, while the addition of a third or more carriers merely drains off corporate resources in an unproductive advertising struggle to redistribute the available market.*

The size question could be met by a general policy declara-

* The Harvard Business School has published a detailed discussion on this point: *Airline Competition* by Gill & Bates (Cambridge; 1949).

tion that no one company should end up with more than 25 percent of the total market. In this way, the airlines themselves would have both the opportunity and the responsibility to realign their own route systems by a series of private trades. The present route structures are acknowledged to be an illogical patchwork resulting from ill-considered or outdated CAB decisions. Route systems established in the days of the DC-3 are now just as obsolete. Under our concepts of free enterprise, it makes sense to give the individual airline managements a chance to work out more efficient route systems privately among themselves.

While some kind of private consolidations seem to offer the most immediate prospects of improvement, they alone are only a partial solution. In a desperate effort to fill the cavernous maws of the high new jets, the bigger airlines have concentrated on the intensely competitive, high-density, long-haul markets, to the neglect of their other route segments. Influenced both by swelling executive egos and limited local traffic, the feeder lines have advanced from their old DC-3's to expensive new turbo-props, and now hope to move on to the richer regional markets (meanwhile running up the intolerable total of $85,000,000 in annual subsidy).

Obviously, this situation can not continue indefinitely. However, it is practically impossible to work out a suitable long-range solution within the limiting context of the CAB as it is presently constituted. Instead, the resolution of the airlines' jet crisis will require a reconsideration of the whole question of national transportation policy.

*CHAPTER XXVII*

# Policy or Politics

Our national transportation system is a national disgrace. While our economy is at its highest levels, our airlines face crippling losses; our highways are choked with traffic; and our railroads are on the point of bankruptcy. Despite the seriousness of the situation, these problems are soluble—but not before there has been a shift from politics to policy in our approach to government regulation. The obstacles are entirely political, not technical. The mechanical means of solution have all been available for some time. Railroads thirty years ago offered superior service. Any boy on a bicycle can often outdistance automobiles in our major cities. The jets which today are losing money have the capacity for substantial profits for the airlines, as well as reduced fares to the public. The fact is that the ingenuity of our engineers and inventors has outdistanced the ability of our transportation executives and government administrators. How ironic that the nation which produced the steamboat, the automobile and the airplane cannot utilize these technical advances more efficiently.

The principal problem is the steady and stultifying growth of government control. Artificial and unnecessary restrictions have all but paralyzed management imagination. Of course, the transportation executives themselves must bear some of the blame for the decline of their industry. All too many have not made any extra effort to work out their own difficulties. Instead, they seem almost schizophrenic, on the one hand blaming the government for all their troubles, while simultaneously demanding more government assistance.*

As of now, our federal rail, highway, shipping and aviation programs are each regulated by separate, jealously independent agencies. (Aviation actually has two distinct agencies, the Civil Aeronautics Board for economic regulation, and the Federal Aviation Agency for safety.) Each agency considers only its own limited segment of the industry. This unrealistic compartmentalization of regulation precludes any overall policy planning or coordination. The only executive, in or out of government, presently permitted by law to formulate policy and operate without restriction throughout the whole transportation industry is Jimmy Hoffa. As a result, his gangster-ridden Teamsters' Union is fast gaining a stranglehold over all U.S. transportation.

This fragmentation of federal transportation authority is not the product of any theory of balanced power. It merely repre-

---

* The dangers inherent in seeking government assistance are, I think, best illustrated by an experience suffered by a friend of mine in the Air Force. His wife was exceedingly fond of her pet cat, which had inexplicably sickened. Distressed, my friend sought the name of a local veterinarian. His fellow officers urged him to consult the Air Force base veterinarian instead. Although deeply suspicious of accepting any favors from the government, my friend finally gave in. After examination, the Air Force vet reported that the cat was suffering from no more than an infected thorn in its paw. Greatly relieved, my friend said he would pick up the animal at once. "Well, not for a day or two," said the vet. "He has to recover from the operation first." "Operation for the thorn?" my friend asked incredulously. "Oh, no," the vet replied, "there's a base regulation that requires that all tomcats be castrated. So, while he was here..."

sents the product of unplanned, cancerlike growth. Historically, governments have always maintained a deep interest in transportation, for the swift movement of mail, troops and tax collectors, as well as for the private commerce of its citizens. The Founding Fathers recognized this fact and empowered Congress in the Constitution "to establish post offices and post roads" and "to regulate commerce with foreign nations, and among the several States, and with the Indian tribes."

It was the spectacular debauchery of the railroad robber barons that brought about the first regulatory agency, the Interstate Commerce Commission, in the 1890's. The railroads were personal playthings to the robber barons, to be used to break a rival or to entertain a mistress. Jay Gould ran the Erie in scandalous fashion from his mistress' apartment and ground out stock on a printing press whenever his control was challenged. Stanford, Crocker & Huntington built fortunes on a succession of swindles and bribed legislatures. When Commodore Vanderbilt said "the public be damned," he seemed to speak for all his contemporaries. Outraged at the arrogance, accidents, bribery, and bankruptcies, the public demanded government regulation—and the ICC came into being. As new means of transport developed, new agencies were formed to regulate them. By the time the airlines came along, the ICC was already heavily encrusted with the moss and mold of bureaucracy. Aviation enthusiasts argued that the dynamic infant industry could not develop properly at the glacial pace of the ICC. So still another agency, jealous of its particular jurisdiction, was added to the existing layers of government regulation.

The underlying theory of the Civil Aeronautics Board was to remove important economic decisions from private hands and place them instead in a government agency. This idealistic approach fails to consider that in both cases decisions are made by human beings. Within government or without, a decision is as good as the man who makes it. In private decisions there exists an explicit, objective standard, measurable in dollars and cents. Within government, however, the standard is vague and nebulous—the public welfare.

In private industry an executive generally has a pretty clear objective, some knowledge of the business, and reasonable access to the facts upon which to base his judgments. None of these conditions obtain for the CAB. So far, over its entire life, the CAB has never formulated any clear or consistent policy.* Critics of the CAB are especially harsh on the lack of experience or knowledge on the part of CAB members, claiming that almost all have been political hacks—such as Congressmen rejected by their constituents, or local attorneys ambitious for the sinecure of a federal judgeship—all without any prior airline experience whatever. In fairness, there are few experienced men to be found without recruiting directly from the airlines themselves. But the lack of background becomes particularly important in view of the procedural difficulties standing between a Board member and the facts in a case. Under present procedures the record of a hearing becomes so vast as to be virtually incomprehensible. Out of the swamp of statistics, evidence might be drawn to support almost any conclusion. Furthermore, the development of a record generally takes so long that its data is out of date when the Board is ready to reach a decision.† As a practical matter, the Board often has to look elsewhere for the factors upon which to base its decision, opening the door to all the dangers of improper influence.

When I was at the CAB, I used to be amazed at the crisis of handwringing created by any telephone call from a Senator.

* Henry Friendly, a long-time and widely respected CAB attorney (for Pan American), now a federal judge, has written a scholarly dissection of the vacillations, inconsistencies and confusion of CAB decisions. 75 Harvard Law Review 1263.

† In recent years the White House has come to have such little regard for CAB data that studies by private research firms are used instead, thereby invaliding the whole basis for the CAB decision.

In most cases, the Senator in question had no strong personal convictions in the case. The calls generally were made to impress a constituent, important either because of employment in the Senator's State or for campaign contributions. Actually, to my observation, such calls were generally self-canceling as far as benefiting any one airline, since every company has a Senator from its home state. The real damage from Congressional pressures seemed to me to be a tendency on the part of the Board to try to give a little something to everybody, rather than seek the best decision regardless.

An equally unworthy reaction was the fear of offending a powerful airline. I recall particularly one situation (which is not intended as a reflection on the parties but is offered merely as an example of typical attitudes). American, after long and strenuous pleading, had persuaded the Board to grant it access as a third carrier nonstop between New York and San Francisco. The airlines already on that route, United and TWA, protested the decision bitterly, claiming that the addition of American would dangerously duplicate existing services without providing any improvement whatever. With the Board decision on the New York–San Francisco nonstop safely in his pocket, C. R. Smith, American's president, publicly delivered a stinging attack on the character and competence of the Board for permitting too much competition in the industry. Of course, Smith then had in mind the pending Southern Transcontinental route which he wanted for American—but his reasoning applied with equal force as a direct contradiction to his sworn submissions in the New York–San Francisco case. Under the circumstances I believed strongly that the Board should not permit his attack to go unchallenged. Accordingly, I recommended that Smith be subpoenaed to explain his position. The proposal was rejected on the grounds that "it might offend Mr. Smith."

It is easy to criticize the CAB and I could cite many other examples. However, it would serve no purpose. Former Board member Louis Hector has already set out a detailed and scathing summary of CAB inadequacies in his memorandum of resignation.* Actually I found the Board members and staff of my acquaintance for the most part to be sincere and honest men working under difficult circumstances and conflicting responsibilities. I mention a few personal experiences only to illustrate my own conviction that the solution to the airlines' problems does not lie in more government regulation. Quite the contrary. I believe that the real remedy is to remove the existing maze of artificial restrictions and fragmented bureaucratic fiefdoms. Only then can management properly exercise the necessary ingenuity to take advantage of the existing technical achievements in transportation for the benefit of the nation as a whole.

Under our present uncoordinated system of federal regulation, we see the sorry spectacle of billions of dollars of taxpayers' funds being spent to build new highways, draining traffic from the railroads which could handle the same loads better, faster, and far safer. It is no answer to say that railroad managements brought it on themselves through complacency and neglect—or that new highways are necessary for trucks and cars to replace the poor service of the railroads. The essential point is that public funds should be invested in that means of transportation which can do the best job. Anyone who has ridden on Japanese railroads has had his eyes opened to new standards of speed and comfort. Per dollar of investment, railroads in this country, with modern equipment, in high density areas such as along the East Coast between Boston, New York, Philadelphia, Baltimore and Washington, could perform far more effectively than equivalent highway or aviation programs. Similarly, from a national (or taxpayer's) point of view it is pure folly to continue the steadily increasing subsidy, presently exceeding 85 million

* 69 Yale Law Journal 931.

dollars annually, for local service airlines to do a job better performed by trains or buses. As of now, there is no attempt of any kind to coordinate air and surface transportation. Even a joint timetable would be an enormous step forward. Yet, as countless thousands of air travelers stranded at lonely airports learn daily, it is almost impossible to get information regarding local train or bus schedules.

Evidence of possibilities inherent in integrated services have already been demonstrated by the growth of truck-rail "piggybacking," where loaded truck trailers are shipped on railroad freight cars for the long haul between major points and then delivered to the destination by truck. This system effectively combines the economies of railroad transportation with the flexibility and door-to-door service of the truckers.

Reason would seem to require an extension of this concept to other areas of transportation. For instance, one of the most pressing problems for airlines today is the high cost of local service. Actually, this problem has two aspects: the local schedules flown by the trunk lines and the separate so-called local service airlines themselves. The difficulties are similar in each instance but they are most apparent in the case of the local service airlines which draw off annually 85 million dollars in subsidy from the taxpayer's pocket. There is also a subsidy involved on the local schedules of the trunk lines but this subsidy comes out of the pocket of the passenger on the longer hops who pays proportionately far more than the real costs of his flight.

The farther the airplane flies, the less its actual costs per mile, since the operating costs are nearly constant and the fixed overhead costs are absorbed over more miles. Allocating actual costs on the basis of the New York–Washington route alone, airlines generally lose money at present fare levels. At the other extreme, actual costs of nonstop flights between New York and Los Angeles are comparatively little more than between

New York and Chicago. Nevertheless, over the years airline fares have been arbitrarily set on an average per mile basis. The original reason for this basic fare structure was to compete with railroad fares which were set on this basis. However, this justification has long since disappeared.

To objective observers it has always seemed unwise to try to force local air service where it cannot pay its own way. Yet there has always been a strong political element in bringing a glamorous new service to a local community. (I have always been fascinated at the success of farm communities and small towns in demanding subsidies of various kinds from the cities, apparently on the dual grounds of moral superiority and preservation of local Americana.)

In the early days of the CAB there was a clear recognition that local service was not a money-making proposition. Accordingly, there grew up a policy of granting each trunk airline some rich intercity routes to offset losses on local service. The separate local service airlines got into business with surplus DC-3's in the exuberant days of airline optimism after World War II. They have been on public subsidy ever since, with constantly increasing requirements.

These local service operators now claim that their problem is the high operating costs per seat-mile of their old DC-3's; and that all would be well if they had new turboprops or jets. However, the reduced operating costs per seat of the new planes are more than offset by the increase in depreciation and interest charges. Furthermore, most local service lines can't fill their DC-3's as it is, and lower seat-mile operating costs mean little unless a lot more passengers suddenly materialize.

Meanwhile, the subsidy mounts steadily. In their hearts, the local service operators believe that, if the criticism gets too hot for the CAB on the subsidy question, the Board will cut the local service lines onto the richer, denser trunk line markets like Chicago–Detroit, New York–Boston, etc. Obviously, this is just what the trunk lines want to avoid, for it was precisely this kind of thinking which brought about the present excesses of competition on many trunk line markets.

The ramifications of this problem extend not only to the local service airlines but throughout the rest of the industry as well. Nearly everyone in the business, excepting naturally the parties themselves, opposes the American-Eastern merger as creating an overwhelming giant without reducing any of the serious areas of overcapacity. It's no secret that the CAB would dearly love to have a good excuse to turn the merger down. The strongest argument in favor of the merger is the marginal financial condition of Eastern. A major element in Eastern's distress is the competition of Northeast on the rich New York–Miami run. The CAB put Northeast on New York–Miami originally in an effort to offset the losses Northeast was suffering on its local service routes. Removing Northeast would thus relieve a lot of pressures all at once, if only adequate transportation could be maintained to the small northeastern towns now served by Northeast.

The most obvious, and only available, alternative method is by means of express bus connections to funnel passengers to central points for economic airplane loads. This approach would also solve the other local service problems as well. Yet, when I brought this proposal to Alan Boyd, chairman of the CAB, he replied, "I can't consider any connecting service with surface transportation. By law the CAB can only consider the promotion of aviation."

Boyd's response illustrates perfectly the fundamental fallacy of our present system of government regulation—the inability to integrate or coordinate existing means of transport. Boyd is not by any means a benighted bureaucrat. He is, in fact, as able and aggressive an administrator as the CAB has had. Yet he regards himself barred by statute from even considering a proposal which could simultaneously improve service and reduce the need for subsidy.

This concept is not limited to local service alone. It has application for the transcontinental markets as well. The more passengers carried per plane, the less the cost per passenger. Therefore, every possible effort should be made to concentrate traffic. Suppose for a moment that New York and Philadelphia were jointly served by a common airport midway between the cities (such as the already existing and available Maguire Air Force Base). The commute by air-conditioned express buses (or helicopter for first-class passengers) would be scarcely longer than the present airport traffic delays. Hourly jet shuttle services to the West Coast could probably be provided at less than half the present fares and still be very profitable for the airlines. Similar concentrations of passengers could occur conveniently at Friendship Airport, almost midway between Baltimore and Washington. (An enterprising reporter will likely discover for himself a scandal of truly epic proportions behind the location and construction of the vast new Dulles Airport in Virginia while the existing Friendship Airport in Maryland is almost as close and relatively little used.) Yet, such apparent and logical economies have always been prevented by the ambition of local politicians who demand a costly separate airport for the greater glory of their own community. Witness the increasing clamor for new jet airports, not only for major cities but also for local communities.

It is unthinkable that the present chaos should continue. But so far Congress has not been forced to face the necessity for reform. Perhaps the jet crisis of the airlines will provide the needed goad. Release from the artificial restrictions of government regulation is long overdue. Not until then can the remarkable achievements in aviation be effectively integrated into improved transportation service for the nation as a whole.

# *Acknowledgments*

This book is the product of many years of professional association and personal interest in the airline industry; but its actual inspiration was a conversation when I was a lawyer with the Civil Aeronautics Board.

A new Board member and I were discussing a pending case. Like each of his four fellow members of the CAB, he had been appointed (by the President, confirmed by the Senate) without any prior airline experience whatever. (This is written not as a criticism but as a matter of record.) Yet very shortly he would vote as one of the five men charged with the responsibility for formulating our national airline policy.

As we talked it became apparent that he was seriously misinformed on several historical facts necessary to any understanding of the pending case. As gracefully as I could, I asked how he had come to his conclusions. "Well," he said, "actually I can't make anything out of the record. It's too damn long and it's full of contradictions. [Perfectly true.] So last night I had a long talk with Mr. X and he filled me in on where all the old bodies are buried."

"Didn't X tell you he is counsel for one of the parties in this case? You can hardly consider him disinterested."

He looked at me, "Yes, I know. But what else can I do? There just isn't any other way to get at the background."

Over the years I have been privileged to know many of the men whose names appear in these pages. Our conversations on various aspects of the airline industry are reflected throughout. It would not be fair to name them, for the conclusions from our conversations are my own responsibility. Nevertheless, my deep appreciation is due to all of them—and to my former associates at the Chadbourne law firm, the CAB and the Department of Commerce.

# *Bibliography*

In the preparation of this manuscript, I have relied for factual detail primarily upon testimony in the files of the Civil Aeronautics Board and upon the following published works.

CHAPTER ONE: By far the best insight into the Wright brothers and the early days of aviation is *The Collected Papers of Wilbur and Orville Wright* (McGraw-Hill; New York, 1958). For a biography, see *The Wright Brothers* by Fred C. Kelly (Harcourt, Brace; New York, 1943).

CHAPTER TWO: Grover Loening, an important early aeronautical engineer, gives his view of the World War I aircraft procurement program in *Our Wings Grow Faster* (Doubleday; New York, 1935). *The Report of the Aircraft Production Inquiry* (to the Attorney General) by Charles Evans Hughes is reprinted in the Congressional Record, 65th Congress, v. 57, pt. 1, pp. 883-914. A critical analysis is found in *The Aviation Business* by E. E. Freudenthal (Vanguard; New York, 1940).

CHAPTER THREE: *The Early History of Air Transport* (Norwich, 1937), by E. P. Warner (a member of the original Civil

Aeronautics Board) is an excellent summary of this period. *The Air Mail* by B. B. Lipsner (Follett; Chicago, 1951) is an account by the first superintendent of the government Air Mail service. For a participant pilot's recollections, see *By the Seat of My Pants,* by D. C. Smith (Atlantic-Little, Brown; Boston, 1961).

CHAPTER FOUR: Out of all the Lindbergh material, nothing compares to his own autobiographical *The Spirit of Saint Louis* (Scribners; New York, 1953). An interesting approach to Lindbergh's impact on our society is *The Hero: Charles A. Lindbergh and the American Dream* by K. S. Davis (Doubleday; New York, 1959).

CHAPTER FIVE: The corporate history of the Boeing Company is *Vision* by Harold Mansfield (Duell, Sloan & Pierce; New York, 1956).

CHAPTERS SIX, SEVEN and EIGHT: The dominant source is the massive testimony contained in *Hearings, Special Committee to Investigate Air Mail and Ocean Mail Contracts,* U. S. Senate, 73d Congress, Second Session, 1934. For background on the New Deal generally and Senator Black in particular, I have relied primarily on Arthur Schlesinger, Jr.'s monumental series, *The Age of Roosevelt,* particularly *The Coming of New Deal* (Houghton, Mifflin; Boston, 1959). H. L. Smith's *Airways* (Knopf; New York, 1940), the only early history of the airlines, contains a fair summary of the various points of view. The account of Farley's and Black's discussion with Roosevelt regarding the cancellation is from *Fortune,* April, 1934. Unfortunately, Justice Black refused to discuss his role in any way.

CHAPTER NINE: Several analyses of the Civil Aeronautics Act of 1938 are to be found in the *Journal of Air Law and Commerce* for 1938 and 1939.

CHAPTER TEN: The early days of Imperial Airways (later BOAC) are detailed in *The Seven Skies* by John Pudney (Putnam; London, 1939). For poetic interpretation of airline pioneering one must read the works of Antoine de Saint-Exupéry, particularly *Night Flight* (Harcourt, Brace; New York, 1942). An account of the formation of KLM appears in *Conquest of the Air* by Hendrik de Leeuw (Vantage; New York, 1960).

CHAPTERS ELEVEN and TWELVE: *Fortune* magazine has two articles on Pan American pioneering; April 1931 and April 1936. Matthew Josephson's *Empire of the Air* (Harcourt, Brace; New York, 1944) is a biography of Trippe and Pan American. W. A. M. Burden's *The Struggle for Airways in Latin America* (Council of Foreign Relations; New York, 1943) covers the activities of the French and German airlines during the twenties. The NYRBA episode from the NYRBA point of view appears in Grooch, *Winged Highway* (Longmans, Green; New York, 1938).

CHAPTER THIRTEEN: The story of the Air Transport Command is told by the official historian of the ATC, Oliver La Farge, in *The Eagle and the Egg* (Houghton, Mifflin; Boston, 1949). Particular aspects appear in H. H. Arnold's autobiography *Global Mission* (Harpers; New York, 1950).

CHAPTER FOURTEEN: The immediate postwar airline problems are recounted by H. L. Smith in *Airways Abroad* (University of Wisconsin Press; 1950). The various antagonisms are set forth in the testimony in the critical CAB route case dockets: Pacific (Docket 547); Latin America (525); North Atlantic (855). See also *Report on the Airlines,* listed below.

CHAPTERS FIFTEEN and SIXTEEN: The bitter nonsked controversy is detailed in various articles in the *Journal of Air Law and Commerce* during the early 1950's. A summary is contained in the *Report on the Airlines,* Antitrust Subcommittee, Committee on the Judiciary, 85th Congress, First Session (G.P.O.; Washington, 1957).

CHAPTER SEVENTEEN: The early British jet development is described in *The Tale of the Comet* by Derek D. Dempster (David McKay; New York, 1958). *Boeing 707* by Martin Caiden (Ballantine Books; New York, 1959) is self-explanatory. For an account of the Convair jet transport debacle, I refer the reader to the series of articles in *Fortune* in 1961 and to the annual reports of General Dynamics.

CHAPTER EIGHTEEN: United Airlines has a corporate history, *High Horizons* by Frank J. Taylor (McGraw-Hill; New York, 1955).

CHAPTERS NINETEEN through TWENTY-FIVE: These chapters are drawn from personal associations, interviews, and biographical data furnished by the individual airlines themselves. *Time* magazine featured C. R. Smith of American in November 17, 1958. *Fortune* has had several articles on the Hughes–TWA situation during 1960. The Harvard Graduate School of Business Administration has published two important studies: *Airline Competition* by Gill & Bates (Cambridge, 1949) and *Airline Price Policy* by Paul W. Cherington (Cambridge, 1958).

CHAPTERS TWENTY-SIX and TWENTY-SEVEN: These chapters are largely drawn from my own experience.

# Index

Adams, Sherman, 183
Aeroflot, 287
Aéropostale, 118, 131
African route, 148-50
*Age of Roosevelt, The* (Schlesinger), 85
Aircraft Production Board, 26-29, 66
Air Force, U. S., 150n., 153, 190, 191, 239, 251, 253, 293n.
Air France, 107, 118, 133, 194, 198, 287
Air India, 194
Air Mail, U. S., 30, 32-42, 44-46, 53, 54-55, 61, 71-72, 73-74, 77, 85-96, 97, 102, 108, 115, 116, 117, 124, 127, 129, 137, 176, 203, 214, 230, 231, 245, 278; *see also* Civil Air Mail routes; Post Office Department
Air Mail Act (1925), 39, 73
Air Mail Act (1930), 74
Air Mail Act (1934), 96, 203, 232
Air Orient, 107
Airports, 109, 121, 125, 160, 225, 301
Air Transport Association (ATA), 101, 146, 154, 176, 182
Air Transport Command (ATC), 146-48, 150-51, 154, 158, 159, 168, 221, 222, 239, 249, 254, 275
Alaskan-Siberian (Alsib) route, 147
Aleutian Islands, 147, 274
"All American Flag Line," 160
Allegheny Airlines, 172
Allen, Bill, 190
Allison Division, General Motors, 65, 224
American Airlines, 12, 96, 98, 117, 145, 147, 159, 161, 163, 165, 168, 175, 184, 192, 193, 199, 200, 205, 206, 208, 209-26, 241-42, 245, 270, 285, 286, 288-89, 296, 300
American Airways, 79, 80, 81, 82n., 90, 98, 216-17, 229
American Export Airlines (AMEX), 156, 157, 158, 159, 222-23
American Export Shipping Lines, 147, 159, 223
American Federation of Labor, 216
American Fokker Company, 64-65
American Overseas Airlines, 223-24
Arctic expeditions, 131-32

309

310  ] INDEX

Armour, Lester, 61
Army Air Corps, U. S., 117, 145
Army Air Force, 206
Army Air Services, 34n., 44, 93, 94-96, 99, 102
Army General Staff, 23-24, 37-38, 47
Arnold, General H. H. (Hap), 117-18, 145, 146, 153, 221
Association of American Railroads, 176
Atlantic routes, 130-33, 137-38, 139
Atlas Corporation, 96, 232, 245, 263
Auburn Motors, 214
Australia, 136
Autogyro, 230
Avianca, 148
Aviation Corporation (AVCO), 67-68, 76, 79, 82, 91, 96, 98, 117, 212-13, 214-16, 218, 219n., 229
Azores, 131, 139, 158

Baker, David, 210
Baker, George, 175, 200, 238, 264-72
Ball, Clifford, 41-42
Barnstormers, 32, 39, 40, 43, 47
Barrett, A. P., 218
Barton, Bruce, 69n.
Bauer, Dr. Peter Paul von, 111-12, 124-25, 148
Bautzer, Greg, 259, 260
Bell, Alexander Graham, 10, 21
Bell, Larry, 104
Bendix Corporation, 65, 79, 261
Berle, Adolf A., Jr., 156, 157
Bermuda, 139, 164
Bermuda Agreement, 164-65
Bevier brothers, 126-27
Big Four carriers, 199-200, 288
Black, Hugo, 85-86, 87-93, 95, 96, 100, 134, 137, 204, 216
Blériot, Louis, 106
Boeing, Bill, 31, 51-57, 61, 71, 89, 96, 103, 194n., 200, 202, 203
Boeing Aircraft Company, 53-55, 57, 145, 146, 189-91, 192, 193, 194, 195-96, 200, 203, 225
Boeing Air Transport Company, 55, 57, 202
Boeing B-1, 54
Boeing B-17 "Flying Fortress," 145, 190, 246
Boeing B-40's, 55, 57, 62
Boeing B-47's, 190

Boeing B-707's, 191, 192, 193, 194, 195, 197, 209, 225, 255, 256, 270, 281
Boeing B-720's, 194, 240, 261, 276
Boeing B-727's, 197, 240
Boeing B-247's, 103, 104, 205, 245
Boeing B-307 "Stratoliner," 146, 246
Boeing B-314 "Clipper," 139, 145
Boeing B-377 "Stratocruiser," 170, 190, 276
Boeing KC-97 tankers, 190
Boeing *Yankee Clipper*, 139
Bolivia, 110, 129n., 148
Bolling, Reynal, 26, 27
Bonanza Airline, 172
Boyd, Alan, 235, 282, 300-01
Braniff, Paul, 98
Braniff, Tom, 98-99
Braniff Airways, 98, 165, 166, 200, 204, 226, 238
Brazil, 110, 148
Breech, Ernest R., 79-80, 231, 232, 233, 244, 259, 261
Brewster, Owen, 251
British aviation, 105-06, 108-09, 130-31, 132, 138, 161, 162-63, 164, 187-89, 286
British Overseas Airways Corporation (BOAC), 166, 188, 192, 193-94, 287
British Royal Navy, 189
Brooks, Harry, 66, 67
Brooks, Joe, 66
Brophy, Gerald, 232
Brown, Walter Folger, 70-82, 85, 87, 88, 89, 90, 91, 96, 97, 98, 99, 128, 129, 214, 219, 231, 278
Burgess, Carter, 254
Burma Road, 143, 154
Byrd, Richard, 48

Cabin pressurization, 189
Canal Zone, 125
Capital Air Lines, 41, 175, 191, 200, 205, 209-10, 226, 278-79
Capone, Al, 264
Caravelles, French, 197, 198, 211
Caribbean, the, 119, 130
Caribbean routes, 122, 130, 148
Carmichael, "Slim," 209-10
Century Airlines, 213, 214, 216
Chadbourne, Thomas, 24, 25, 232
Chamberlain, Clarence, 48
Chambers, Reed, 41, 117
Chandler, Harry, 41

INDEX [ 311

Chanute, Octave, 18
China, 133, 135-36, 137, 143, 150
China National Aviation Company (CNAC), 134, 135, 154
Chrysler, Walter, 66
Churchill, Winston, 155
Civil Aeronautics Act (1938), 102, 160, 183n.
Civil Aeronautics Authority, 102n.
Civil Aeronautics Board (CAB), 102n., 104, 134, 157, 159, 160, 161, 163, 165-66, 168, 172-73, 174, 176, 177, 178, 180, 181, 182, 183, 184, 205, 206, 207, 210, 222, 225, 226, 235, 237, 239, 241, 262, 263, 265, 267, 268-69, 270, 271, 275, 282, 284, 285, 286, 288, 289, 290, 291, 293, 294-97, 299, 300-01
Civil Air Mail routes, 40-42, 44, 116, 204, 265, 267-68, 269, 270
Coach service, 174-75, 179-83, 286
Coffin, Howard, 25-26, 27, 28, 29, 53
Cohu, Lamont, 215-16
Colombia, 111-12, 123, 124-25, 148
Colonial Airways, 40, 68, 116-17, 269
"Columbia" route, 40, 54
Commerce Department, U. S., 49, 77, 100, 102n., 176
Commodore flying boats, 126, 128
Consolidated-Vultee, 126
Continental Airlines, 200, 271, 281-82
Convair, 126n., 194-96, 198, 255-56
Convair 240's, 171, 223
Convair 340's, 224
Convair 880's, 255, 261
Convair 990's, 255, 261
Cook, Ray, 259
Coolidge, Calvin, 38, 49, 69
Cord, Errett Lobban, 213-16, 217, 219, 229
Crissey Field, 202
Crop-dusting, 277, 278
Crowley, Carl, 92
Cuba, 118, 122
Curtiss, Glenn, 10, 20, 21-22, 52
Curtiss Aircraft Company, 220
Curtiss Condors, 76n., 218-19, 231, 232
Curtiss JN-4's, "Jennys," 31, 32, 43
Curtiss-Wright Company, 25, 60
Customer hostility, 237

Daimler Company, 109
Damon, Ralph S., 219, 220, 222, 254
Daniels, Josephus, 37

Dayton, Ohio, 25, 48
Dayton Electric Laboratory Company (Delco), 25, 28
Dayton-Wright Airplane Company, 25, 27, 28, 56
Deeds, E. A., 25, 26, 27, 28, 29, 53
DeHavilland Comet, 188-89, 192, 196, 224, 238
DeHavilland DH-4's, "Flaming Coffins," 10, 27, 31, 34, 44, 45, 108
DeHavilland DH-9's, 107-08
Delta Airlines, 200, 226, 241, 277-79
Denny, Harmar, 182
Depression of 1930's, 83, 96, 100, 230n.
Dietrich, Noah, 249-50, 253
Dillon Reed, 257
Dirigibles, 110-11
Doolittle, Jimmy, 64, 126
Dornier DOX flying boat, 111
Douglas, Donald, 194n., 245
Douglas Aircraft Company, 65, 170, 191, 193, 194, 195-96, 197, 209, 225
Douglas DC-2's, 94, 99, 102, 104, 108, 205, 220, 231, 232, 245
Douglas DC-3's, 102-03, 104, 108, 130n., 144, 145, 169, 170, 171, 191, 207, 223, 225, 232, 234, 245, 265, 285, 291, 299
Douglas DC-4's, 145-46, 154, 169, 170, 225, 246, 265, 266, 276
Douglas DC-5's, 170
Douglas DC-6's, 170, 171, 189, 195, 208, 223, 224, 225, 267
Douglas DC-7's, 180, 195, 208, 224, 225, 254
Douglas DC-8 jets, 108, 191, 192, 193, 194, 195, 209, 225, 238, 255, 270, 276, 279
Drinkwater, Terrell C., 207
Dulles Airport, 160n., 301
Du Pont, Pierre, 231
Dutch aviation, 105, 107-08, 161

Earhart, Amelia, 169
Eastern Airlines, 12, 86, 98, 145, 147, 175, 184, 191, 192, 193, 199, 212, 226, 227, 229-42, 263, 265-66, 270, 271, 278, 279, 288-89, 300
Eastern Air Transport, 65, 86-87, 88-89, 94, 98, 116, 231
Ecuador, 148
Egypt, 162
Eisenhower, Dwight D., 25, 26n., 38n., 79, 183, 184

312 ] INDEX

Embry-Riddle, 68
Equitable Life Insurance Company, 257, 258
Eurasia, 133, 134

Fares policy, 280-82, 292, 299
Farley, James A., 92, 95, 97, 99, 136, 137
Federal Aviation Agency, 102n., 260, 293
Feeder carriers, 171-72, 173
Field, Marshall, II, 61
Financial problems, 283-88
Fischgrund, 181
Fiske, Jim, 214
"Five Freedoms of Flight," 164
Florida Airways, 117, 118
Flying boats, 53-54, 109, 111, 120, 126, 128, 131, 138, 139, 145, 146, 154, 250, 285
Flying Tigers Line, 173, 174, 181
Fokker, Anthony, 64-65, 108, 110, 116-17
Fokker Aircraft Company, 229
Ford, Henry, 10, 21, 42, 66-67
Ford Air Services, 62
Ford Trimotor transports, 42, 66-67, 119, 120, 274
Foreign competition, 286-87
*Fortune* Magazine, 185
Foulois, Brig. General Benjamin, 93
French aviation, 105, 106-07, 131, 132, 161, 197, 198
Friendly, Henry, 295n.
Friendship Airport, 160, 301
Frontier Air Lines, 172, 272
Frye, Jack, 94, 99, 231, 244-46, 248, 249-50, 253

Gander Air Base, 154
Gardner, George, 275
Gates, Samuel P., 157
General Aviation, 229, 231, 233
General Dynamics, 253
General Electric Company, 255
General Motors Corporation, 64, 65-66, 79, 224, 229, 231, 232, 233, 244, 245
Genghis Khan, 105
German aviation, 109-12, 118, 148
Germany, 143, 153
Gibson, Harvey D., 24
Glass, Carter, 157
Gorst, Vernon, 41, 201, 202, 203
Gould, Jay, 63, 294
Governmental control, 293-301

Grace, Peter, 268
Grace & Company, W. R., 123-24, 165
Grace Line, 124, 268, 269
"Grandfather" carriers, 102, 168, 171, 172, 173, 174
Great Circle route, 132, 133, 134, 135, 165, 166-67, 169, 273-74, 275, 276, 290
Green, William, 216
Greenland, 131, 154
Gross, Robert, 169-70, 192, 256
Guggenheim, Harry F., 48, 49
Gypsy pilots, 39, 40

Haggarty, Harry, 258
Halliburton, Earl, 81, 90
Halliburton, Richard, 81
Hambleton, John, 115, 116, 117, 118, 140
Hamilton Propeller Company, 57
Handley-Page bombers, 108
Hanshue, Harris M., 41, 76, 77, 78, 79, 202
Harding, Warren G., 35, 36
Harding, William Barkley, 234
Harlow, Jean, 248
Harmon Trophy, 150
Harriman, W. Averell, 67, 176, 213
Hart, 181
"Hat-in-the-Ring" Squadron, 228
Hawaiian Islands, 38n., 136, 166
Hearst, William Randolph, 87
Hector, Louis, 262, 297
Helicopters, 230n.
Herring, Augustus M., 18-19
Himalaya route, "The Hump," 147-48, 150, 154
Hoffa, Jimmy, 293
Holliday, Raymond, 259-60
Hong Kong, China, 136
Hooven-Owen-Rentschler Company, 55
Hoover, Herbert, 69-70, 71, 83
Hoover, Herbert, Jr., 81n.
Hoover Commission, 177
Hopkins, Harry, 156, 164
"Hornet" engines, 103
Hostesses, airline, 266
Hoyt, Richard F., 24, 25
Hubbard Gold Medal, 49
Hughes, Charles Evans, 28
Hughes, Howard, 170, 195, 199, 243-44, 246-63
Hughes Aircraft Company, 247, 250-54, 256

INDEX [ 313

Hughes F-11 pursuit plane, 250
Hughes Tool Company, 246, 247, 250, 255, 256, 257, 258, 259, 262
"Hump, The," 147-48, 150, 154
Hunter, Croyl, 274, 275-76

Iceland, 131
Imperial Airways, 109, 131, 133, 136, 138
International aeronautical law, 121-22
International Air Transport Association (IATA), 162, 164, 286
International aviation, 105-12
Interstate Commerce Commission, 100, 101, 294
Irving Trust Company, 257-58, 259
Israel, State of, 162

J-57 engines, 191, 279
J-75 engines, 191, 193, 279
Japan, 134, 135, 143, 147, 148, 150, 153, 165
Japanese Airline, 166
Jet engines, 187-98, 208-09, 255, 279
Johnson, Phil, 203
Jones, Jesse, 220
Junkers Company, 109

Kaiser, Henry J., 250
Kellogg-Olaya Pact, 125
Kelly, Clyde, 39, 73-74
Kelly Field, 44
Kennedy, John F., 26 n., 178, 251
Kennedy, Robert, 289
Kettering, Charles F., 25
Keys, Clement, 41, 60-62, 63-65, 116, 215, 230-31
Kindelburger, Dutch, 233
Kingsford-Smith, 169
Kitty Hawk, North Carolina, 9, 15-16, 17, 18
Knight, Jack, 36
Knudson, William, 66
Korean War, 178, 180, 182, 252
Kuhn, Loeb & Company, 234
Ku Klux Klan, 85

Lafayette Esquadrille, 24
La Guardia Airport, 225
Lambert Field, 45
Langley, Samuel Pierpont, 17, 18, 19, 21-22
Latecoere, Pierre, 106

Lazard Frères, 257
Le Bourget Field, 43, 48
Lehman, Robert, 67
Lehman Brothers, 96, 213, 232, 245, 253, 257
Leland, Henry, 25
Lend-lease program, 147
Lewin, 181
Lewis, Fulton, Jr., 86, 87
Lewis, Roger, 253
"Liberty" engines, 26-27, 28, 34, 54, 56, 66
Licenses, pilot's, 31-32
*Life* magazine, 182
Lindbergh, Anne Morrow, 123, 132, 133
Lindbergh, Charles Augustus, 11, 15, 38, 41, 43-50, 59, 67, 68, 71, 94-95, 112, 120, 123, 126, 132, 133, 169, 214, 233, 244, 275
*Listen, the Wind* (Lindbergh), 132
Litton Industries, 253, 256
Lloyd Aéreo Boliviano, 110
Lobbying activities, 90, 157, 176, 222
Lockheed Aircraft Company, 169-70, 191, 192, 225, 248, 256
Lockheed Constellations, 154, 169, 170, 171, 180, 248, 249, 254, 266
Lockheed Electras, 170
Lockheed Electra turboprops, 191, 192, 209, 225, 226, 238-39, 240, 274, 276
Lockheed F-94's, 252
Lockheed 14's, 248
Lockheed P-38 pursuit plane, 248
Lockheed Vega, 169
Loening, Grover, 27, 31, 103
Long Island Airways, 115
Loughead brothers, 169
Lovett, Robert A., 156
Luce, Clare Boothe, 161
Luce, Henry, 114
Ludington Line, 86-87, 88-89, 241
Lufbery, Major Raoul, 228
Lufthansa, 133
Lyautey, Marshal Louis, 106

Macao, 135-36, 139
Machado, President, of Cuba, 118
Mach 2 airplane, 198
MacIntyre, Malcolm, 226, 239-42, 279, 282
Maclay, Hardy, 181
Maguire Air Force Base, 301
Mailwings, 230

314 ] INDEX

*Man Nobody Knows, The* (Barton), 69n.
Martin, Glenn L., 20, 24, 25, 27, 31, 52, 104, 208
Martin Aircraft Company, 207-08
Martin *China Clipper*, 136-37
Martin 202's, 171, 276
Mayo Composite aircraft, 138
Maytag, Lewis, Jr., 271-72
McAdoo, William P., 81
McCarran, Patrick, 160
McDonnell F2H, 252
McNamara, Robert S., 26n., 251
Mellon, Andrew, 78
Mercedes engine, 65
Merchant Marine, U. S., 86
Mergers, 12, 78-79, 200-01, 206, 210, 226, 227, 241-42, 263, 271, 279, 288-91, 300
Merman, Ethel, 281
Metropolitan Life Insurance Company, 257, 258
Midway Airport, 225
Military Air Transport Service (MATS), 150n.
Military aviation, 23-29, 31, 37-38, 53
Misr Airwork, 162
Mitchell, Charles, 84
Mitchell, General William (Billy), 37-38, 47, 93, 117
Mohawk Airlines, 172, 263
Monopoly charge, 184-85
Montgomery, Captain John, 117-18
Morgan, John Pierpont, 10, 20-21, 84
Morgan, John Pierpont, the Younger, 84
Morrow, Dwight, 38-39, 123
Musick, Captain, 137

National Airlines, 175, 200, 238, 263, 264-72
National Airlines Taxi Service, 265
National air sovereignty, doctrine of, 121-22
National Air Transport (NAT), 41, 61, 62-64, 116, 215
National Geographic Society, 49
National Mediation Board, 267
Naval Air Transport Service (NATS), 146, 150n.
Naval Reserve Flying Corps, 114
Navy, U. S., 37-38, 57, 112, 114, 115, 122, 125, 134, 145, 146, 150n.

New Deal, 11, 83-96, 97, 99, 100, 102, 200, 204, 278
New York, Rio, and Buenos Aires (NYRBA), 126-29
New York Stock Exchange, 63, 84
*New York Times, The*, 54, 63
*Night Flight* (Saint-Exupéry), 35, 106
Night flights, 35-37, 80, 93
Niles-Bement-Pond Company, 56
94th Pursuit Squadron, 228-29
"Nonsked" airlines, 88, 173, 175, 176, 177, 178, 179, 180-81, 184
North American Airlines, 181, 215
North American Aviation, 60, 61, 63, 65, 76, 79, 91, 96, 230, 231, 232, 233, 244
North American F-86, 252
North Central Airlines, 172
Northeast Airlines, 241, 262-63, 269, 300
Northrup Alphas, 233
Northrup F-89, 252
Northrup Gammas, 99, 245
*North to the Orient* (Lindbergh), 133
Northwest (Orient) Airlines, 41, 134, 165-66, 167, 183, 208, 226, 238, 241, 273-76, 290
Nyrop, Don, 276

Oates, James, 258
O'Connell, chairman of CAB, 178, 235
Ohio Transport, 78
Olds, Irving, 259
O'Neill, Ralph, 126-29
Orteig, Raymond, 47
Orteig Prize, 47
O'Ryan, General John F., 116
*Ostfriesland*, German battleship, 37
Ozark Airlines, 172

Pacific Airline, 172
Pacific Air Transport, 41, 201-02, 203
Pacific routes, 133-36, 138-39, 165-67
Packard Motor Car Company, 66
Panama, 123, 124
Panama Canal, 112, 119, 122, 125
Pan American, Inc., 117-18, 126
Pan American Building, 113
Pan American-Grace Airways (Panagra), 124, 147, 165, 166, 268, 269
Pan American-Imperial Airways Corporation, 131
Pan American World Airways, 12, 40, 49, 68, 112, 113, 118-29, 130-41, 144,

INDEX [ 315

145, 146, 147, 148, 149, 153-67, 169, 178, 183, 190, 192, 199, 222-23, 224, 238, 243, 253, 263, 268, 270, 271, 274, 275, 276, 285, 286, 289-90
Paschall, Nat, 194n.
Passenger market, 283-84
Patterson, William A., 154, 192-93, 199, 200-11, 212, 281
Paulhan, Louis, 52
Payne Field (Cairo), 162
Pennsylvania Central Airlines, 205
Pennsylvania Railroad, 62
Pershing, General John J., 228
Peru, 148
Peruvian Airways, 123
Philippine Islands, 137, 165
Piedmont Airlines, 172
Pitcairn, Harold F., 229-30, 232
Pitcairn Aviation Company, 230-31
Pittsburgh Airways, 77-78
Pittsburgh Aviation Industries Corporation (PAIC), 77-78, 79, 205
Plesman, Albert, 107, 108
Pogue, L. Welsh, 156
Poindexter, Governor, of Hawaii, 136
Portland, Maine, 49
Portugal, 131, 135-36, 138-39, 158
Post, Wiley, 169
Postage stamps, air mail, 32-33
Post Office Department, U. S., 32-33, 34, 35, 37, 39, 40, 53, 71, 87, 100, 115, 117, 127, 216, 229, 230
Pound, Roscoe, 206
Pratt & Whitney Corporation, 56, 57, 89, 96, 103, 170, 191, 200, 223, 225
Prescott, Bob, 173
Priester, André, 120
Prudential Life Insurance Company, 257

Quantas Empire Airways, 166, 194
Quebec Conference (1943), 155
Quezon, President, of Philippines, 137

R-2800 engines, 170
Radar surveillance, 236n.
Railroads, 39, 62, 72-73, 105, 176, 179, 292, 294, 297-98
Ramo, Dr. Simon, 251, 252, 253
Rand, James, 126, 128
Reconstruction Finance Corporation, 220

Regulatory agencies, 100-01, 293-301
Remington Rand Company, 126
Rentschler, Frederick, 55-58, 62-64, 89-90, 200
Rentschler, Gordon, 57
Republic Rainbows, 223
Reynolds, Earle H., 61, 62
Reynolds, Richard, 277
Rickenbacker, Eddie, 32, 41, 94, 191, 199, 227-39, 265-66, 269, 270
Rickenbacker Motor Company, 229
Ripley, Joseph, 57, 63, 64
Rizley, Ross, 183, 184
RKO movie studios, 246, 248, 253, 263
Robertson, Frank and William, 40
Robertson Aircraft Corporation, 40, 44, 45, 213
Rockefeller, David, 242
Rockefeller, Laurance, 234, 239, 242
Rockefeller, Nelson, 234
Rockne, Knute, 80
Rolls-Royce engines, 193, 224
Rooney, Congressman, 178
Roosevelt, Eleanor, 182
Roosevelt, Franklin D., 22, 83, 85, 92-93, 94-96, 97, 102, 146, 148, 155-56, 217
Roosevelt, Jimmy, 101
Roosevelt, Theodore, 19
Roosevelt Field, 48
Royal Dutch Airlines (KLM), 65, 107-08, 133, 287
Russell, Jane, 250
Russia, see Soviet Russia

Saint-Exupéry, Antoine de, 35, 106-07
Satellites, 122n.
*Saturday Evening Post*, 182
Scandinavian Airlines System, 194, 287
SCADTA (in Colombia), 111-12, 123, 124-25, 148
Schlesinger, Arthur, Jr., 85
Science Museum (London), 22
Seaboard Airline, 181
Sessel, Ben-Fleming, 258
Short flying boats, 138
Shuttle service, 241
Signal Corps, U. S. Army, 26, 55
Sikorsky, Igor, 120, 131, 230n.
Sikorsky Airplane Company, 20, 58, 120
Sikorsky Clippers, 131-32, 135
Sindicado Condor, 110, 111
Six, Robert, 200, 271, 281-82

## INDEX

Slick Airline, 181
Smith, C. R., 168, 191, 193, 199, 200-26, 239, 242, 254, 270, 281, 296
Smithsonian Institution, 10, 17, 21-22
South American routes, 123-29, 130, 166, 234-35
Southern Air Transport, 68, 218, 278
Soviet Russia, 134, 147, 287
Spaatz, Major Carl, 117-18, 228
Spanish Armada, 105
Sperry, Elmer, 64
Sperry Gyroscope Company, 64, 230
*Spirit of St. Louis, The* (Lindbergh), 44
*Spirit of St. Louis, The* (Ryan monoplane), 48
Standard Steel Propeller Company, 58
"Star" flights, National's, 267
State Department, U. S., 100, 125, 132, 134, 135, 138, 148, 155, 157, 158, 164
Stettinius, Edward R., Jr., 123, 156
Stinson trimotor planes, 86, 98, 274
Stock market crash of 1929, 83, 128
Stout, William, 66-67
Stranahan, Robert, 66
Strategic Air Command, 190
Strikes, airline, 225n., 267, 269
Subsidies, government, 98, 102, 107, 110, 118, 166, 173, 175-76, 177-79, 235, 293, 297-98, 299
Sud-Aviation Company, 197, 198
Surplus planes, *see* War-surplus planes
Swift, Philip, 61

Taft, William Howard, 19
Talbott, Harold, 25, 191, 253, 261
Teamsters' Union, 293
Technical advances, 102-04, 121, 154, 169, 187-98, 225, 248-49, 283, 292
*Temps, Le*, 106
Texas Air Transport, 218
"Thirteen Black Cats," 244
Thomas, Charles, 256, 257, 258
Thornton, Charles B. "Tex," 251, 253, 256
Tillinghast, Charles, 261-62, 282
*Time* magazine, 114, 182
Tipton, Stuart, 182
Trans American Airline, 181
Transatlantic flight, 43-50, 130-32, 144, 150-51
Trans-Canada Airlines, 194
Transcontinental Air Transport (TAT), 62, 76, 77, 79, 206n., 230, 244, 245

Transcontinental and Western Air, Inc., 79-80, 81, 82, 90, 94, 96, 100, 104, 244, 249
Transcontinental flight, 34-35, 64, 74
Trans-Pacific Airway, 137
Transportation policy or politics, 292-301
Trans-World Airlines (TWA), 12, 145, 146, 147, 159, 161, 163n., 167, 170, 175, 180, 184, 197, 199, 204, 205, 206, 208, 226, 231, 232, 233, 241, 243-63, 270, 276, 285, 286, 289, 296
Trippe, Elizabeth Stettinius, 123
*Trippe, John C.*, schooner, 114
Trippe, Juan Terry, 40, 68, 107, 113-29, 130-41, 145, 148, 149-50, 153-67, 169, 192, 199-200, 207, 224, 243, 268, 269, 270-71, 277, 285-86, 289-90
Truman, Harry S., 150, 178
Turboprops, 190-91, 192, 193, 209, 210, 224-25, 291
TV Channel 10 (Miami), 269

U-2 flight, 122n.
Umbaugh Company, 230n.
United Aircraft and Transport Corporation, 57-58, 60, 62-63, 64, 68, 73, 74, 75, 89-90, 91, 96, 99, 120
United Air Lines, 41, 42, 96, 100, 104, 145, 147, 154, 159, 175, 184, 192, 197, 199, 200-01, 203-11, 212, 223, 226, 245, 279, 285, 296
United Avigation, 78, 80, 81, 90
United States Airways, 78, 80
Universal Aviation Corporation, 68, 98, 213

Vanderbilt, Cornelius, 214, 294
Vanderbilt, William H., 115, 116
Varney Air Service, 41
Versailles Treaty, 31, 109
Vickers Company, 263
Vickers Viscount turboprops, 191, 210, 263
Vincent, Jesse, 25, 28
Vultee, 126n.

Wacos, 274
Wall Street, role of, 59-60, 67-68, 84, 88
*Wall Street Journal*, 60
War Department, U. S., 17-18, 19, 23, 100, 148, 149, 150, 157

INDEX [ 317

War-surplus planes, 29, 31-32, 43, 53, 115, 153, 171, 222, 224, 299
"Wasp" engines, 57, 103
*We* (Lindbergh), 48
Weeks, Sinclair, 183
Weiss, 181
Western Air Express, 41, 55, 65, 76, 77, 79, 82, 200, 202, 206, 207, 244, 245
Western Airlines, Inc., 206n.
"Whirlwind" engine, 56, 57, 65
Whitney, Cornelius Vanderbilt, 115, 116, 139-41
Whitney, Richard, 84
Whittle, Sir Frank, 187
Whiz Kids, 251
Wiggins, Albert H., 84
"Wildcatters," 81
Wilkins, Sir Hubert, 169
Willys, John North, 25, 60
Wilson, Charles E., 26n., 79
Wilson, Woodrow, 23, 24, 25, 28, 30, 32, 33
*Wind, Sand and Stars* (Saint-Exupéry), 106

*Winnie May*, 169
Woolbridge, Dr. Gene, 251, 252, 253
Woolman, C. E., 277-79, 288
*World's Work*, 60
World War I, 10, 23-29, 30-31, 53, 55, 64-65, 228, 244
World War II, 11, 49, 117, 120, 140, 143-51, 153, 187, 221, 229, 234, 239, 274-75
Wright, Orville and Wilbur, 10, 15-16, 17-18, 19, 20-22, 24, 25, 48
Wright Aeronautical Corporation, 56
Wright-Martin Aircraft Corporation, 24, 55
Wright Whirlwind, *see* "Whirlwind" engine
Wrigley, Philip, 61
Wynter, Dana, 259


Yale Flying Club, 114-15
Young, Robert, 62


"Zero" fighters, Japanese, 148

# Literature and History of Aviation

AN ARNO PRESS COLLECTION

Arnold, H[enry] H.
**Global Mission.** 1949.

Bordeaux, Henry.
**Georges Guynemer:** Knight of the Air. Translated by Louise Morgan Sill. 1918.

Boyington, "Pappy" (Col. Gregory Boyington).
**Baa Baa Black Sheep.** 1958.

Buckley, Harold.
**Squadron 95.** 1933.

Caidin, Martin.
**Golden Wings.** 1960.

"Contact" (Capt. Alan Bott).
**Cavalry of the Clouds.** 1917.

Crossfield, A. Scott and Clay Blair, Jr.
**Always Another Dawn.** 1960.

Fokker, Anthony H. G. and Bruce Gould.
**Flying Dutchman:** The Life of Anthony Fokker. 1931.

Gibson, Guy.
**Enemy Coast Ahead.** 1946.

Goldberg, Alfred, editor.
**A History of the United States Air Force 1907-1957.** 1957.

Gurney, Gene.
**Five Down and Glory.** Edited by Mark P. Friedlander, Jr. 1958.

Hall, Norman S.
**The Balloon Buster:** Frank Luke of Arizona. 1928.

Josephson, Matthew.
**Empire of the Air:** Juan Trippe and the Struggle for World Airways. 1944.

Kelly, Charles J., Jr.
**The Sky's the Limit:** The History of the Airlines. 1963.
  New Introduction by Charles J. Kelly, Jr.

Kelly, Fred C., editor.
**Miracle at Kitty Hawk.** 1951.

La Farge, Oliver.
**The Eagle in the Egg.** 1949.

Levine, Isaac Don.
**Mitchell: Pioneer of Air Power.** 1943.

Lougheed, Victor.
**Vehicles of the Air.** 1909.

McFarland, Marvin W., editor.
**The Papers of Wilbur and Orville Wright.** 2 volumes. 1953.

McKee, Alexander.
**Strike From the Sky:** The Story of the Battle of Britain. 1960.

Macmillan, Norman.
**Into the Blue.** 1969.

Magoun, F. Alexander and Eric Hodgins.
**A History of Aircraft.** 1931.

Parsons, Edwin C.
**I Flew with the Lafayette Escadrille.** 1963.

Penrose, Harald.
**No Echo in the Sky.** 1958.

Reynolds, Quentin.
**The Amazing Mr. Doolittle.** 1953.

Saunders, Hilary St. George.
**Per Ardua:** The Rise of British Air Power 1911-1939. 1945.

Stilwell, Hart and Slats Rodgers.
**Old Soggy No. 1.** 1954.

Studer, Clara.
**Sky Storming Yankee:** The Life of Glenn Curtiss. 1937.

Turnbull, Archibald D. and Clifford L. Lord.
**History of United States Naval Aviation.** 1949.

Turner, C. C.
**The Old Flying Days.** 1927.

Von Richthofen, Manfred F.
**The Red Air Fighter.** 1918.

Werner, Johannes.
**Knight of Germany:** Oswald Boelcke, German Ace. Translated by Claud W. Sykes. 1933.

Wise, John.
**Through the Air.** 1873.

Wolff, Leon.
**Low Level Mission.** 1957.

Yakovlev, Alexander.
**Notes of an Aircraft Designer.** Translated by Albert Zdornykh. n.d.